# STUDIES IN
# ROMAN GOVERNMENT AND LAW

*Studies in*

# ROMAN GOVERNMENT
# AND LAW

*By* A. H. M. JONES

BARNES & NOBLE
NEW YORK
1968

First printed 1960
Reprinted 1968

PRINTED IN
GREAT BRITAIN

# PREFACE

SEVEN of the articles contained in this book have been previously published elsewhere; I have made a few alterations and additions where new evidence has confirmed or modified my views, or for the sake of consistency or completeness. Two, the second and seventh, are new, and another, the eighth, is substantially new, being a radical revision of what I wrote in the *Journal of Roman Studies*, XXVI (1936), pp. 223-35. They have been assembled because they have a certain unity in that they are all concerned with the constitutional law and practice of the Roman Empire, and all endeavour to trace the continuity of the institutions of the late Republic with those of the Principate. The first two deal with the basic constitutional powers of Augustus and their Republican precedents, the third with the modification of the old electoral system under the new régime. The fourth and fifth trace the evolution of jurisdiction from the Republican to the Imperial system. The sixth and seventh deal similarly with the development of the financial system and provincial administration. The eighth and ninth treat the legal status of the provincials and of provincial land during both periods. The last traces the evolution of the civil service from the Republic to the age of Justinian.

I have to thank the editors of *Studies presented to David Moore Robinson* and the editors of *Historia* for allowing me to republish the fourth and fifth articles in this book. I owe a particular debt of gratitude to the Roman Society for permission to reproduce no less than five articles (the first, third, sixth, ninth and tenth in this book) published in the *Journal of Roman Studies*. Finally I must thank Sir Basil Blackwell for once again venturing to republish articles of mine.

*Jesus College*                                             A. H. M. JONES
CAMBRIDGE
October, 1959

# CONTENTS

Pages

I. The Imperium of Augustus . . . 1-17
(*Journal of Roman Studies*, XLI (1951), pp. 112-19)

II. The Censorial Powers of Augustus . 19-26

III. The Elections under Augustus . . 27-50
(*Journal of Roman Studies*, XLV (1955), pp. 9-21)

IV. 'I Appeal unto Caesar' . . . 51-65
(*Studies presented to David Moore Robinson*, II, pp. 918-30)

V. Imperial and Senatorial Jurisdiction in the Early Principate . . . . 67-98
(*Historia*, III (1955), pp. 464-88)

VI. The Aerarium and the Fiscus . . 99-114
(*Journal of Roman Studies*, XL (1950), pp. 22-9)

VII. Procurators and Prefects in the Early Principate . . . . . 115-125

VIII. The Dediticii and the Constitutio Antoniniana . . . . 127-140

IX. 'In eo solo dominivm popvli Romani est vel Caesaris' . . . . . 141-149
(*Journal of Roman Studies*, XXXI (1941), pp. 26-31)

vii

Pages

X. The Roman Civil Service (Clerical and Sub-
    Clerical Grades)   .     .     .     .   151-175
    *Journal of Roman Studies*, XXXIX (1949),
    pp. 38-55)

Notes      .       .       .       .       .       .   177-216

Index of Passages Cited   .       .       .   217-239

General Index   .       .       .       .       .   241-243

# I

## *THE IMPERIUM OF AUGUSTUS*

B

# The Imperium of Augustus

THERE has been a tendency among some modern scholars to regard the constitutional position of Augustus as of negligible importance. This is a natural reaction from the excessive legalism of Mommsen and his school, and has had valuable results in elucidating extra-constitutional elements in the position of the first Princeps, such as his outstanding *auctoritas* and his huge *clientela*. I do not think however that we can lightly brush aside the constitutional basis of his power. I do not wish to suggest that the restored Republic was intended to be genuine, or even that Augustus meant to share his power with the Senate and People: never for one moment did he part with his control over the great bulk of the legions. But I would suggest he would not have created the elaborate façade of Republican legitimacy, and moreover have subjected his original scheme to at least one radical revision, unless there had been some important element in the State to which the constitution mattered, and mattered so profoundly that its dissatisfaction would endanger the stability of the régime.

This element was not, I think, primarily the nobility. They were too hard boiled to be put off by Augustus' sham Republic, and it was not the Republic that they so much lamented as their lost power. Moreover they had been decimated in the Civil Wars, and Augustus never trusted what was left of them: they did not hold high military commands as his *legati*. For them the restored Republic only meant that they could without loss of self respect hold office under the new régime and thus maintain their ancestral dignity. Nor do I think that it was the Roman People, if by this is meant the *plebs urbana*: the events of Augustus' reign prove that they wanted a popular dictatorship like Caesar's, and from time to time they broke out, demanding that Augustus accept a life-long consulship or dictatorship. Nor was it the rank and file of the army, who followed him because he was Caesar's son, and were to continue for generations to give blind allegiance to any Caesar, even a Nero. Who then were the republicans? The greatest republican constitutionalist of the last days of the Republic was Cicero, a new man from an Italian town. Velleius Paterculus, the enthusiastic panegyrist of the restored Republic, came from an Italian family enfranchised in the Social War. Livy, the Pompeian historian, who glorified the stern fathers of the Republic, came from Padua. If we look a little later, Thrasea Paetus and his fellow admirers of Brutus and Cassius were worthy bourgeois from the *municipia et coloniae*, and Tacitus himself came from the same milieu. It was, I think, the great Italian middle class, most of whom were Roman citizens of the third generation only, who venerated the republican traditions of Rome. And they were important politically; for from them were drawn the centurions and equestrian officers of the army, and picked men from among them were promoted to the Senate and held the higher army commands, in so far as these were not monopolised by the imperial family. Finally they were quite content with the form of the Republic, for their republicanism was sentimental and anti-quarian: they had never tasted power under the old régime and had rarely even aspired to do so.

To turn to the events. In 27 B.C., having purged the Senate, Imperator Caesar restored the Republic with a great flourish of trumpets and was rewarded with the *cognomen* of Augustus by the grateful Senate. The legal powers enjoyed by the Princeps at this moment were somewhat limited. He possessed the sacro-sanctity of a tribune, granted in 36 B.C., and the tribunician power of *auxilium*, conferred in 30 B.C. He was moreover one of the consuls of the year. Of what happened next we have only Dio's account, and according to him Augustus was voted a number of provinces for ten years. These provinces Dio enumerates according to their later boundaries: in 27 B.C. they could have been summed up as Hither Spain, Transalpine Gaul, Syria, and Egypt.[1]

It has been argued *ad nauseam* whether Augustus' *imperium* at this stage was consular or proconsular. I do not believe that the question arose. Augustus was consul, and the Senate assigned him a *provincia*: no grant of *imperium* was required, for, to quote Appius Claudius Pulcher, speaking as consul, about to depart for his province at the end of 54 B.C., 'se quoniam ex senatus consulto provinciam haberet lege Cornelia imperium habiturum quoad in urbem introisset.'[2] It is true that the Lex Pompeia de provinciis had since then modified the position by inserting a five years' interval between magistracy and promagistracy, but this law had evidently either been abrogated or fallen in abeyance before 27 B.C., since Augustus either re-enacted or revived it in that year.[3] The revival of the Lex Pompeia would naturally have come after the assignment of Augustus' province, which, as an extra-ordinary command, would in any case have been (and of course was) exempted from its provisions. The grant of the provinces must have included the right to appoint numerous *legati*, which Pompey and Caesar had received before. It was probably at this date also that Augustus was given the right to declare war and make treaties which is mentioned by Strabo and by the Lex de imperio Vespasiani.[4] There were Republican precedents for this in the Lex Manilia and the Lex Trebonia[5] and it was a not unnatural privilege for the magistrate who was to control most of the frontiers for the next ten years; it also incidentally gave Augustus control over the numerous and powerful kings of the Empire. Though this right proved to be lifelong as Strabo describes it, I think that it was probably originally linked with the *provincia*, as in the cases of Pompey and of Crassus.

We tend, I think, knowing what did happen next, to assume too readily that it was an open secret at the time that Augustus was going to be consul year after year. Dio, for what he is worth, represents the majority of the Senate as being in the dark,[6] and if this is true many of them may have hoped and expected that

Augustus would, like Caesar in 59, go and govern his provinces, or at the worst, like Pompey in 55, hang about in Italy as proconsul, governing his provinces through his legates. But if so they were disappointed; for Augustus stood for, and was naturally elected to, the consulship in 26, and again in 25, and in 24, and in 23.

He thus placed himself in a position which could hardly be called republican. The only recent precedent for a continuous series of consulships was Marius, hardly a reputable figure. Moreover, in addition to ruling the great *provincia* which the Senate had assigned to him, he possessed the vast and undefined powers of a consul, which he could stretch to include an ultimate control over all proconsuls; for according to that excellent republican jurist, Cicero, 'omnes in consulis iure et imperio debent esse provinciae' and to the consuls 'more maiorum concessum est vel omnes adire provincias'.[7] That Augustus (conjointly with his fellow consul) used this prerogative is proved by a recently published inscription: it records a decree of Augustus and Agrippa, consuls (that is in 27 B.C.), ordering the restitution of sacred property in the provinces, and a consequential judgment of the proconsul of Asia, who refers to it as *iussu Augusti Caesaris*.[8] The incident of Primus, proconsul of Macedonia, charged with making war on the Odrysae without authorisation, proves that Augustus was suspected of ordering proconsuls about in more important matters; for Primus claimed in defence that he had acted on Augustus' orders, and when Augustus, questioned by the praetor, denied this, Primus' counsel Murena asked him what he was doing in court in that case, implying that he doubted his word.[9] And Augustus, besides interfering with other proconsuls, was from time to time in Rome, where as consul he could dominate the Senate. Matters were made worse by the too obvious parade of Marcellus as heir apparent, which suggested a hereditary tyranny: Primus at his trial exploited this suspicion by claiming that Marcellus had given him instructions, and Augustus after Marcellus' death thought it prudent to offer to publish his will to prove that he had no intention of founding a hereditary monarchy.[10]

That this state of affairs caused bitter dissatisfaction is proved by the conspiracy of Caepio and Murena, misplaced by Dio in 22, really belonging to the previous year:[11] this conspiracy was all the more serious in that Murena was what Velleius calls a good man, that is a Caesarian, and it must have been a sharp reminder to Augustus that, if he was to avoid his adoptive father's fate, something must be done. This, I think, is the true explanation of Augustus' abrupt resignation from his consulship in 23. He had, it is true, been very ill, and had even made arrangements envisaging the possibility of his death, handing his seal to Agrippa, and the accounts of the Empire to his colleague Piso.[12] But his weakened health was no more than a convenient excuse for the constitutional change which he now made, a change which did not effectively reduce the amount of work or responsibility which he had to undertake.

For what happened in 23 we are again dependent on Dio.[13] Augustus resigned his consulship, and to prove his good republican principles, filled its remaining term by L. Sestius, an open admirer of Brutus, who had fought on his side in the Civil Wars. To compensate for the abandonment of the consulate the Senate voted 'that he should hold the *imperium proconsulare* once for all, so as neither to lay it down on entering the pomerium nor to renew it again, and that he should have greater power in the subject territory than the governors of the several areas' (τὴν ἀρχὴν τὴν ἀνθύπατον ἐσαεὶ καθάπαξ ἔχειν, ὥστε μήτε ἐν τῇ εἰσόδῳ τῇ εἴσω τοῦ πωμηρίου κατατίθεσθαι αὐτὴν μήτ' αὖθις ἀνανεοῦσθαι, καὶ ἐν τῷ ὑπηκόῳ τὸ πλεῖον τῶν ἑκασταχόθι ἀρχόντων ἰσχύειν). Dio is wrong if he meant that the Senate gave Augustus an *imperium*: he had already had it as proconsul of his province. That there was no break in his provincial command is proved by the fact that it was renewed at the end of the original ten years.[14] What the Senate did was to modify that *imperium* in two ways; by enacting that it should not lapse when Augustus re-entered the *pomerium* as did an ordinary proconsul's *imperium*, so that Augustus could when he wished attend to affairs in the capital, leaving his provinces to his legates, without having to have his *imperium* renewed each time; and secondly by making his *imperium maius* in relation to that of other proconsuls. This latter point has been the subject of infinite debate, and I have nothing new to say on it. I can only say that I do not rate Dio so low as to think he made up this clause, and that in my view some of the Cyrene edicts, and also an edict to Asia preserved by Josephus, display Augustus exercising a *maius imperium*.[15] The opponents of the idea seem to me to be tilting against windmills. They transform a *maius imperium* whereby one proconsul's will prevails over the wills of other proconsuls in case of a clash into the revolutionary *imperium* whereby the triumvirs claimed to appoint all magistrates and promagistrates and treat them as their delegates, and then quite truly assert that Augustus claimed no such power. The *maius imperium* was perhaps intended as some compensation for the loss of the vague overriding powers which Augustus had held as consul, or may have been initially voted to enable Augustus to undertake the tour of the provinces upon which he did in fact next year embark.

Dio's statement that the *imperium* was granted once for all seems to conflict with his later statements that the provincial command was renewed for terms of five or ten years. Technically I think that Dio is correct. According to the Lex Cornelia de provinciis a proconsul held his *imperium* not for any fixed time, but 'quoad in urbem introisset'.[16] The Senate had removed this limitation and Augustus' *imperium* became thereby perpetual. But the *imperium* without any *provincia* in which to exercise it was a tenuous conception—it was in fact merely the capacity to assume a *provincia* when assigned without waiting for a law conferring *imperium*. It could only be actualised by the grant of a *provincia*, and this was done from time to time so as to make Augustus perpetual proconsul. In my view from 23 Augustus was a proconsul exercising his *imperium* in the province assigned to him, but with power to exercise it in other provinces if he disagreed with their proconsuls.

As far as the provinces were concerned Augustus was thus placed by formal grant in the position which he had occupied hitherto in virtue of his undefined powers as consul. In Rome and Italy he had no *locus standi*. As this point is important, I had better elaborate it. A proconsul possessed *imperium* from the passing of his *lex curiata* (whether as consul, or, if he were a *privatus*, when his province was assigned to him) till he re-entered the city; but he could exercise his *imperium*, except by special authorisation, only in his province. The later imperial lawyers are explicit on this point. As Ulpian says 'proconsul ubique quidem proconsularia insignia habet, statim atque urbem egressus est: potestatem autem non exercet nisi in ea provincia sola quae ei decreta est'.[17] That this rule goes back to Sulla at any rate is indicated by Cicero's remark in the *in Pisonem*: 'mitto exire de provincia, educere exercitum, bellum sua sponte gerere, in regnum iniussu populi Romani aut senatus accedere, quam cum plurimae leges veteres, tum lex Cornelia maiestatis, Iulia de pecuniis repetundis planissime vetat'.[18] There are two exceptions to this rule. A proconsul might exercise a jurisdiction 'non contentiosam sed voluntariam', e.g. manumit slaves, outside his province.[19] Secondly, a proconsul on his way to or from his province might be authorised by the Senate to perform some particular task, as it was proposed that Verres should round up some insurgent slaves at Tempsa, and that Cicero should take charge of Sicily: it was sometimes more convenient to revive the dormant *imperium* of a passing proconsul than send someone with *imperium* from Rome.[20] But such an exercise of *imperium* could, it would seem, be undertaken only 'iussu populi Romani aut senatus'.

To provide Augustus with a modest position in Rome the Senate, and no doubt the People, voted that he should possess *tribunicia potestas* for life. I believe this to have been the first occasion that the *tribunicia potestas* was granted to him, for the good reason that Augustus numbers his tenure of it from this year. It may also be noted that Augustus distinguishes a perpetual grant of *sacrosanctitas* from a grant of *tribunicia potestas* for life.[21] Appian and Orosius must therefore be wrong in speaking of a grant of *tribunicia potestas* in 36, when Dio speaks only of *sacrosanctitas*,[22] and Dio must be wrong in implying that Octavian accepted the *tribunicia potestas* voted to him in 30 B.C. (when he apparently accepted only the power of *auxilium*).[23] The additional rights which Augustus acquired with the full power of a tribune would have been *intercessio*, the *ius agendi cum plebe*, and the *ius consulendi senatus*.

These powers were useful but neither very essential nor very adequate. The power of *intercessio* was very occasionally used by Tiberius and Nero to quash sentences by the Senate,[24] but it was scarcely essential: on the rare occasion when a defiant magistrate flouted him he could surely have relied on one of the ten tribunes exercising his veto on his behalf.   The *ius agendi cum plebe* Augustus himself used to put through some of his social legislation.[25]   But it was hardly necessary for him to be the formal mover: for the rare occasion when a law was called for he could always find an obliging consul, and in fact for several of his major social laws—the Lex Junia, the Lex Fufia Caninia, the Lex Aelia Sentia, the Lex Papia Poppaea—not to speak of the Lex Valeria Cornelia[26] which remodelled the electoral procedure, and such minor measures as the Lex Quinctia de aquaeductibus,[27] he did use the consuls.   The *ius consulendi senatus* was more practically useful, but here also it was always possible to use the consuls, and in point of fact it so happens that all the surviving *senatus consulta* of the reign were moved by the consuls.[28]   Moreover a tribune enjoyed a very low priority in summoning or consulting the Senate, which was hardly consonant with the dignity of Augustus, and from the very start he was accorded the special right of putting one question in each session even if not consul, and in the following year the special right of summoning the Senate when he wished: these rights are recorded in the Lex

de imperio with others of a similar kind.²⁹   It is to my mind
suggestive that, when Tiberius on Augustus' death summoned
the Senate by virtue of his *tribunicia potestas* (not yet possessing the
special prerogatives), he explicitly stated, in a somewhat apologetic
fashion, that he was using this power.³⁰   This surely implies that
Augustus had not normally so used it.   Augustus in fact hardly
needed to use his *tribunicia potestas* at all, since he could achieve
the same ends by his *auctoritas*.   A formal veto was not needed
when a hint would suffice: it was not necessary to make proposals
to the Senate or the People when others acting on his advice
would carry through his measures.

Yet Augustus made the tribunician power, as Tacitus puts it,
'summi fastigi vocabulum,'³¹ numbering the years of his reign by
it and granting it most sparingly to his colleagues to mark them
out as his potential successors.   One reason why he did so was, no
doubt, the very fact that it did convey so little power; by making
it appear that his position rested on so harmless a prerogative he
could conceal the real constitutional basis of his power.   Another
reason was, I suspect, that the tribunate was popular.   We do not,
I think, sufficiently appreciate the sentimental associations of the
tribunate in the minds of the common people.   In the optimate
tradition, which we mainly hear, the tribunate was a baneful
institution and the great tribunes were villains.   But contrast
Cicero writing for an upper class audience, and Cicero addressing
the people: in his public speeches the Gracchi are heroes;³² and
Caesar could find no better *casus belli* to inflame his troops with
wrath than the violation of the tribunes.³³   By posing as tribune
of the plebs Augustus hoped to rally this popular sentiment for
himself, and to represent that he occupied his high position
'ad tuendam plebem'.³⁴   The assumption of the tribunician
power was in short a gesture, and a gesture to two parties
in the State.   To the plebs, it was a guarantee—which as sub-
sequent events proved they did not consider adequate—that
Augustus was not abandoning them to the optimates, to the
optimates a threat that Augustus might revive the popular

tradition of his adoptive father if they would not play ball with him.

The text books usually represent the settlement of 23 B.C. as the final step, after which they all lived happily ever after. It was in fact the signal for a prolonged and violent agitation. In the following year there were riots, and Augustus was pressed to accept a dictatorship or a perpetual and annual consulship, and according to Dio a perpetual censorship and a *cura annonae* with sweeping powers like that given to Pompey in 57 B.C.; Augustus admits that he accepted a *cura annonae* as a temporary measure, and he had censors elected, which suggests that Dio is right in saying that the censorship was pressed upon him.[35] After Augustus had left for the East, the people insisted on electing him consul for 21 B.C. and for long refused to fill the vacancy when he would not accept office.[36] In 21 B.C. Agrippa was sent to Italy, and succeeded in getting a second consul elected for that year, and in arranging the consular elections for the next year. But after his departure, when the elections for 19 B.C. came on, the people again insisted on reserving one consulship for Augustus. The situation grew so serious that in the summer of 19 B.C. the Senate passed the SC *ultimum*, and the one consul begged Augustus to return, which he did on 12th October: the Senate's relief was revealed by its sending a special delegation to meet him in Campania and voting an altar of Fortuna Redux.[37]

These disturbances are of course susceptible of two explanations, and I think that there may be some truth in both. They would hardly have been so sustained unless there had been some popular feeling behind them, and it looks as if the populace took Augustus' resignation of the consulship very seriously, and feared that its champion was going to abandon his dominating position and that the anarchy of the Republic would begin again: the people, it seems, cared little for the constitution but wanted a strong man to rule. On the other hand Augustus was probably not ill pleased to prove to the constitutionalists that if he withdrew to his provinces and abandoned control of Rome to them, ruin would follow. In his nervousness in 23 he had jumped back further than he wanted; now he could step forward once more, and the Senate would be only too thankful to give him the necessary powers.

Dio says that these were 'the *imperium* of the consuls for life, so that he should use the twelve *fasces* always and everywhere and should sit on his *sella curulis* between the consuls for the time being' (τὴν δὲ τῶν ὑπάτων (sc. ἐξουσίαν) διὰ βίου ἔλαβεν, ὥστε καὶ ταῖς δώδεκα ῥάβδοις ἀεὶ καὶ πανταχοῦ χρῆσθαι καὶ ἐν μέσῳ τῶν ἀεὶ ὑπατευόντων ἐπὶ τοῦ ἀρχικοῦ δίφρου καθίζεσθαι).[38] These words of Dio have been interpreted so that the consecutive clause defines and qualifies the opening sentence; that is, Augustus received so much of the consular *imperium* as consisted in the twelve lictors and the seat between the consuls. Dio's words will bear this interpretation, but other facts seem to me to indicate that he is right in assigning to Augustus from this date a consular *imperium* which was valid in Rome and Italy. The chief objection brought against this view is that Augustus never mentions such an *imperium* in his *Res Gestae* or his titulature. But this is rather naïve. Augustus may have told nothing but the truth, but he certainly did not feel it necessary to tell the whole truth. I challenge any impartial reader to find in the *Res Gestae* any allusion to the main basis of his power, his *imperium* in his own *provincia*. From the *Res Gestae* one would infer that Augustus had held many consulates and other honours and waged many wars, but never that for forty-one years continuously he had been proconsul of half the empire: that would not have looked well. And in his imperial titles similarly Augustus blazoned the number of his consulates and imperial salutations, the years of his tribunician power, and harmless offices and titles such as *pontifex maximus* and *pater patriae*, but never mentioned his proconsular *imperium*.

On the other hand there are many powers which Augustus exercised in Italy and even in Rome which could only be based on the *imperium*. And here I think that I must pause to draw a distinction between what could be done by *auctoritas* and what by *imperium*. By *auctoritas* Augustus could get many important things done: he could get a *senatus consultum* passed in the sense which he wished or he could get A and B elected consuls instead of C and D. But to give commands to soldiers and to exercise jurisdiction he required *imperium*; one could not say 'C. Seium gladio animadverti placet' in virtue of *auctoritas*. Now Augustus did command troops, the Praetorian cohorts, stationed in Italian towns, and the three Urban cohorts and the *vigiles* actually in the city.[39] He exercised a civil and criminal jurisdiction within the city which Dio at any rate derives from the *imperium*.[40] He exercised magisterial *coercitio* not only against actors,[41] but also against a Roman Knight, Ovid, whom he relegated to Tomi.[42] He also apparently levied troops by conscription both in Italy and Rome.[43] What is most significant he appointed a *praefectus urbi*, a specifically consular prerogative,[44] and delegated *imperium* within the city to him.[45]

The chronology of the urban prefects is particularly interesting. Augustus first appointed a *praefectus urbi*, Messalla Corvinus, in 26 or 25 B.C. when he was consul, but had to be absent to look after his province.[46] Between 22 and 19 he was again away but he appointed no *praefectus* and there seem to have been no troops available to keep order in Rome. All that Augustus did was to send Agrippa to Rome in 21, apparently without any official position.[47] It is perhaps noteworthy that the attempt of the consuls to appoint a *praefectus urbi* for the Latin festival occasioned riots and had to be abandoned:[48] the populace perhaps resented what looked like an attempt by the consuls to arrogate to themselves an appointment which the people wished Augustus to exercise. But when Augustus next left Rome in 16 B.C. he appointed a *praefectus urbi*, Statilius Taurus.[49] By what power unless he now held a consular *imperium*? Another less striking but specifically consular prerogative which Augustus exercised in the latter part of his reign was that of receiving *professiones* (or making *nominationes*) for the consular and praetorian elections, concurrently with the consuls.[50] Finally Augustus himself explicitly states that on two occasions he used a *consulare imperium* in Italy, to conduct the censuses of 8 B.C. and A.D. 14.[51] This is generally explained away as an *ad hoc* grant, but such an explanation is most implausible. If special powers had to be voted to him, it would have been more economical and more modest to ask for a *censoria potestas*: a *consulare imperium* was a very heavy tool for the conduct of a census, which needed no *imperium* at all. If on the other hand Augustus possessed a consular *imperium* already, it was natural that he should use it for conducting his censuses, instead of applying for special powers.

What precise form the enactment of 19 B.C. took it is scarcely possible to say. I find it rather difficult to believe what Dio appears to say, that Augustus received a consular *imperium* in addition to his existing *imperium* in the provinces. It would seem more plausible that the Senate declared Augustus' *imperium* to be equal to that of the consuls, thus releasing it from its territorial limitations. The titles given to the *imperium* are not very helpful in solving this question. The *imperium* in Italy was in Augustus' day called consular, as Augustus himself testifies; but so, no doubt, as Pelham has argued, was the *imperium* which Augustus held *pro consule* in the provinces.[52] By Claudius' day terminology seems to have changed, if Tacitus is accurate in saying that the young Nero was in 51 granted 'proconsulare imperium extra urbem'.[53] This phrase implies that Claudius' *imperium* (which presumably would have been valid *intra urbem* also) was deemed to be proconsular not only in the provinces, but in Italy. And indeed Claudius seems to have thought that his position was not quite that of a consul when he asked for 'some power of a consul' (ὑπάτου τινὰ ἐξουσίαν) to celebrate his triumphal games.[54] For what it is worth I think that this evidence suggests that the emperors possessed one *imperium* only which was earlier called consular, later proconsular. But whatever the technicalities it seems to me clear that from 19 B.C. Augustus exercised his *imperium* not only in his own provinces, and when occasion arose in the public provinces, but also in Italy and Rome itself.

Augustus shared his *imperium* with various colleagues from time to time, but not, it would appear, his *imperium* over Italy. Agrippa's position in 23-13 B.C. is a well-known tangle; it is perhaps sufficient for my purpose to note that he exercised his *imperium* in Gaul and Spain, and in the eastern provinces, but that in Italy, where he was in 21, his position seems to have been unofficial. In 13 B.C. his *imperium* was renewed and is explicitly stated to have been *maius* outside Italy (μεῖζον αὐτῷ τῶν ἑκασταχόθι ἔξω τῆς Ἰταλίας ἀρχόντων ἰσχῦσαι ἐπιτρέψας).[55] For Augustus' later colleagues no very clear evidence exists until we come to the renewal of Tiberius' powers in A.D. 13. On this occasion our authorities imply that Tiberius was granted a position more nearly equal to Augustus than any colleague had hitherto enjoyed, 'ut aequum ei ius in omnibus provinciis exercitibusque esset quam erat ipsi' according to Velleius; according to Suetonius, 'ut provincias cum Augusto communiter administraret, simulque censum ageret'.[56] But even now nothing is said of Italy, and it is indeed implicitly excluded by the special powers granted to Tiberius to hold the census concurrently with Augustus.

This circumstance may explain the awkward situation which arose on Augustus' death. I find Tacitus' narrative very confusing, and I doubt whether he grasped the niceties of the constitutional position. He seems for instance to regard Tiberius' action in continuing to issue orders to the provincial armies as illegal. On the generally accepted view, on the other hand, no problem would have presented itself at all. Except for a few ornamental offices and titles, like *pontifex maximus*, *Augustus* and *pater patriae*, and a few minor powers, like the special right to convoke and consult the Senate, Tiberius would have stood in precisely the same position as Augustus without any further ado. If my view is correct, however, Tiberius was back where Augustus had been in 23 B.C.; he had command over his provinces and their armies and a *maius imperium* over other proconsuls, but in Italy he had only the tribunician power, which he used to summon the Senate.

His assumption of command over the Praetorian and Urban cohorts was probably *ultra vires*, but what else could he do? And it would seem that the office of prefect of the city temporarily lapsed, since the magistracy which had delegated the *imperium* to it had disappeared. This would explain the well-known puzzle of Lucius Piso, who is stated to have served as prefect of the city for twenty years down to his death in A.D. 32, but in A.D. 14 is conspicuously absent from the group of high officials who take the oath.[57]

The general picture that I would draw of the reign is then that after the restoration of the Republic it falls into three phases. In the first Augustus attempted too blatant an exhibition of power; checked by the fear of assassination he next made a sharp retreat, and let the Senate realise that they could not do without his guiding hand in Rome; in the third he recovered, but in a less obtrusive form, much of the same power that he had possessed before 23 B.C.

# II

## THE CENSORIAL POWERS OF AUGUSTUS

# The Censorial Powers of Augustus

AUGUSTUS himself in his *Res Gestae* speaks of his censorial activities and powers in two chapters. In Chapter 8 he states 'patriciorum numerum auxi consul quintum (29 B.C.) iussu populi et senatus'. This was done, as we learn from Tacitus,[1] in virtue of a special law, the Lex Saenia. He goes on to say with tantalising brevity: 'Senatum ter legi'. He then recounts his three censuses, the first 'in consulato sexto . . . conlega M. Agrippa' in 28 B.C., the second 'consulari cum imperio' and 'solus' in 8 B.C., and the third also 'consulari cum imperio' but 'conlega Tib. Caesare filio meo' in A.D. 14. Finally he speaks briefly of his social legislation. In Chapter 6 he states that in 19, 18 and 11 B.C. when pressed by the senate and people 'ut curator legum et morum summa potestate solus crearer, nullum magistratum contra morem maiorum delatum recepi', but carried out the wishes of the Senate through his tribunician power: this is clearly another allusion to his social legislation.

The natural inference from these statements, which most historians have made, is that Augustus never held any special censorial powers, but took action either as consul or in virtue of his consular *imperium* (for the censuses and presumably for the *lectiones senatus*), or through his tribunician power (for the social legislation). Suetonius gives quite a different account in his life of Augustus. In one passage, after mentioning his tribunician power, he says, 'recepit et morum legumque regimen aeque perpetuum, quo iure quamquam sine censurae honore censum tamen populi ter egit, primum ac tertium cum collega, medium solus'.[2] In another context he speaks of two *lectiones senatus*, 'prima ipsorum arbitratu quo vir virum legit, secunda suo et Agrippae'.[3] Elsewhere he describes the social legislation[4] and

Augustus' *recognitiones* of the equestrian order,[5] which were normally a censorial function.

Finally Dio gives abundant, if sometimes rather inaccurate and confused, information about various censuses and *lectiones senatus* and the powers under which Augustus conducted them. It will simplify the issue if we first endeavour to fix the dates of the *lectiones*. There is no doubt about the first, which took place in 29 B.C. in preparation for the restoration of the Republic and is fully described by Dio.[6] Nor is there much doubt about the second which is again fully described by Dio under the year 18 B.C.[7] It was on this occasion that Augustus endeavoured to revise the roll of senators 'ipsorum arbitratu, quo vir virum legit'. Suetonius appears to know only of these two *lectiones* and to have inverted their order. After this Dio appears to record three more *lectiones*, in 13 B.C., in 11 B.C. and in A.D. 4.[8] The last, which is very fully described, was not conducted by Augustus himself, but by a triumvirate of senators[9] and is therefore not to be counted among Augustus' three. His third *lectio* must then have been either in 13 or in 11 B.C.; one of these two must be eliminated, for apart from Augustus' own statement, it is incredible that the roll of the Senate should have been revised twice in three years. Dio's account of 13 B.C. is highly confused. He begins by stating that 'after this there was again an examination of the senators' (ἐκ δὲ τούτου ἐξέτασις αὖθις τῶν βουλευτῶν ἐγένετο). He goes on to explain that the senatorial census, having originally been 400,000 sesterces, had been raised to 1,000,000 and that as a result many sons and descendants of senators had not claimed senatorial rights and had even resigned when already senators, and that as a consequence a decree had been passed whereby the *vigintiviri* were no longer enrolled in the Senate. He finally states that Augustus then examined them all himself (τότε δὲ αὐτὸς πάντας αὐτοὺς ἐξήτασε), and did not bother those over 35, but compelled those under that age who had the property qualification to be senators, unless they had any bodily defect, examining their persons himself, but accepting sworn declarations of their property.

An upper age limit of 35 is very odd for admission to the Senate: on the other hand it is appropriate for equites, and Suetonius expressly states that Augustus 'reddendi equi gratiam fecit eis qui maiores annorum quinque et triginta retinere eum nollent'. Physical deformity was no bar to senatorial rank, but might well be so for membership of the equestrian *turmae*; Suetonius in the same passage says that Augustus allowed equites to absent themselves from the *travectio* if 'senio vel aliqua corporis labe insignibus'.[10] It would appear that Dio has misunderstood his sources, who after discussing the effects of the increased senatorial census, and the resultant decree that the *vigintiviri* should no longer be enrolled in the Senate but remain equites, went on to describe a *recognitio equitum*. It follows then that Augustus' third *lectio senatus* was that briefly described under 11 B.C.

Dio records the census of 28 B.C.[11] but ignores those of 8 B.C. and A.D. 14; the latter is, however, mentioned by Suetonius not only in the passage already cited but in two others.[12] Dio appears to speak of two other censuses. In 11 B.C. he states that Augustus 'held registrations, registering all his own property like a private citizen, and revised the roll of the Senate' (ἀπογραφάς τε ἐποιήσατο, πάντα τά ὑπάρχοντά οἱ καθάπερ τις ἰδιώτης ἀπογραψάμενος, καὶ τὴν βουλὴν κατελέξατο).[13] In view of the recent raising of the senatorial property qualification and the emphasis laid on Augustus' personal declaration this is probably to be understood as a registration of senatorial property. In A.D. 4 Dio speaks more definitely of a census, even talking of the *lustrum* (καθάρσιον), but he specifically states that it was limited to those domiciled in Italy who owned over 200,000 sesterces.[14] This was clearly, then, not a normal census, but is to be connected with the creation of the judicial decury of the *ducenarii*, whose property qualification was 200,000 sesterces and who had to be resident in Italy.[15]

We may now consider the powers under which Augustus acted on these various occasions. Dio opens his account of the *lectio* of 29 B.C. with the statement that Augustus held the censorship with

Agrippa (τιμητεύσας σὺν τῷ ’Αγρίππᾳ).¹⁶ This is wrong, for
Augustus never held the office of censor, as Suetonius rightly
says, but perhaps not entirely wrong. For a semi-official and more
or less contemporary document, the Fasti Venusini, states: 'imp.
Caes. VI, M. Agrippa II, idem censoria potest. lustrum fecer.'¹⁷
It is difficult to resist the conclusion that Augustus was slightly
disingenuous in the Res Gestae: it is quite true that he held a
census in his sixth consulship with his colleague Agrippa, but he
appears to have passed over the fact that he and his colleague
simultaneously held censoria potestas.

After this one may look at Dio's further statements with a less
prejudiced eye. Although Augustus does not mention the
incident, there seems no particular reason to doubt Dio's story
that a life censorship was offered to Augustus in 22 B.C. and that
he refused it, and instead had censors elected:¹⁸ the election of the
two censors is elsewhere attested.¹⁹ Next Dio states that in 19 B.C.
Augustus, while refusing the offer of extravagant powers to
reform the state, including the right to enact at his discretion laws
to which the Senate would swear obedience in advance, nevertheless did accept a cura morum and censoria potestas for a term of
five years.²⁰ In 12 B.C. Dio mentions that at Agrippa's funeral a
veil was hung between Augustus and the corpse, and that various
explanations were given, either that Augustus feared pollution as
pontifex maximus, or because he was conducting censorial
business:²¹ as the former alternative is fairly certainly right,²² this
is not good evidence. Later in the same year, however, he records
that Augustus accepted the same powers as in 19 for another
period of five years, 'for he took it like his sovereign powers
by instalments' (καὶ γὰρ τοῦτο κατὰ προθεσμίας, ὥσπερ που τὴν
μοναρχίαν, ἐλάμβανε).²³ This last phrase has sometimes been taken
to mean that Augustus henceforth went on receiving periodic
renewals of censorial powers, but in fact what Dio says is that
he accepted them only for limited periods, and he records only
these two grants, in 19 B.C. (for 19-14) and in 12 B.C. (for 12-7).

Now Augustus, as we have seen, records the refusal of extravagant censorial powers in the second half of 19, in 18 and in 11 B.C. It might be, and has often been, argued that Dio wrongly assumed that these offers were accepted. On the other hand there are reasons for believing that Dio was accurate. In 19 B.C. he does distinguish the extravagant powers which Augustus refused, and the ordinary *cura morum* and *censoria potestas* which he accepted. Furthermore it is curious that each alleged grant of censorial powers, in 29, 19 and 12, is immediately followed by a *lectio senatus*. Finally it may be noted that Augustus does not explicitly deny that he received a *cura morum* or *censoria potestas*. He only states that when it was proposed that he should be created 'curator legum et morum summa potestate' he refused any office which was contrary to ancestral custom. His statement is certainly disingenuous, if he did accept a *cura morum* and *censoria potestas*, but it cannot be called a lie, for the normal powers of a censor could not be said to be 'contra morem maiorum'.

I would suggest that Augustus did accept censorial powers in 29, 19 and 12, and with the specific aim of strengthening his hand in view of a forthcoming *lectio senatus*.

It was apparently only for this purpose that he felt he needed special authority. The grants of censorial powers have no obvious connection with the census. The first census and *lectio* coincided in date, but the second census, though it fell within the quin-quennium of 12–7 B.C., came near its end, and, since Augustus states that he held this census 'consulari cum imperio', he had probably already resigned his *censoria potestas* after completing the *lectio* in 11 B.C. Since he managed to get the fourth *lectio* conducted by others, he received no censorial powers in A.D. 4, and Dio expressly notes that he carried out the partial census of that year in virtue of his *consulare imperium* (ἀνθύπατον ἐξουσίαν as Dio calls it).[24] There is no record that he took any special powers for the census of 14 A.D. Nor again does he seem to have felt the need for special censorial powers in dealing with the equites, though of course when the *recognitio equitum* was entrusted to others, they had to receive *censoria potestas*.[25] At any rate the only datable *recognitio equitum*, if I am right, falls in 13 B.C. in the interval between his two terms of *censoria potestas*.

Why, it may be asked, should Augustus have taken these powers, and why should he have so carefully avoided allusion to them in the *Res Gestae* ? Constitutionally they were not necessary; he could have relied on his consular *imperium*, But the revision of the roll of the Senate was a task which Augustus evidently found extremely invidious and embarrassing. This is shown by the lurid anecdotes told by Suetonius [26] and by his many attempts to get the senators to do the work themselves—by pressing them to anticipate expulsion by voluntary resignation in 29 B.C., by an elaborate scheme of nomination and sortition (which broke down) in 18 B.C., and finally by the creation of a triumvirate of senators (which actually did the work) in A.D. 4. In these circumstances it would be natural that Augustus should have wished to fortify himself for execution of this painful and unpopular duty by the solemn grant of censorial powers. For the very same reason he did not wish to revive memories of them when he wrote his *Res Gestae*. He dismissed his successive purges of the Senate with the three words 'senatum ter legi', and he let his readers infer that he never held a *censoria potestas*.

# III

## THE ELECTIONS UNDER AUGUSTUS

# The Elections under Augustus

THE *Tabula Hebana* already has a bibliography more than six pages long, in which figure the names of most of the eminent scholars of Europe.[1] It may seem, therefore, both superfluous and presumptuous to add to it. But very few of the studies hitherto produced have attempted to deal with the political implications of the document, and of these few only one, Professor Tibiletti's monograph, *Principe e magistrati repubblicani*, has tackled them seriously. As will appear, I owe much to Professor Tibiletti's acute analysis of the procedure laid down in the *Tabula*, but as I differ profoundly on several points from his interpretation of the political background, I have thought it worth while to propound my views.

It is almost accepted doctrine that Augustus throughout his reign systematically gerrymandered the elections, those at any rate for the higher offices, especially the consulate. What I may call the prosopographical school of historians, in particular, assume that the consuls were *de facto* the nominees of Augustus, and regard the consular *fasti* as a barometer of his personal policy or that of the narrow group which controlled affairs. I would challenge this view. The liberty of the elections was, I would agree, to some extent limited by the predominant influence of the Princeps, but the evidence, I maintain, strongly suggests that genuine electoral contests continued, not only for the lower offices, but for the praetorship and the consulate, with which alone the *Tabula Hebana* is concerned.

Competition for entry to the Senate was no doubt somewhat reduced by the formal enactment of a property qualification, which was at least once raised. The exact figures are variously given in our authorities. According to Suetonius[2] the qualification

was at first 800,000, later 1,200,000 HS. Dio[3] says that in 18 B.C.
Augustus laid down the figure of 400,000 HS, the equestrian
census, in fact, which must always have been in practice required,
and that this was raised before 13 B.C. to 1,000,000 HS.[4] He later,
however, mentions that Augustus in A.D. 4 made up the census
of certain impoverished senators to 1,200,000 HS,[5] Suetonius'
higher figure. Tacitus,[6] on the other hand, speaks of grants of
1,000,000 HS in similar cases under Tiberius. Whatever the figure
it was hardly likely to prove an impediment to the kind of new
men whom Augustus favoured, 'omnem florem ubique coloniarum ac municipiorum, bonorum scilicet virorum et locupletium'.[7] The census qualification was useful rather in eliminating
impoverished and disreputable scions of noble families; Augustus
could and did maintain the status of families of which he approved
by private benefactions.

In one passage, it is true, Dio[8] does speak of the census qualification as being a deterrent. In 13 B.C. owing to the increase of the
senatorial census from 400,00 to 1,000,000 HS, 'no one was any
longer to be found willing to be a senator, but even some sons
and descendants of senators, some genuinely poor, others humbled
by their ancestors' misfortunes, not only did not claim the rank of
senator, but resigned when already enrolled'. This may be
accepted as a rather exaggerated statement: the emphasis is, it
may be noted, on impoverished members of old families. Dio's
further statement that Augustus compulsorily enrolled men
under thirty-five possessing the requisite census appears to be an
error.[9]

It is usually stated that aspirants to the Senate, if not sons of
senators, had to obtain the *latus clavus* from the emperor before
they could stand for the quaestorship. This is certainly true for the
Flavian period, and, if we accept a scandalous story told by
Suetonius[10] of Vespasian, for Nero's reign. But it is very doubtful
if any such rule existed under Augustus. Suetonius[11] tells us that
Augustus allowed senators' sons to assume the *latus clavus* and
attend sessions of the Senate—as spectators—as soon as they

came of age. Dio[12] found in his authorities a statement that Gaius filled up the equestrian order, depleted under Tiberius, with provincials, and gave to some of them the *latus clavus* as an indication that they might stand for the quaestorship. He adds his own inference that hitherto presumably only sons of senators had been allowed to wear the *latus clavus*.

Contemporary evidence is difficult to reconcile with this picture. In the early years of the 'restored Republic' Ovid[13] and his brother, who were of equestrian family, assumed the *latus clavus* on coming of age—

> liberior fratri sumpta mihique toga est
> induiturque humeris cum lato purpura clavo.

He then held one of the minor magistracies—his brother died prematurely—and

> curia restabat: clavi mensura coacta est:
> maius erat nostris viribus illud onus.

It is perhaps possible that, if the *latus clavus* was a gift from Augustus, Ovid could have failed to record this fact, but it is extremely unlikely, and the passage implies that young men who aspired to the Senate normally advertised their ambition by assuming the *latus clavus*. An anecdote told of Augustus himself[14] suggests that, for senators' sons at any rate, this practice went back to the later Republic; for we are told that when the young Octavius came of man's estate, the tunic with the broad purple stripe which he then first put on slipped from his shoulders. I suggest that under the late Republic the custom had grown up whereby the sons of senators and others who aspired to the Senate put on the *latus clavus* with their *toga virilis*, and that Augustus confirmed this practice for senators' sons, but banned it for others. He thereby made it understood that it was the right—and perhaps the duty—of senators' sons to follow in their fathers' footsteps, as had, of course, been the normal practice in the past. But it can hardly be inferred that he thereby deprived *novi homines* of their right to stand for the quaestorship. It is, however, not unlikely

that ambitious young men not of senatorial family may have
applied to Augustus for special leave to wear the *latus clavus*, and
so a custom may have grown up, which later hardened into a
rule.[15]

Whatever the effect of the property qualification, and whether
or no the *latus clavus* existed in its later sense, it may be asked
whether in fact there was a sufficient number of candidates to
make the elections a reality. Dio on various occasions records an
insufficiency of candidates to fill certain offices. In 13 B.C. there
was trouble over the vigintivirate,[16] and in 13 and 12 B.C. and
again in A.D. 12 over the tribunate of the plebs,[17] and in A.D. 5
over the aedileship.[18] Now these offices had not been necessary
steps in the *cursus honorum* under the Sullan Lex annalis. By A.D. 23
the vigintivirate had become obligatory,[19] and in the later
Principate either the tribunate of the plebs or the aedileship had
to be held by a plebeian between the quaestorship and the praetorship.[20] It is a reasonable inference that under Augustus these three
offices were still, as in the late Republic, optional. That in these
circumstances there should have been little competition for them
under the 'restored Republic' is understandable. They were not a
necessary step to the real prizes, the praetorship and above all the
consulate, and they gave little opportunity under the new régime
for their holders to win popularity. Tribunes of the plebs could
no longer endear themselves to the people by proposing attractive
bills, the aediles had surrendered the conduct of the games, their
main source of popularity, to the praetors as early as 22 B.C.,[21]
and had by A.D. 5, when a shortage of candidates is first recorded,
lost most of their other duties, including the control of the fire
brigade—whereby Egnatius Rufus had made his name, and
secured his praetorship, and aspired to the consulate in 19 B.C.[22]

There is no indication that there were not always enough
candidates for the quaestorship. Dio[23] tells us that in 24 B.C. there
were not enough quaestors for all the provinces, but this was
presumably because too many of the twenty were occupied with
other duties at home. There was certainly no shortage of

candidates for the praetorship. The number of praetors was raised from eight in 27 B.C. to ten in 23 B.C.[24] and twelve in the last years of the reign;[25] the Senate pressed Tiberius to increase the number further.[26] In A.D. 11 there were sixteen candidates for the twelve places, and the struggle was so bitter that Augustus allowed them all to hold office.[27] There was naturally even greater pressure for the consulate. It is significant that it proved impossible to keep to the old rule, revived in 27 B.C., of having two consuls only; inconsistent though they were with 'prisca illa et antiqua reipublicae forma', suffect consuls became regular again from 5 B.C.[28]

That the Princeps exercised a certain influence over the elections no one, of course, can deny. As consul from 27 to 23 B.C. and, as I hold, from 19 B.C. in virtue of his *consulare imperium*, Augustus possessed, concurrently with his colleague in the earlier period, and with the consuls in the later, the right of *nominatio*, that is of receiving the *professiones* of candidates to the magistracies of the Roman people;[29] he presumably had similar rights with regard to the tribunate and aedileship of the plebs in virtue of his *tribunicia potestas* from 23 B.C. This power of accepting *professiones* was sometimes held to imply the right of refusing them; but this negative power was, it would seem, rarely exercised, and the candidates and the assembly did not always accept the consul's ruling; when Sentius Saturninus in 19 B.C. forbade candidates whom he considered unworthy of the quaestorship to make their *professio*, they declared that they would stand none the less, and he had to threaten to use his *consularis vindicta* if they appeared on the Campus. Egnatius Rufus, a candidate for the consulship, also insisted on standing, and in his case Saturninus was reduced to swearing that he would not return him, even if he were elected by the votes of the people.[30] Augustus' outstanding *auctoritas* would no doubt have enabled him to exercise a more effective censorship on candidates, had he wished, but there is no evidence that he did so, still less that he used his power of *nominatio* to make the elections a mockery by accepting only so many *professiones* as there were places to fill.

D

There remains the Princeps' power of *commendatio*. This is first explicitly mentioned immediately after Augustus' death, when Tiberius confined himself to commending four candidates for the twelve praetorships—'moderante Tiberio ne plures quam quattuor candidatos commendaret sine repulsa et ambitu designandos'.[31] Later emperors are recorded to have exercised a similar right in respect of the quaestorship, aedileship, and tribunate of the plebs[32]—under Augustus it would hardly have been required for the two latter offices, which it was difficult to fill at all. It was apparently only very exceptionally applied to the consulate: it is in fact only mentioned once in an inscription,[33] where the words 'per [commendation.] Ti. Caesaris [Augusti] ab senatu [cos. dest.]' depend on a sixteenth-century transcript.

Here again as with the *latus clavus* we probably have to deal with a custom hardening into a rule. According to Suetonius,[34] Augustus 'quoties magistratuum comitiis interesset tribus cum candidatis suis circuibat supplicabatque more solemni'. He acted, in fact, as any Republican *suffragator* had always done. According to Dio,[35] he continued this practice until A.D. 8, when owing to his failing health, he abandoned a personal canvass, and instead posted a list of candidates whom he specially recommended to the plebs and populus. Candidates whom Augustus thus 'commended' to the Roman People, or to whom he gave or promised his *suffragatio*—this is the phrase used in the Lex de imperio Vespasiani[36]—were no doubt in fact pretty sure of being elected, but it is a little difficult to see how their return *sine repulsa* could have been formally guaranteed in an election where voting was by secret ballot. Yet by the end of the reign this was apparently the case. The wording of the Lex de imperio Vespasiani may give the clue, 'eorum comitis quibusque extra ordinem ratio habeatur'. A practice was established, I suggest, that at each *comitia* the presiding officer first read out the names of Caesar's candidates, and that a vote was taken on them *extra ordinem*; when they had been elected *nem. con.* the genuine election for the remaining candidates and places followed. It is noteworthy that no precedent is cited for this privilege in the Lex de imperio Vespasiani. This may be because the unlimited power of *commendatio* granted by this law was unprecedented, but it is, I think, more likely that no previous formal grant was on record because *commendatio* had hitherto been a matter of custom.

Be that as it may, it would seem that Augustus used his *auctoritas* as a *suffragator* sparingly, commending to the populus and to the plebs only a small number of candidates for the lower magistracies, and rarely if ever bringing his weight to bear on the consular elections. Occasionally, as the result of serious disorders, he intervened decisively. In 19 B.C. he appointed Quintus Lucretius to the vacant consulship,[37] and in A.D. 7 owing to prolonged disorders, he appointed all the magistrates.[38] But these were exceptional cases, noted as such by Dio. Dio also records that in 28 B.C. and often afterwards Augustus appointed the urban praetor.[39] This is so uncharacteristic of Augustus' general policy, and in particular of his policy at this date, when he was carrying through the restoration of the Republic, that one may legitimately ask whether Dio has not misunderstood his authority. May it not be that the *iurisdictio urbana*, instead of being allocated by lot, was assigned to one of the praetors designate 'extra sortem auctoritate Augusti ex senatus consulto'?

We may now trace what is recorded of the elections themselves. The regular procedure for the election of magistrates was certainly restored in 27 B.C.: as Suetonius[40] says, 'comitiorum quoque pristinum ius reduxit'. Dio[41] gives a fuller account, which is, however, to be taken rather as a description of electoral procedure under the early Principate generally. 'The populus and the plebs again met for the elections. Nothing, however, was done of which he did not approve. He himself chose and commended some of the future magistrates, others he left to the choice of the populus in the old way, but took precautions against the election of unsuitable persons and against canvassing and bribery.'

It has been argued [42] that between 27 and 23 B.C., when Augustus himself was chosen consul each year with a reliable adherent as a colleague, the consular elections at any rate must have been carefully stage-managed. I see no reason to assume this. To take the most cynical view, it is likely that Augustus' propaganda—the war in defence of Italian traditions against the threatened oriental invasion, crowned by the victory at Actium, the clemency with which that victory was followed, and finally the restoration of the Republic—was during these years highly successful, and that the *comitia* were spontaneously eager to elect the great leader and the colleague of his choice. This view is confirmed by the events which followed his resignation of the consulate in 23 B.C., the repeated offer by the people of a dictatorship or a perpetual consulship,[43] and their insistence on electing him consul though he was not a candidate.[44] No one could claim that the elections were 'managed' between 23 and 19 B.C., when disorders were so violent that the State was twice left with only one consul; it was in these years that Egnatius Rufus, having made himself a popular hero as aedile, in defiance of constitutional rules pressed on not only to the praetorship but almost to the consulate.[45]

When Augustus returned in 19 B.C., order was restored, but in the following year he thought it necessary to pass the Lex Iulia de ambitu, which greatly increased the penalties for electoral corruption.[46] Candidates would hardly have wasted money on bribing the electorate, if the elections were *de facto* managed by Augustus. And bribery was still rife in the consular elections, which Augustus is supposed to have controlled absolutely, as late as 8 B.C., when Augustus demanded a deposit from all candidates, to be forfeited if they employed corrupt practices.[47] Suetonius[48] records that Augustus regularly tipped the members of his own two tribes, Scaptia and Fabia, 1,000 HS per head on election days, in the hope that they would feel less inclined to accept bribes from the candidates. Finally in A.D. 7 electoral riots were so violent that Augustus had to nominate all the magistrates himself.[49] But this brings us down to a date later than the Lex Valeria Cornelia of A.D. 5, whose existence the *Tabula Hebana* has revealed.

The *Tabula Hebana* is a piece of legislation by reference, and in some vital sections a very large proportion of the text is lost. It is therefore doubly difficult to reconstruct the Lex Valeria Cornelia to which it so often refers. I need not enter into details, since Professor Tibiletti has to my mind elucidated the major issues so far as the condition of the text allows. The law created ten centuries of C. and L. Caesar, in which senators and 'equites omnium decuriarum quae iudiciorum publicorum causa constitutae sunt erunt' voted 'de consulibus praetoribus destinandis'. Professor Tibiletti has, I think, demonstrated two points. First,[50] the ten centuries having all voted, the result of the vote of each century, that is, the two consuls and twelve praetors which it had 'destined', was announced in an order determined by lot. But as each candidate secured an absolute majority, that is six centuries, he was declared 'destined' by the ten centuries, so that finally a list of two consuls and twelve praetors 'destined' by the ten centuries of C. and L. Caesar was produced. This argument depends on the peculiar procedure of Roman elections, whereby the declaration of the votes ceased when a sufficient number of the candidates to fill the places had been elected by a bare majority of the voting units. The result of this procedure was that the order in which the votes of the units was declared might in marginal cases be decisive, and that order was therefore fixed by lot. If no consolidated result of the vote of the ten centuries was declared, it would have been natural to declare the separate votes of each century in their order of precedence—the first of C. Caesar, the second of C. Caesar, and so on, and then the first of L. Caesar down to the fifth of L. Caesar. The fact that results were declared in an order fixed by lot proves that they contributed to a final consolidated vote.

Secondly,[51] Professor Tibiletti has demonstrated that the vote of the ten centuries of C. and L. Caesar was somehow fitted into a vote of a larger number of centuries, presumably a vote of the *comitia centuriata* as a whole. This argument depends on the interpretation and reconstruction of the very defective and much disputed sentence 'isque numerus centuriarum qui h. r. adicitur in nu[merum . . . pro]inde cedat atq. eum numerum qui X centuriarum est cedere ex lege quam Cinna e[t Volesus cos. tuler. cautum est] comprehensumve est uti cedat': Professor Tibiletti convincingly argues that this clause must mean that the five centuries of Germanicus Caesar are counted among the whole total of centuries in the same way that the ten centuries of C. and L. Caesar are counted in that total. It follows from this that the vote of the ten centuries was not decisive, that the two persons 'destined' by them as consuls, and the twelve 'destined' as praetors, were not the only candidates presented to the *comitia centuriata*, whom they were therefore bound to elect. The vote of the ten centuries was rather a reinforced *praerogativa*, whereby a preselected list of candidates came before the *comitia* with the double advantage over all others that each already had ten votes in his pocket, and that these votes represented the choice of the two highest orders in the State, the Senate and the equites.

Professor Tibiletti [52] propounds the hypothesis that *destinatio* of this type had been exercised by the Senate (without the equites) as early as 5 B.C., and indeed from the original settlement in 27 B.C. This view is based on the statement in the *Res Gestae*:[53] 'Gaium et Lucium Caesares honoris mei causa senatus populusque Romanus annum quintum et decimum agentis consules designavit ut eum magistratum inirent post quinquennium.' But it is surely pressing Augustus' exact words too strictly to insist that the Senate must have taken part in the actual election. The Senate would have had to contribute to the result by voting that Gaius and Lucius should be released from the Lex annalis, and would furthermore have had to vote that their *designatio* should take place five years before they would enter on office. This is surely enough to justify Augustus' mention of the Senate in this passage. And while the language of the *Tabula Hebana* does not prove that *destinatio* was first introduced by the Lex Valeria Cornelia, it strongly implies it.

I take it that in A.D. 5 Augustus introduced a new stage into the procedure for electing the consuls and praetors. Henceforth there was a preliminary vote by ten special centuries, composed of senators and equites of the judicial decuries, which would give a strong lead to the *comitia centuriata*. The method employed for introducing this reform, by making it a part of the honours paid to the recently deceased princes, Gaius and Lucius, is curious, but I hope that what I have already said will have convinced readers that the electoral provisions of the Lex Valeria Cornelia are not likely to have been mere pious flummery to keep their memory green. These provisions dealt with a living and actual problem, and are likely to have been politically important. That they excited violent controversy is shown by the commotions which only two years later, in A.D. 7, prevented the elections from being completed.[54] I venture to suggest that Augustus had the electoral reform inserted into the honours paid to Gaius and Lucius with the precise object of stifling opposition. Respect for the feelings of the bereaved father would have forbidden any controversy over the bill.

To understand the political significance of the reform it is necessary to consider the composition of the ten centuries, and in particular the number and character of the equites, to whom most commentators have hitherto given scant attention. It may be noted in the first place that the equites who voted in the ten centuries were not the *equites equo publico* who were enrolled in the eighteen centuries or six *turmae*. This was only natural, for the *equites equo publico* were mostly young men under thirty-five,[55] ill fitted for grave political responsibility. But it has generally been held, on the strength of a sentence in Pliny the Elder,[56] 'equitum nomen subsistebat in turmis equorum publicorum,' that under Augustus there were no equites save the *equites equo publico*. Pliny is, however, certainly wrong. A clause in the *Tabula Hebana* distinguishes between 'ii qui equom pub. habebunt' and 'ii qui ordini [equestri adscripti nec publicum eq]uum habebunt'; however one restores the second phrase, it clearly implies the existence of members of the equestrian order other

than the *equites equo publico*.[57]  Another inscription which records
the careers of two men, P. Vergilius Laurea and P. Vergilius
Paullinus, probably brothers, is even more relevant to our
purpose.[58]  For the former is described as 'praef. fabr. iudici de
IIII decuriis equiti selectorum publicis privatisq.' and the latter as
'equo publico iudici de IIII decur. praef. fabrum'.  If Laurea had
held the public horse like his brother, he could hardly have
omitted to state the fact; yet he describes himself as *eques
selectorum*.

The qualifications for ranking as an eques without the public
horse may be inferred from a *senatusconsultum* passed in A.D. 23
reaffirming and perhaps tightening up the qualifications for
wearing the gold ring; for the gold ring was known as the *anulus
equester*.[59]  They are: 'qui ingenuus ipse ingenuo patre avo
paterno HS $\overline{\text{CCCC}}$ census fuisset et lege Iulia theatrali in
quattuordecim ordinibus sedisset.'  A seat in the first fourteen
rows of the theatre was an equestrian privilege—

> sedilibusque magnus in primis eques
> Othone contempto sedet,

as Horace[60] remarks of a wealthy freedman—and this privilege
was conditional, as the Horatian passage shows, on free birth, and
also on an 'equester census': Suetonius [61] tells us how a number of
equites, impoverished in the civil wars, were afraid to sit in the
first fourteen rows until Augustus ruled that the 'poena theatralis'
should not be exacted from those 'quibus ipsis parentibusve
equester census umquam fuisset'.  When Strabo [62] says : 'I have
heard that at one of the censuses in our time five hundred men of
Gades were assessed as equites,' he is clearly referring not to men
given the public horse, but to men of a certain census qualification.

The equites in the ten centuries had then to be citizens of free
birth—perhaps for three generations back—and assessed at
400,000 HS at least.  We must turn to the other half of the
qualification, 'omnium decuriarum quae iuduciorum publicorum
causa constitutae sunt erunt'.  Under the late Republic there had

been three *decuriae*, consisting of senators, equites, and *tribuni aerarii*;[63] Caesar had abolished the third;[64] but under Augustus there were again three. To these Augustus added a fourth 'ex inferiore censu quae ducenariorum vocaretur iudicaretque de levioribus summis';[65] this was in A.D. 4, when Augustus held a census of all citizens resident in Italy who were assessed at 200,000 HS or more.[66] This fourth decury then does not concern us, since it did not contain equites, and moreover, since it dealt with minor monetary cases, cannot have been 'iudiciorum publicorum causa'. Did the three older decuries consist, as under the late Republic, of senators, equites, and *tribuni aerarii* respectively? Probably not, for Suetonius'[67] statement that Augustus, to relieve the burden on the *iudices*, allowed each decury in rotation a year off duty, strongly implies that the three decuries—the system of rotation cannot of course, have applied to the fourth decury of *ducenarii*—were uniform in composition; for it would be very odd if in one year capital cases were tried by a jury of, say, senators and equites, and the next by one of equites and *tribuni aerarii*.

Our major witness on the composition of the *decuriae iudicum* under Augustus, Pliny the Elder,[68] is unfortunately very confused. The passage in question is primarily concerned with the use of the gold ring, the *anulus equester* which, Pliny says, was formerly granted for a military horse, but now for a monetary qualification. This, he asserts, was a recent change. 'Divo Augusto decurias ordinante maior pars iudicum in ferreo anulo fuit, iique non equites sed iudices vocabantur; equitum nomen subsistebat in turmis equorum publicorum.' This is, as we have seen, false; the gold ring and the title of Eques were in fact in Augustus' day shared by all citizens of free birth and equestrian census. Pliny goes on to say that in Augustus' day there were only four decuries, and barely a thousand in each decury, and that provincials were not yet admitted. 'Decuriae quoque ipsae,' he continues, 'pluribus discretae nominibus fuere, tribunorum aeris et selectorum et iudicum. praeter hos etiamnum nongenti vocabantur ex omnibus selecti ad custodiendas suffragiorum cistas in comitiis, et divisus hic quoque ordo erat superba usurpatione nominum cum alius se nongentum, alius selectum, alius tribunum appellaret.'

It is difficult to make much of this jumble of garbled information. The 900 *custodes* of the ballot boxes at the elections, who were, according to Pliny, chosen from all the decuries—their number implies from the three senior—need not detain us.[69] The term *selecti* seems in late Republican[70] and Augustan[71] usage to denote the whole body of *iudices* who served in the *iudicia publica*. They are sometimes mentioned in later inscriptions as if they were an elite among the 'iudices ex quattuor'—from Gaius onwards 'quinque'[72]—'decuriis'. This is suggested by such variants from the usual 'iudex ex V decuriis' as 'iudex selectus ex V decuriis'[73] or 'iudex ex V decuriis inter selectos'.[74] Especially significant are 'ex V decuriis decuriarum III'[75] and 'iudex selectus decuriis tribus'[76] (at a date when there were five decuries), which strongly suggest that the *selecti* were the members of the three superior decuries, as opposed to the plain *iudices* of the later fourth and fifth decuries, one of which, and probably both, had a lower census qualification. Finally 'iudex CCCC Romae decuriarum V'[77] or 'ex quinque decuriis iudicum inter quadringenarios'[78] together with 'iudex CCCC selectus'[79] suggests that the distinguishing mark of the *selecti* was the equestrian census. This is confirmed by the early inscription already quoted 'iudex de IIII decuriis eques selectorum publicis privatisque', and almost clinched by a sentence in Seneca,[80] 'iudex ex turba selectorum quem census in album et equestris hereditas misit'. In Nero's reign the qualification for a *iudex selectus* was the equestrian census.

Pliny would appear to be right therefore in asserting that in the Augustan decuries there was a distinction between the *selecti* and the other *iudices*, and that not all *iudices* were equites, but the evidence suggests that the members of the three superior decuries were all *selecti* and equites, in the sense of holding the equestrian census, and that only the fourth decury consisted of mere *iudices* of a lower *census*. But he mentions yet another distinction, the *tribuni aerarii.* They never appear again. They may perhaps have been revived after their suppression by Caesar, but if so the revival seems to have been short-lived: it is perhaps more probable that Pliny is confusing late Republican with Augustan memories.[81]

Finally it may be asked did senators still serve as *iudices*? There is no record of their doing so under the Principate, and Mommsen[82] inferred *ex silentio* that they did not. The inference is by no means certain. Pliny does not, it is true, speak of them in the passage discussed above, but as this is primarily concerned with the gold ring, they were not strictly relevant to his argument. In the inscriptions senators never record membership of the decuries, as do persons of lower degree; but for them it was no distinction, and for others it was. In literature the *decuriae iudicum*, which is always the official term, are sometimes called *decuriae equitum*;[83] but senators would have been a small minority if distributed, as they must have been if they served at all, among three decuries each a thousand strong. It seems at first sight uncharacteristic of Augustus, who did so much to restore the prestige of the Senate, to take from the order the judicial powers to which it had attached so much importance in the last century of the Republic. But judicial service came during his reign to be regarded as a burden rather than a privilege,[84] and he may well have relieved senators, who found regular attendance at the sessions of the House a nuisance,[85] of the additional obligation of serving as jurors. The Lex Iulia iudiciaria[86] (or the leges Iuliae iudiciorum publicorum et privatorum)[87] may have included in its provisions a thorough reorganisation of the *iudices selecti*, and what it did, I suggest, was to establish the three *decuriae*, each a thousand strong, consisting of equites, in the sense of ingenuous citizens with a census of at least 400,000 HS.

This, in my opinion, was the body which shared with the senators the right of voting in the ten centuries of C. and L. Caesar. It was admirably adapted for the purpose. The equites of the decuries were not only by definition men of substance.

They were of mature years—the minimum age limit was at first 35, later reduced to 30.[88] They were picked, by the emperor himself[89] or a small senatorial commission,[90] for their probity and judgment. They could therefore be expected to exercise their franchise responsibly. They had, moreover, to be domiciled in Italy,[91] and, from the nature of their duties, had to spend much of their time in Rome. They could therefore be counted upon to attend the elections. They would thus be the preponderating body in the ten centuries: at full strength they would outnumber the senators by five to one; and even if under the later system of rotation[92] only two-thirds were in Rome to record their votes, it must be remembered that at any given time something approaching a sixth of the senators would be absent in the provinces.[93] It was clearly the equites who, under the new system, if Augustus' hopes and wishes were to be realised, would dominate and direct the praetorian and consular elections.

These equites were, it may be noted, the very type of men whom, according to Claudius, his uncle the divine Augustus wished to see in the Senate—to quote his words once again, 'omnem florem ubique coloniarum ac municipiorum, bonorum scilicet virorum et locupletium.'[94] Merely to enter the Senate was probably not very difficult for them, and the Princeps could by *commendatio* push a selected few as far as the praetorship, as Velleius Paterculus and his brother were pushed in the last year of the reign.[95] Augustus seems, however, to have been reluctant to commend to the consulate. The new voting procedure seems admirably designed to get over this difficulty. The ten centuries, dominated by *equites municipales*, would be able to give a strong *praerogativa* to the *comitia centuriata* in favour of candidates from their own ranks who aspired not only to the praetorship, but to the consulate itself. The Lex Valeria Cornelia would have achieved in another way much the same result as the other electoral reform which Augustus contemplated, according to Suetonius,[96] but did not put into force, of enabling the decurions of his twenty-eight Italian colonies to record their votes by post. By this means, too, close on 3,000 voters from the Italian upper class would have been given a privileged position in the elections.

How far do the known results of the consular elections bear out this analysis? This is a problem of prosopography and as I am not an adept in that science, I would hesitate to attack it, were it not that experts in that field have already provided an answer. They have noted[97] that in the middle years of Augustus' reign, from 18 B.C. to A.D. 4, *nobiles* preponderate to a marked degree in the consular *fasti*: *novi homines* very rarely appear, and there are not many consuls from the new nobility which had been created in the triumviral period. This they attribute to the policy of Augustus. It is rather, I submit, to be attributed to the normal working of the electoral system. During the late Republic the *nobiles*, by means which are not altogether clear, but included patronage and bribery, had been consistently able to manage the *comitia centuriata*: it was only by a concerted effort that in a few isolated years the First Triumvirate had been able to put through the election of their candidates. When normal elections had been restored, and Augustus' initial popularity had worn off, the *nobiles*, I submit, regained their hold.

From A.D. 4 to the end of the reign, the prosopographical experts[98] note that *novi homines* and men of recently ennobled families are noticeably commoner in the consular *fasti*. This again they attribute to direct intervention. According to one view, Professor Syme's, the change was due to the return of Tiberius, who according to the tradition of the Claudii favoured new men. According to another, that of Professor Marsh, Tiberius favoured the *nobiles*, but being away on the frontiers, was unable to make his influence felt until the last year or two of the reign, when Professor Marsh detects a swing towards the *nobiles*. The author of the change was, according to him, Augustus himself, who felt the need for consulars better fitted than the *nobiles* for the urgent military tasks of this decade. A simpler explanation is, I suggest, the operation of the new electoral procedure enacted by the Lex Valeria Cornelia in A.D. 5.

It remains to consider what happened in A.D. 14, when on Augustus' death, according to Tacitus, 'tum primum e campo comitia ad patres translata sunt.'[99] That the Lex Valeria Cornelia was still in operation is shown by the fact that it was amended by the *Tabula Hebana* after Germanicus' death in A.D. 19, five additional centuries being created in his honour, and fragments survive of yet another law which added five more centuries in honour of Drusus on his death in A.D. 23.[100] No more is heard of *centuriae Caesarum* after this date, but there seems no reason why the formal procedure should not have continued as long as the *comitia centuriata* went on holding the ceremonial of elections.[101] But this is no reason for doubting the truth of Tacitus' statement that in the first year of Tiberius the real election was transferred from the *comitia* to the Senate. Here I agree with Professor Tibiletti[102] that Tacitus cannot have been mistaken on so important and public a change, but I would go further than he in my faith in Tacitus. Professor Tibiletti thinks that in A.D. 14 the vote of the ten centuries of the Caesars was made binding on the *comitia*, in that henceforth the presiding magistrate nominated to it only the candidates 'destined' by the ten centuries, which in default of others it was bound to elect. This he thinks is what Tacitus rather loosely describes as 'a campo comitia ad patres translata sunt'. To this view I would object that the ten centuries, in which equites outnumbered senators by about five to one, could hardly be termed 'patres', and that the narrative of Tacitus clearly implies that the elections were held at a regular session of the Senate in which other business was transacted, including a decision that tribunes of the plebs should celebrate the newly established *ludi Augustales*, and should receive a treasury grant for the purpose.[103]

What did happen in A.D. 14 was, I suggest, that Tiberius proposed to the Senate that they should settle among themselves who should be candidates for the various magistracies: that the House itself should reduce the number of candidates to equal the number of places to be filled, so that the elections both by the ten centuries and by the full *comitia* would become a formality. For the majority of the offices—the aedileship, tribunate of the plebs, praetorship, and consulate—where the candidates were necessarily members of the House, this procedure would present no difficulty. But for the vigintivirate and the quaestorship also the majority of the potential candidates would be senators' sons, for whose obedience their fathers could answer, and the few outsiders would no doubt be under some senator's patronage. In the last resort the presiding magistrate could refuse to nominate candidates not approved by the Senate. The change could thus have been brought about without any formal legislation.

Tacitus gives us a few details of the new electoral procedure. Tiberius limited himself to commending four candidates for the praetorship, who were to be elected without canvass, and without the possibility of rejection. He also, according to Tacitus, 'candidatos praeturae duodecim nominavit, numerum ab Augusto traditum; et hortante senatu ut augeret, iure iurando obstrinxit se non excessurum'. What Tacitus intended these words to mean, I am not certain, but what his source must have stated was that Tiberius refused to raise the number of praetorships above twelve, the figure fixed by Augustus.[104] More than twelve candidates might be, and commonly were, nominated for the twelve places; under Nero competition was so embittered that the emperor had to resolve the conflict by appointing the three disappointed candidates to legionary legations.[105] For the lower offices likewise elections were often, if not normally, contested. Under Gaius, Vespasian failed in his first candidature for the aedileship, and only scraped in sixth in his second.[106] The younger Pliny in his letters solicits support for candidates whom he was backing[107]—in one case for the tribunate of the plebs—and speaks of corrupt practices by candidates,[108] and of the unseemly uproar of the elections in his day, which he contrasts with the dignified procedure of the past:[109] he also records the introduction of the secret ballot in the elections.[110] Up to and including the praetorship the elections in the Senate were a reality down to the early second century at least.

The consulate, on the other hand, had by then, and indeed as early as Nero's reign,[111] come to be managed by the emperor, who in effect commended for all the places. Tacitus evidently assumed that this was already the case in Tiberius' reign, but he frankly states that the evidence appears to be incompatible with this view. He had read Tiberius' speeches on the occasion of the elections,[112] and found that sometimes without mentioning the names of the candidates he described the birth and education and service of each, so that it could be gathered who they were. On other occasions he merely urged the candidates, without indicating who they were, not to disturb the elections by canvassing. He often stated that only those had made their *professio* to him whose names he had communicated to the consuls, but that others might also make a *professio*, if they had confidence in their popularity or their merits. Tacitus regards all this as Tiberian hypocrisy, but to an impartial reader Tiberius' speeches would surely have revealed that there were genuine contests for the consulship, and that the emperor studiously avoided giving any lead.

Cassius Dio gives an interesting picture of the elections under Tiberius under A.D. 32.[113] He, too, assumes that the Emperor then as in his own day himself arranged the consulates. 'Of those who competed for the other magistracies,' he goes on, 'he picked as many as he wished, and sent them to the Senate, commending some to it (who were elected unanimously) and leaving the others to their merits, or to agreement or sortition. And after this the appropriate candidates went to the populus or the plebs respectively, for the ancient ceremonial, as today, to be carried out in form, and were declared.' The first stage is here the *nominatio* by the emperor, who weeds out some of the competitors. The rest he sends to the Senate, a few with his *commendatio*, who are automatically elected. The picture which Dio gives of the process whereby the superfluous candidates for the remaining places were eliminated is interesting. The choice might be made on the merits of the candidates, that is by discussion and vote. But alternatively candidates might draw lots or strike bargains among themselves. A might agree to stand down to B, if next year B's brother would stand down to him, for instance. These informal arrangements were eased, as Dio explains in the next sentence, by varying the number of magistracies from year to year. 'If ever there were not enough candidates, or there was a bitterly contested election, fewer were elected'; and here I would suggest that the words 'or more' have been omitted from our text, for electing a smaller number would be no remedy for a superfluity of obstinate candidates, and in the next sentence Dio specifically states that fifteen praetors were elected in the next year, and that their number varied at this period, being sometimes as many as sixteen, sometimes as few as thirteen or fourteen. By this time Tiberius had evidently released himself from his oath to keep the praetorship at twelve.

Dio's account of Gaius' abortive attempt to revive genuine popular elections fits in well with this picture.[114] The attempt failed partly, he says, because the voters were inexperienced, but also because usually no more candidates presented themselves than there were places to fill, and if there were more aspirants than places, they made agreements among themselves. Gaius evidently prohibited a formal debate in the Senate, such as Tiberius had introduced with a view to producing an agreed list for presentation to the *comitia*, but the candidates none the less got together privately and arranged things as they had done previously.

What were Tiberius' motives in transferring the effective elections to the Senate, or what Augustus had had in mind, if Tiberius was merely posthumously carrying out a change planned by his predecessor, it is difficult to divine. The result of the change seems to have been nil. Professor Tibiletti,[115] who has carefully analysed the *fasti* from A.D. 5 to A.D. 14, and from A.D. 14 to A.D. 31, can detect no difference between them in the proportion of *nobiles* and *novi homines* elected. This is perhaps not surprising. The *nobiles* always formed numerically a small minority in the

E

full house of 600 members and it was by their *auctoritas* that they swayed its vote. It would seem that by now, with several representatives among the consulars, the new and modest senators had acquired sufficient confidence to elect one of themselves to the consulate from time to time. Senators were no doubt, as Tacitus says, glad to be relieved of the trouble and expense of canvassing and bribery, and the electorate was apathetic. If by the new system the aim of imperial policy could be achieved in a way which gratified the Senate, and at the same time eliminated the scandals of electoral disorders and corruption, so much the better.

It is generally agreed that it was one of Augustus' main objectives—and also one of his major achievements—to broaden the basis of the ruling oligarchy by the admission not only to the Senate, but to the inner ring of the *nobiles*, of new men drawn from the length and breadth of Italy. It has hitherto been held, and on the evidence available no alternative view was possible, that Augustus achieved this objective by *commendatio*, or by other less overt uses of his *auctoritas* at the elections. I have endeavoured to prove that Augustus found it impracticable or impolitic to exercise strong pressure on the elections, and the *fasti* suggest that during the middle years of his reign, when his initial popularity had receded, the *nobiles* reasserted their monopoly of the consulate. The *Tabula Hebana* has, I believe, revealed Augustus' counter-measures against the nobility, in the ingenious electoral machinery of the Lex Valeria Cornelia, whereby, although the freedom of the *comitia* was theoretically left untrammelled, a strong lead was given to it by ten centuries composed in the main of the very class whom Augustus wished to see elected to praetorships and consulates. This electoral machinery remained in effective use for less than ten years, but it seems during that period to have achieved its object. By the accession of Tiberius the monopoly of the *nobiles* had been broken, and a sufficient number of new men had been promoted to the higher ranks of the Senate to make it possible to entrust the elections to the Senate itself.

# IV

## *I APPEAL UNTO CAESAR*

# I Appeal unto Caesar

IT would appear that in the last century of the Republic Roman citizens possessed the right of *provocatio ad populum* against sentences of death or flogging not only in Rome but abroad, in Italy and the provinces, even when on military service. The best evidence for this is the fact that the right of appeal was on several occasions offered to the Latins or allies as an alternative to the citizenship. Under Flaccus' abortive bill of 125 B.C. the allies were to have the option of *civitas* or *provocatio*.[1] In 122 B.C. Livius Drusus proposed as an alternative to C. Gracchus' citizenship bill a measure which would have made it illegal to flog a Latin even on active service.[2] In the Lex Acilia successful prosecutors of Latin status were rewarded with *provocatio* if they preferred it to *civitas*.[3] Now the right of appeal would have been of very little use to Latins and allies if it could be exercised only in Rome. They must have felt the need of it mainly when on active service, on visits to the provinces, and in their own home towns as a protection against such abuses of the *imperium* by travelling magistrates as Gracchus recounted in his speeches.[4] To be an effective alternative to the citizenship the right of appeal must have afforded protection over a wider area than the city of Rome, and in one case, as we have seen, Latins were to be protected even on military service. If the right of *provocatio* offered to Latins and allies was one which would protect them wherever they went, *a fortiori* Roman citizens must have possessed as extensive a right.

If the facts were not so obscure and the text of Sallust in the crucial passage so corrupt, a test case would be that of Turpilius, who was flogged and executed for a military offence in Africa during the Jugurthine war, 'nam is civis ex Latio erat.'[5] These words must mean that the penalty could be inflicted because he was merely a Latin (and not a Roman) citizen. To interpret them as meaning that Turpilius was liable to summary punishment because he was a Roman citizen from a Latin town (and not a Latin) is absurd, since it implies that Latins were at this time more highly privileged than Romans in this vital matter.[6] The fact that Roman commanders still occasionally decimated Roman units guilty of cowardice proves only that, in moments of crisis, they ignored the law.[7] Nor does the fact that Verres executed numerous Romans and even crucified one in Sicily[8] prove that citizens in the provinces had no legal protection against the *imperium* of the governor. It has been argued that since Cicero does not in so many words assert that Verres was acting illegally, Verres' action must have come within the letter of the law.[9] But to this argument it has been justly objected that if the citizen's right of appeal existed it was unnecessary for Cicero to give chapter and verse for so obvious a fact, and would have marred the rhetorical effect of the passage.[10] Verres' defence, it appears, was to assert that the men whom he had executed were Sertorians, that is *hostes*, and that Gavius, whom he crucified, was not a citizen but a spy of the rebel slaves under Spartacus: he did not assert that he had a perfect right to execute Romans in Sicily.[11]

This privilege of the Roman citizen was reaffirmed by the Lex Iulia de vi publica, which forbade anyone vested with *imperium* or *potestas* to kill, scourge, torture, condemn or put in bonds a Roman citizen who appealed to the people, or to prevent a defendant from presenting himself in Rome within a certain time.[12] Under the Principate, appeal to the people was converted into appeal to Caesar, perhaps by the law of 30 B.C., whereby Octavian was, according to Cassius Dio, granted the *ius auxilii* of a tribune and the right to judge on appeal.[13]

The scanty evidence on the exercise of this right of appeal is conflicting. The most famous case is that of Paul. When flogged and imprisoned by the magistrates of Philippi he protested, 'They flogged us publicly, uncondemned, being Romans, and imprisoned us, and now do they let us out secretly?'[14] When threatened with flogging by the tribune at Jerusalem, he again protested, 'Are you allowed to flog a Roman, and uncondemned?'[15] Finally when Festus, the procurator, proposed to try him on the charges made by the Jews, he appealed to Caesar, and Festus, having consulted his *consilium*, allowed the appeal to go forward, and after investigating the case sent him under military escort to Rome, where he was handed over to the Praetorian Prefect.[16] From these facts it would seem that a Roman citizen was protected against arbitrary flogging without trial, and if accused could refuse to submit to trial by appealing to Caesar. If, however, he consented to be tried and was condemned, it would appear that he could lawfully be flogged and executed.

By the beginning of the second century it does not seem to have been necessary for Roman citizens to make a formal appeal; Pliny, as governor of Bithynia, sent up to Rome for trial all Christians who were citizens.[17] Later in the century it seems to have become the practice for a provincial governor to refer capital charges against Roman citizens to the emperor, keeping the accused in custody meanwhile, and to execute the emperor's sentence when it was received. This emerges from the story of the persecution at Lyons under Marcus Aurelius told by Irenaeus.[18] Here the legate on his own authority condemned to the beasts some of those who confessed. One of the prisoners, Attalus of Pergamum, was actually being marched round the amphitheatre when the legate was informed that he was a Roman. He was forthwith removed and put into custody in the company of others about whom the legate had written to the emperor and was awaiting his reply. It would appear that these prisoners included other Romans, and also persons who had denied Christ, but had been rearrested, probably on charges of cannibalism and incest which came up later in the investigation. The emperor's reply was to uphold Trajan's ruling, that those who confessed should be executed but those who denied should be released. Accordingly the legate re-examined the accused and when they remained obdurate beheaded the Romans and condemned the

others to the beasts. Attalus, though a Roman, was condemned
to the beasts as a favour to the crowd. There is no suggestion in
this case or in that of the Bithynians that the prisoners lodged any
appeal: in their eagerness for martyrdom it is most unlikely that
they did.

The law was not always observed. Josephus records that
Florus, the procurator of Judaea, flogged and crucified even
Roman knights; it is clear from his comment that this action was
illegal.[19] Galba, as legate of Spain, crucified a guardian who had
poisoned his ward, 'implorantique leges et Romanum se testifi-
canti' gave him an extra high whitewashed cross;[20] here also it is
implied that Galba was exceeding his powers. Fonteius Capito,
legate of Lower Germany, when a prisoner appealed, mounted
to a higher seat, and saying, 'Plead your cause before Caesar,'
proceeded to condemn and execute him;[21] but Capito died for
this act of lèse majesté.

There are however two cases where a Roman citizen was
condemned on a capital charge by a proconsul, and the sentence
executed, but the legality of the proceedings was not challenged.
Marius Priscus, proconsul of Africa in 98-9, flogged, condemned
to the mines and finally executed a Roman knight. Pliny, who
was appointed to prosecute him in the Senate for extortion,
insisted on criminal proceedings being taken against him largely
on the strength of this case. But it is notable that Pliny does not
say that Priscus' action was a breach of the Lex Iulia de vi publica:
his charge is that Priscus had been guilty of corruption in the trial,
having been bribed by the prisoner's enemies to condemn him.[22]
The other case is that of Flavius Archippus, who was condemned
to the mines for forgery by Velius Paulus, proconsul of Bithynia
in Domitian's reign. Here again, Archippus did not challenge
the legality of his condemnation, but alleged that Domitian
had subsequently pardoned him.[23] In both these cases the accused
had every reason to appeal to the emperor, seeing that Priscus'
victim was falsely accused, and Archippus was clearly viewed with
favour by Domitian, who, if he did not, as Archippus alleged,

shortly pardon him, certainly granted him lands purchased from his privy purse.

It would seem therefore that in the second century provincial governors could in certain circumstances condemn and execute Roman citizens without appeal, but in other circumstances reserved the decision on Roman citizens for the emperor, whether they appealed or not. The distinction did not depend on the status of the accused, for one of those condemned without appeal was a Roman knight, whereas the majority of the Christians referred to the emperor were probably humble folk. The status of the governor may be more relevant, for both the judges who condemned without appeal were proconsuls, while all those against whom appeals were made or who remitted cases for trial to Rome were procurators or legates of Augustus. But one of the legates, Pliny, was specially invested with the consular power,[24] and had therefore presumably authority to do what proconsuls had done.

To explain the apparent anomaly it is necessary to turn to the lawyers of the early third century. These lawyers write of a world in which everyone—except a slave—is a Roman citizen. Appeal to the emperor is, except in the case of notable brigands, ring-leaders of sedition, or leaders of factions, when there is a threat to public order,[25] universally allowed. But this appeal is something very different from the old *provocatio*. It may be exercised in either civil or criminal cases in exactly the same form,[26] and is normally made after sentence within two or three days.[27] The judge now tries the case and gives his sentence, and then the condemned party appeals, whereas in the earlier period the judge either did not try the case at all, or at most made a preliminary investigation and left the issue to be decided by the emperor. This last procedure is now limited to decurions[28] and to cases where *deportatio in insulam* is the appropriate penalty[29]—that is, to *honestiores*. Immunity from flogging is now a privilege of decurions and no longer a right of all Roman citizens.[30] The Lex Iulia de vi publica seems in fact to have become a dead letter.

Roman citizens may be flogged, apparently without trial, and may be condemned to death, although they can appeal against this sentence, as they can against almost any judicial decision.

This result has been achieved by grant of special powers by law, *senatusconsultum* or imperial constitution to certain judges. Unlike the ordinary *imperium*, these special powers cannot be mandated by their holder, and thus a proconsul to whom they are granted cannot delegate them to his legates.[31] A legate (of a proconsul) thus possesses only the normal *imperium*, which, now that his subjects are all Roman citizens, amounts merely to *iurisdictio* with 'imperium quod jurisdictioni cohaeret'. The special powers which convey criminal jurisdiction are sometimes described in somewhat vague terms by the lawyers, as 'merum imperium', that is undiluted *imperium*,[32] 'animadvertendi coercendi vel atrociter verberandi ius' or the like,[33] but two technical terms are also used, *ius* or *potestas gladii*,[34] and *publici iudicii exercitio*.[35]

The second, it appears from Papinian, means the power which was conferred on certain magistrates by law or *senatusconsultum* to try cases coming under certain statutes, of which he cites the Lex Iulia de adulteriis. The statutes to which he alludes are the series which defined a number of crimes and set up *publica iudicia* for their trial, the Leges Corneliae de veneficiis et inter sicarios, de falso and so forth.[36] Papinian evidently believed that this practice was already current at the very beginning of the Principate, for he cites a clause of the Lex Iulia de vi, 'ut is cui optigerit exercitio possit eam si proficiscatur mandare,' as proof that magistrates could not delegate this jurisdiction in other circumstances. Whether Papinian was right it is impossible to say, since we do not know the context of the clause. The magistrate vested with these powers tried cases coming under the laws by *cognitio*, and was not bound by the procedure or the penalties enacted in them.[37]

This derogation from the citizen's right of *provocatio* would be an eminently reasonable step, and one which would naturally suggest itself as the number of Roman citizens in the provinces increased. The creation of the *iudicia publica* had effectively abolished the right of *provocatio* for certain legally defined categories of crime. It would, however, have become increasingly difficult, when there came to be large communities of Roman citizens in the provinces, to try all charges at Rome, and therefore certain magistrates were specially invested with power to try these statutory crimes without *provocatio*. Citizens both in Italy and in the provinces would be protected against arbitrary magisterial *coercitio*, but liable to trial for statutory crimes. This will explain why Paul and the Christians in Bithynia and Lugdunum could not be condemned by provincial governors, since they were not guilty of any statutory crime,[38] while on the other hand Flavius Archippus could be condemned by the proconsul of Bithynia for *falsum* under the Lex Cornelia. Marius Priscus presumably acted under similar powers: the alleged offence of his victim is not recorded.

These powers were certainly exercised by proconsuls in the reign of Domitian. The case of Galba against whom an appeal was made—though to no effect—in a case of *venificium*, implies that he had no such powers in the reign of Nero. The explanation may be that the grant of powers to provincial governors was introduced between Nero's and Domitian's reign, or that the powers were granted to proconsuls and not to *legati pro praetore*.[39] If Papinian is correct the latter alternative is to be adopted. It is not inconceivable that the empowering act, particularly if it were passed very early in the Principate, may have conveyed authority to those who held an *imperium pro consule*, including the emperor, of course, but may not have permitted the emperor, any more than any other proconsul, to delegate it to his *legati pro praetore*.

On the *ius gladii* it is difficult to reconcile the statements of the authorities. Ulpian states that it was held by all 'qui universas provincias regunt,'[40] that is proconsuls, *legati Augusti pro praetore* and praesidial procurators, as opposed to *legati pro praetore* of proconsuls, and *legati iuridici* and *legionis*, who often had charge of parts of provinces. In two passages he either closely associates or identifies it with a *merum imperium* or a general right of *animadversio* or *coercitio*.[41] Cassius Dio, on the other hand, states that the right of wearing a sword was conceded to such *legati Augusti pro praetore* as 'have the right of punishing even soldiers' ('or soldiers also'). He adds that no one, either proconsul, *legatus pro praetore* or procurator, is allowed to wear a sword 'who has not the legal right of killing even a soldier' (or 'a soldier also') and that not only senators but also knights who have this right are allowed to wear a sword.[42] As in the next chapter Dio states that proconsuls, as opposed to their legates and quaestors, have the right of putting their subjects to death, it would appear that he conceives of soldiers as a privileged class not subject to the ordinary powers of a provincial governor, and of the *ius gladii* as a special power to deal with them.

A preliminary difficulty is caused by the statement of Paulus that *tribuni militum, praefecti alarum* and *praefecti classium* were exempted from the provisions of the Lex Iulia de vi publica in order that they might be able to punish military offenders.[43] For if these junior officers could execute soldiers without appeal, why was a special grant of *ius gladii* required for army commanders? It appears also, from another passage of Dio, that even legionary legates had no power of executing *gregarii*, but had to send up their cases to the consular.[44] The explanation would seem to be that tribunes and prefects were empowered to employ the lesser means of *coercitio*—flogging and putting in irons—without appeal: actors, whom Paulus mentions in the same passage as being outside the protection of the Lex Iulia, were liable to flogging, but not, so far as we know, to summary execution.[45]

This passage indicates that soldiers were not, under the early principate at any rate, a privileged class. They were on the contrary, in the interest of military discipline, denied some of the rights of Roman citizens. The *ius gladii* will therefore have been in origin a power granted to army commanders to execute Roman soldiers, but not civilians under their jurisdiction. This conclusion is borne out by the story of the Lyons persecution. The legate of Lugdunensis had under his command an urban cohort, whose tribune and men are mentioned in the narrative, and would presumably therefore have possessed *ius gladii*; yet he could not summarily execute civilian Roman citizens.

*Ius gladii* is first mentioned in an inscription of the reign of Domitian.[46] It is however very rarely mentioned at all in inscriptions, and never in connection with those who would normally hold it, *legati Augusti pro praetore* in command of legions—and presumably the prefect of Egypt. Those who record the grant are sometimes praesidial procurators,[47] who would presumably have received it because citizen troops were temporarily stationed in their province, or officers given a special command, such as the praetorian legate who during Marcus' wars on the Danube was 'praepositus legionibus I Italicae et III[I Flaviae cum omnibus copiis] auxiliorum dato iure gladi.'[48] Since the inscriptions evidently record only extraordinary grants, we are justified in conjecturing that *ius gladii* was far older than Domitian and may well go back to the beginning of the Principate. It may be that the power μέχρι τοῦ κτείνειν which was according to Josephus[49] bestowed on the first prefect of Judaea was the *ius gladii*. If the troops under his command included the 'Italian band' (*Cohors II Italica civium Romanorum voluntariorum*)[50] it would have been desirable for him to possess the *ius gladii*.

Down to the reign of Marcus Aurelius the citizen's right of appeal would therefore seem to have suffered two derogations only, both of which are firmly attested as early as the reign of Domitian, but may well go back to the beginning of the Principate. Provincial governors, or perhaps only proconsuls, had been granted the right of trying citizens on charges covered by *leges* (or some *leges*) and of executing those whom they sentenced without appeal. Provincial governors, and in exceptional circumstances other officers, in command of Roman troops, had been granted an unlimited right of *coercitio* over citizen soldiers. In the period after the Constitutio Antoniniana all provincial governors were granted an unlimited right of *coercitio* over civilians (with the exception of decurions and other privileged categories) and some governors, presumably those normally in command of troops, possessed a similar power over soldiers (once again with the exception of the higher grades from centurion upwards).[51]

Ulpian speaks of the *merum imperium* or general power of *coercitio*, which every governor possessed over civilians, as *ius gladii*, while Dio appears to restrict this term to provincial governors who had authority over soldiers as well as civilians. Dio cannot be mistaken in his statement that not all governors possessed the right of executing soldiers.[52] He does not, however, it may be noted, expressly say that this power was called *ius gladii*, but that those governors only who possessed this right had the privilege of wearing a sword as part of their official dress. Ulpian and Dio can be reconciled on the assumption that the power of *coercitio* over civilians which was granted to all provincial governors was called *ius gladii* on the analogy of the power of *coercitio* over soldiers already held by commanders of armed provinces, but that the right of wearing the sword was restricted to those governors who possessed in addition the old *ius gladii* over soldiers.

It is, however, rather more probable that Dio is strictly correct and that Ulpian is speaking in untechnical language. For, though in popular language *ius gladii* was used to denote the power of *coercitio* against civilians—Saint Perpetua was tried and executed by 'Hilarianus procurator qui tunc loco proconsulis Minucii Timiniani defuncti ius gladii acceperat'[53]—in inscriptions *ius gladii* continues after the Constitutio Antoniniana to be used in the military sense. P. Sallustius Sempronius Victor records that he was *praeses ducenarius* of Sardinia, and that he 'held command of the peace over the whole of the sea' with *ius gladii*:[54] he claims *ius gladii* only in connection with this extraordinary naval command, not his governorship of Sardinia. T. Licinius Hierocles claims *ius gladii* in two inscriptions, once in connection with a special military command, and once as *praeses* of Mauretania.[55] The special mention of *ius gladii* in connection with his governorship is to be explained by the fact that it was rather exceptional at this date (under Severus Alexander) for a procurator to be in command of troops.[56]

The most plausible date for the universal grant of a *merum imperium* over citizens to all governors would be A.D. 212. The Constitutio Antoniniana would have made the old rules for the protection of Roman citizens quite unworkable. The *Acta* of Saint Perpetua are, however, quite definite evidence that in some provinces at any rate the *merum imperium* was granted earlier. The *Acta* are generally accepted as contemporary with the martyrdom, which took place in A.D. 203. The author assumes that the proconsul of Africa normally at this date possessed special powers (which are called *ius gladii*) under which he could try and execute Roman citizens on a charge of Christianity—which came under no *lex*—and incidentally also flog them without trial.[57] There is however no reason to believe that all provincial governors possessed this power at this date. *Merum imperium* may well have been granted to those governors whose provinces included, as did Africa, a large number of *oppida civium Romanorum*, and who therefore had to control large groups of citizens of humble status. It would hardly have been needed in the majority of provinces, where Roman citizens were relatively rare and mostly of the higher order of society.

In order to estimate the effect of the Constitutio Antoniniana and the probably concurrent grant of *merum imperium* to all provincial governors it is first necessary to discuss two developments in criminal law which had begun in the second century. One is the growth of *appellatio* in the form known to the classical jurists. An appeal could be made against a civil judgment or a capital sentence alike, under the same rules of procedure, within a time limit of two or three days. In pecuniary cases an appeal did not lie to the emperor unless the sum at issue exceeded a certain minimum,[58] and the appellant had to deposit a sum (*poena appellationis*) which he forfeited if his appeal was rejected.[59] There is no indication that there were any such checks on capital appeals, and indeed Ulpian declares that not only the prisoner but anyone was entitled to enter an appeal.[60] Paulus however states that appeals intended merely to cause delay and those by redhanded or confessed criminals were not accepted.[61] Similarly if there was a danger to public order, brigands, ringleaders of riots and such like might be executed despite appeal.[62] This right of appeal does not seem to have existed in Domitian's reign—not at any rate against the sentence of a proconsul under the *leges publicorum iudiciorum*. It is mentioned in a rescript of the Divi Fratres and a speech of Marcus Aurelius.[63] It would be interesting to know if it was available to other than Roman citizens, but here evidence is lacking.

The other development is the growing discrimination between *honestiores* and *humiliores*. In the third-century lawyers there is a different scale of penalties for every offence according to the rank of the offender. *Humiliores* are liable to be flogged, and may be burned alive, thrown to the beasts or sent to hard labour in the mines: *honestiores* are in general immune from any penalty severer than deportation to an island and confiscation of property.[64] Moreover, since (apart from the prefect of the city) only the emperor could pass sentence of *deportatio*, *honestiores* were in effect secured from the capital jurisdiction of the provincial governor, who merely investigated the charge and reported to the emperor, holding the accused in custody meanwhile. For decurions it is specifically laid down that in all capital cases the final decision must be reserved for the emperor.[65]

This discrimination did not exist in Domitian's reign, when a Roman knight was condemned to the mines, a penalty later reserved for *humiliores*. It first appears under Hadrian, who ruled that decurions should not undergo capital punishment (presumably under the Lex Pompeia de parricidiis) except for the murder of a parent, but be subject to the penalty of the Lex Cornelia (presumably de sicariis et veneficiis), that is *deportatio*.[66]

In a similar spirit Antoninus Pius decided that in cases of 'crime passionnel' *honestiores* should be relegated to an island for a limited period, *humiliores* sentenced to exile or penal servitude for life.[67] Marcus and Verus laid down the general rule that decurions of cities should be deported for capital crimes.[68] Here again one cannot be certain whether this privileged status was accorded only to Roman citizens of the rank of decurions or to all city councillors whether Romans or *peregrini*. A letter of Hadrian to Terentius Gentianus, proconsul of Macedonia, on the penalties appropriate for those who removed boundary stones, rather suggests the latter.[69] The emperor suggests *relegatio* for varying periods in the case of upper class delinquents, *opus publicum* or flogging for lesser persons: the last mentioned penalty is inapplicable to Roman citizens; and the letter therefore refers to *peregrini*.

If this is the case, the Constitutio Antoniniana will not have improved the status of those *peregrini* who were *honestiores*, since they already in virtue of their rank were immune from flogging and could not be condemned to any capital penalty without reference to the emperor. If the right of *appellatio* was reserved to Roman citizens, *peregrini* who were *humiliores* gained something by the Constitutio Antoniniana. *Humiliores* who were already Roman citizens on the other hand, by the grant of the *merum imperium* to all governors, lost their immunity from flogging and their right to have any capital charge against them referred to the emperor. Roughly speaking the final result of the series of changes which culminated in the Constitutio Antoniniana was that *honestiores* retained the privileges which had once belonged to all Roman citizens, and *humiliores* were degraded to a status slightly if at all superior to that which *peregrini* had held.

F

# V

## *IMPERIAL AND SENATORIAL JURISDICTION IN THE EARLY PRINCIPATE*

# Imperial and Senatorial Jurisdiction
# in the Early Principate

UNDER Augustus, or at any rate in the Julio-Claudian period, several forms of jurisdiction affecting Roman citizens came into existence, or into prominence, which either did not exist or were rarely to our knowledge exercised under the late Republic. Appeals (*appellationes*) to the emperor against civil judgments from both Italy and the provinces were already common under Augustus, and similar appeals to the Senate are recorded under Nero. Augustus also occasionally exercised a primary civil jurisdiction, and so apparently did the consuls in his day. In capital cases both the emperor and the Senate exercised a primary jurisdiction against which there was, it would seem, no *provocatio ad populum*: these jurisdictions are well attested under Tiberius and can be traced back to Augustus' reign. Finally in some capital cases the accused was entitled to appeal to the emperor; this right apparently replaced the ancient *provocatio ad populum*. The only attested case in the Julio-Claudian period is the appeal of Paul of Tarsus to Nero.

## Civil Appeals in the Late Republic

The judicial *appellatio* of the Principate was, as its name implies, derived from the Republican practice, whereby a citizen could appeal to (*appellare*) a tribune of the plebs or a magistrate of the Roman people to give him aid (*auxilium*) against the action of another magistrate. The tribune or magistrate thus invoked was not, of course, compelled to accede to the citizen's request, but if he did so, he exercised his *auxilium* by vetoing, either *qua* tribune or in virtue of *par maiorve potestas*, the action of the magistrate against whom the appeal had been made.

It is questionable how far this procedure was applicable to civil jurisdiction. In the formulary process, which seems to have been normally followed both in Italy and in the provinces under the late Republic, the part of the magistrate (the praetor at Rome and the governor or his delegates in a province) was limited to issuing executive orders (*decreta*), such as *missio in possessionem*, to determining the *formula* under which a case was to be tried and appointing the *iudex* who was to try it.[1] When these preliminary proceedings (*in iure*) were concluded by the *litis contestatio*, the magistrate's part was finished, and the *iudex* tried the case and gave judgment. The judgment of the *iudex*, it is generally held, was not liable to *appellatio*, since he was not a magistrate, nor strictly speaking a delegate, but, in theory, an arbitrator to whom the litigants had submitted their dispute.

There were various means whereby the judgment of the *iudex* could be annulled or rectified. It was possible for the defeated party to contest the *actio iudicati* whereby the successful party sought to obtain execution: if he was unsuccessful in thus impugning the judgment he was liable to pay double the sum in which he had been originally condemned.[2] In certain circumstances an unsuccessful litigant could apply to the magistrate for *restitutio in integrum*, whereby the trial was annulled. He might allege that the trial was vitiated by *metus*,[3] that is that the judge had been intimidated, or by *dolus*,[4] as, for instance, when the witnesses had been bribed. He might also sometimes claim *restitutio* if he had lost his case by some technical error, such as *plus petitio*.[5]

Cicero in a sentence obscure from its brevity, 'decrevit ut si iudicatum negaret, in duplum iret; si metu coactos diceret, haberet eosdem recuperatores', seems to allude to both these remedies as alternatives: the case was between two *peregrini* and took place in the province of Asia, but the proconsul—Quintus Cicero—was clearly using Roman procedure.[6] A litigant could also bring an action against the *iudex* for corruption, malice or favour, or even negligence. In such circumstances the *iudex* was said *litem suam facere*, and if condemned was liable in damages to the litigant.[7]

It may be noted that some of the procedures mentioned above resulted, or might result, in a retrial of the case, and what was in effect a reformatory judgment.[8] If a defeated litigant brought an action against the *iudex*, the court had presumably to determine whether and in what matters the *iudex* had erred in his judgment in order to assess the damages. *In integrum restitutio* was technically purely cassatory, but was often followed by a new trial. Quintus Cicero in the case mentioned above, where the defeated party alleged that *metus* had vitiated the original trial, decreed that the case should be retried by the same *recuperatores*. A litigant who had failed in his suit owing to *plus petitio* applied for *restitutio* precisely in order that he might be able to reopen his suit with a revised *formula*.[9]

None of these remedies, however, were obtained by *appellatio*. They continued to exist under the principate side by side with *appellatio*—indeed most of our information about them is derived from the imperial lawyers—and are distinguished from it.

But if no *appellatio* was possible against the decision of the *iudex*, it could be exercised against the preliminary proceedings of the magistrate, and it was at this stage, it may be argued, that an appeal was most likely to arise. By his *decreta* and by his *formula* the magistrate gave his decision on the points of law involved, and the part of the *iudex* was to find the facts and apply the law. Appeals generally arise on legal rather than on factual issues, and against corruption or unfairness on the part of the *iudex* the litigant had other remedies. The case is not quite so simple as this, for the division of the proceedings into those *in iure* and those *apud iudicem* corresponded only imperfectly with the division into issues of law and of fact. The magistrate had to make some preliminary investigation into the facts of the case in order to determine the legal issues. On the other hand the *formula* was a very brief document, and the *iudex* had often to decide complex legal issues in applying it to the case before him.

Nevertheless the proceedings *in iure* were no formality, and we know in fact of several cases in the late Republic in which appeals were made at this stage. In the complicated preliminary proceedings to the trial in which Cicero defended P. Quinctius, the latter's *procurator* Alfenus appealed to the tribunes against a decree of the praetor, and obtained partial satisfaction in that one of them, M. Brutus, threatened to interpose his veto unless the plaintiff Naevius came to a reasonable agreement with Quinctius to enable the latter to appear and plead his case.[10] In the case in which Cicero spoke on Tullius' behalf, the defendant P. Fabius, dissatisfied with the *formula* which the praetor Marcellus proposed, to which he wished the word *iniuria* to be added, appealed to the tribunes, but without success.[11] In both these cases the *auxilium* of the tribunes would have had a purely negative effect in theory, merely putting a stop to the trial, but the real object of the *appellatio* was by threatening to hold up the action to force the praetor to withdraw his decree or modify his *formula*.

In other cases appeals were made to, or *auxilium* was offered by, a praetor against another praetor in virtue of their *par potestas*. In 48 B.C. 'M. Caelius Rufus took up the cause of debtors and at the beginning of his magistracy placed his judgment seat next to the official chair of C. Trebonius, the urban praetor, and promised that if anyone appealed (*appellavisset*) on the payments which were to be made on the basis of a valuation by an arbitrator, as Caesar had ruled in person, he would come to their rescue (*fore auxilio*)'.[12] According to Caesar no one did appeal. If they had, Caelius would no doubt have been content to veto the proceedings: no further action would have been required, as he would have achieved his object of preventing creditors from collecting their debts.

Another and more interesting case is Verres' urban praetorship. Cicero tells how L. Piso, probably the *praetor peregrinus*, 'filled large numbers of ledgers with the cases in which he interceded (*intercessit*) because Verres had made a judicial ruling (*decrèvisset*) not in accord with his own edict. You have not forgotten, I expect, the crowd, the procession that used to converge on Piso's official seat when Verres was praetor. If he had not had him as a colleague, he would have been stoned in the forum. But his injuries seemed the lighter because there was in the equity and learning of Piso a ready refuge, which people used without toil or trouble or expense, without even an advocate.'[13]

Piso's action may, like that of Caelius, have been purely negative. But Cicero's praise of his equity and learning would seem to be somewhat exaggerated if all he did was in appropriate cases to hold up proceedings until his and Verres' term of office had expired. It may be that, like the tribunes, he used his power of veto to exercise pressure on Verres to change his rulings. But it does not seem impossible that he himself issued *decreta* and *formulae* to dissatisfied litigants in substitution for those of Verres which he vetoed. Whether he was entitled to do so depends on a dubious point in Roman constitutional law—or perhaps rather practice. When in the *sortitio provinciarum* C. Verres obtained the *iurisdictio inter cives* and L. Piso the *iurisdictio inter peregrinos* did this inhibit Verres from trying a case where a foreigner was involved, and Piso from acting where both parties were citizens? Or did both retain the full power of *iurisdictio* inherent in their *imperium*, and accept a *de facto* division of duties? I know of no evidence against the latter view, in which case Piso was entitled not only to veto Verres' acts, but to issue *decreta* and *formulae* of his own on the same cases. Verres could, of course, have in his turn vetoed Piso's acts, but perhaps he was not such a fool as to expose himself to ridicule by so doing.

We know also of one case where an appeal was made from a praetor to a consul. In 77 B.C. the urban praetor Orestes granted *bonorum possessio secundum tabulas testamenti* to one Genucius, a Gallus of the Magna Mater, whom Naevianus, a freedman, had made his heir. Naevianus' patron, Surdinus, appealed to Lepidus, one of the consuls, who vetoed the praetor's decree (*praetoriam iurisdictionem abrogavit*), on the ground that Genucius was neither a man nor a woman.[14] Valerius Maximus, who tells the story, speaks of Lepidus making a *decretum*. He may not be speaking technically for, as the appellant Surdinus would inherit as Naevianus' patron if the latter's will were invalidated, it would only be necessary for Lepidus to annul the praetor's decree and no further action was required. But here again there seems to be no reason to doubt that a consul could if he wished issue a decree in substitution for that which he vetoed. It seems unlikely that when the office of praetor was created to relieve the consuls of the task of administering justice, the consuls were thereby deprived of the *iurisdictio* inherent in their *imperium*. One act of jurisdiction, *manumissio vindicta*, they continued to exercise regularly as long as the consulate survived.[15] Otherwise, their powers of *iurisdictio* were normally dormant, but could, it would seem, be brought into action if a citizen appealed to them to intervene in what was normally the business of their junior colleague, the praetor.

Two other more general allusions to appeal may be cited. Cicero, applying legal terms metaphorically to a philosophical argument, says of his opponents: 'tribunum aliquem censeo adeant: a me istam exceptionem numquam impetrabunt.'[16] The imaginary case is that of the praetor whom one of the parties is urging to insert an *exceptio* in the *formula*: he refuses, and they appeal to the tribunes, who by vetoing the *formula* will bring pressure on the praetor to make the emendation. The author of the *ad Herennium*, discussing the various kinds of *ius*, distinguishes that created by judicial decisions. 'Iudicatum est id de quo sententia lata est aut decretum interpositum: ea saepe diversa sunt, ut aliud alii iudici aut praetori aut consuli aut tribuno plebis placitum sit; et fit ut de eadem re saepe alius aliud decreverit aut iudicaverit.'[17] The list of persons who thus create law is interesting in that it includes not only the praetor and the *iudex*, who interprets the *formula*, but the consul and the tribune. These two can only have acted on appeal. The tribune, it is true, possessed no formal power of *iurisdictio*,[18] and his intervention could modify the law only indirectly. The consul probably could make legal decisions, but would only do so on appeal. Both passages suggest that appeal to the tribunes was common in civil litigation, and the second provides further evidence for appeal to the consuls.

We have so far spoken only of appeals in the city of Rome. Here the process would be simpler than elsewhere, for the consuls, the tribunes and the other praetors were normally available on the spot to veto the action of the urban praetor. It may be asked whether *auxilium* might not be given at greater range to ligitants who appealed from Italy and the provinces.

In Italy all important cases had to go *ab initio* to the urban praetor at Rome. The municipal magistrates had in general jurisdiction only in minor cases, when the sum at issue was less than 15,000 sesterces.[19] In these cases there was presumably an appeal from one municipal magistrate to another. But it also seems to have been possible for a litigant to obtain a *revocatio Romae*. This is implied in a clause preserved in the *Fragmentum Atestinum*[20] which is probably part of the Lex Rubria whereby the jurisdiction of the magistrates of all newly enfranchised communities of Transpadane Gaul was regulated. The clause is retrospective, and lays down that in any private suit, whatever the amount involved, in which a duovir, or other person vested with jurisdiction by law, treaty, *senatus consultum* or custom, possessed *iurisdictio* before the Lex Roscia, the present law should not have the effect 'quo magis privato Romae revocatio sit quove minus quei ibei iuri dicundo praerit de ea re ius dicat.' This apparently means that cases already initiated under the local magistrates, when the towns were still Latin communities and therefore judicially independent, were to be carried to their conclusion by the local magistrates. And it implies that in the future, it would be possible for a litigant in a case initiated before a local magistrate of a Roman *municipium* to obtain *Romae revocatio*.

In a province the only magistrates possessing *iurisdictio* were the governor and those to whom he delegated his powers—normally his legates and his quaestor, sometimes also his *praefecti*. An appeal would naturally lie from these delegates to their chief, but, as Cicero remarks in the Verrines, there was no very practicable remedy against a 'praetor improbus, cui nemo intercedere possit', if he issued arbitrary decrees, pronounced inequitable *formulae* or appointed corrupt *iudices*.[21] In the provinces also, however, a litigant who took prudent precautions could secure a *revocatio* or *reiectio Romae*. It was not a right, it would seem. P. Scandilius, a Roman knight, instituted a *sponsio* against Apronius before Verres; objecting to the latter's choice of *recuperatores*, he demanded a *reiectio Romae* ('postulat abs te ut Romae rem reicias'), but Verres refused outright.[22] But in another case the litigant took precautions beforehand. L. Mescinius, Cicero's former quaestor, was heir to the estate of a deceased cousin, M. Mindius, a *negotiator* at Elis. Anticipating legal difficulties he got Cicero to write to Servius Sulpicius, the proconsul of Achaea, asking him to expedite his affairs. In particular Cicero asks Sulpicius to send back to Rome (*Romae reieceris*) any troublesome opponents of Mescinius. Finally, he tells Sulpicius, 'to enable you to do this with less hesitation, I have obtained a letter to you from the consul M. Lepidus, not to give you any orders ('non quae aliquid te iuberent'), for that I thought would not accord with your dignity, but if I may so put it, a letter of advice.'[23]

This letter gives a clue to the true nature of *Romae revocatio*. In asking for it a provincial litigant announced his intention of appealing from the proconsul to the consul at Rome, whose *imperium* extended to all provinces and was *maius* in relation to that of their proconsuls; for as Cicero remarks, 'omnes in consulis iure et imperio debent esse provinciae'.[24] A reasonable proconsul would no doubt usually allow the litigant to go to Rome and make his appeal, but as it was not physically possible for him to make the actual appeal except after a long delay, a stubborn proconsul would ignore his request and proceed with the trial. A litigant could only make sure of securing a *revocatio Romae* by approaching the consul beforehand, as Mescinius did through Cicero's agency, and getting from him a letter in which he informed the proconsul that he would give his *auxilium* if an appeal were made to him, and ordered him in that case to remit the case to Rome. This seems to have been the practice in the provinces. In Italy, it would appear, the Lex Rubria gave a statutory right to the litigant to obtain *Romae revocatio*: the local magistrates were in effect given standing orders to allow appeals to Roman magistrates.

There seems thus to have existed under the later Republic a rudimentary form of appeal. The appeal was made against the magistrate's acts *in iure*, against his *decreta* or the *formula* or the choice of *iudex*. In Rome, to judge by the number of cases which occur in our very limited body of evidence and by the way in which the procedure is taken for granted both in these cases and in more general allusions to ligitation, appeal was quite a common practice. In some cases the appeal was purely cassatory, but in others it caused the magistrate against whom the appeal was made to revise his decision. And in some cases it is probable that the magistrate to whom the appeal was made substituted a new decision for that which he vetoed. In Italy appeals from the local magistrates to the magistrates at Rome were apparently guaranteed by statute. In the provinces the appeal was less developed. A litigant could ask leave to appeal to the consuls, and the average proconsul would probably give him leave. But a proconsul could only be forced to allow an appeal by application in advance to the consuls.

## Civil Appeals in the Principate

Civil appeals to the emperor, both from Italy and the provinces, were already very common under Augustus. So common were they that, according to Suetonius, Augustus was unable to deal with them personally, but regularly each year delegated this appellate jurisdiction, assigning provincial appeals to men of consular rank specially appointed to deal with cases from each province, and those of *urbani litigatores* to the urban praetor.[25] Nero, according to Tacitus, ruled in A.D. 60 that those who appealed from private judges to the Senate should incur the same pecuniary risk as those who appealed to the emperor.[26] This statement shows that the emperors had already protected themselves against a deluge of frivolous appeals by demanding a *poena appellationis*, that is a deposit which was forfeited if the appeal was rejected.[27] Secondly it proves that appeals might at this date—and probably from the beginning of the Principate—be made either to the emperor or to the consuls; for, as only a magistrate could possess jurisdiction, the Senate in this context must mean the consuls using the Senate as their *consilium*.

The constitutional basis of these appeals is most naturally explained by the Republican precedents discussed above. The consuls had under the late Republic received appeals from the urban praetor and from proconsuls, and they continued to do so. Augustus, in virtue of the *consulare imperium* which he received in 19 B.C.,[28] and his successors after him, had all the powers of the consuls, and therefore could like them receive appeals from the praetor and from proconsuls. They furthermore as proconsuls of their own group of provinces received appeals from the *legati* to whom they mandated their jurisdiction in them. All appeals from the imperial provinces would thus naturally be made to the emperor. Appeals from Italy and the public provinces might constitutionally be made either to the emperor or to the consuls. Nero, indeed, on his accession announced, 'consulum tribunalibus Italia et publicae provinciae adsisterent', and his words probably allude to appeals among other things: Suetonius' statement that he ruled, 'ut omnes appellationes a iudicibus ad senatum fierent', may well be an exaggerated version of the same announcement.[29] But this was not a ruling on constitutional law, but a statement of policy. In fact most litigants preferred the emperor, and Augustus, as we have seen, did receive appeals from Italy and from the provinces in general—Suetonius makes no distinction, and in fact most appeals would have come from the public provinces, where Roman citizens were numerous, and relatively few from the imperial provinces, where they were scarce.

The increased volume of appeals must be put down to the

policy of Augustus. It must be presumed that he made it known to the public, by edict or more informally, that he and the consuls were willing to receive appeals. He no doubt definitely instructed his *legati* to allow appeals from themselves to him, and his *auctoritas*, backed by his *maius imperium*, will have been sufficient to make proconsuls yield to any litigant who expressed a wish to appeal from themselves to Augustus or the consuls. So far no constitutional or legal innovation need be assumed except the grant of *consulare imperium* to Augustus. The change is only one of practice, that the volume of appeals increases and the right of appeal becomes automatic, and this change is achieved by Augustus through his *auctoritas*.

What is to all appearances novel is that the appeals to the Senate come from *iudices* and no longer from magistrates. There can be little doubt that when Tacitus speaks of *privati iudices* (and Suetonius of *iudices*) he means the *privati iudices* of the formulary procedure, and not *iudices extra ordinem dati*. It is true that in the early Principate, as will be recorded later, the emperor, the consuls and certain special praetors had begun to try exceptional cases, or special categories of cases like *fideicommissa*, by the process of *cognitio*. It may be that they already had so much jurisdiction of this kind brought to them that they sometimes delegated a case to a *iudex extra ordinem datus*, whose sentence was appellable. It is also probably true that in the provinces *cognitio* was employed more freely: even under the Republic a provincial governor was apparently entitled to reserve cases for his personal *cognitio*,[30] and he may have delegated some *extra ordinem* to *iudices*. But it seems very unlikely that by the time of Nero—or even by that of Trajan, assuming that both Tacitus and Suetonius are being anachronistic—*cognitio* and the appointment of *iudices extra ordinem dati* can have been a regular practice, particularly in Italy and the public provinces, to which their remarks primarily refer. Gaius, writing under Antoninus Pius, assumes that the formulary procedure is invariably followed, save for such exceptional matters as *fideicommissa*.[31] In his Institutes he is

writing primarily about the praetor's court at Rome, but in the
occasional references which he makes to provincial procedure,
he assumes it to be the same;[32] and enough of his work on the
Provincial Edict survives to indicate that the procedure which
Gaius there describes was the formulary.[33] In some provinces,
it is true, *cognitio* seems to have been prevalent; the papyri have
revealed few if any examples of the formulary procedure in
Egypt, despite the fact that the prefect had the jurisdiction of a
Roman magistrate.[34] But it was probably in the more recently
acquired imperial provinces that the new procedure prevailed.
Under the Republic the formulary procedure had been generally
used in the provinces, both for Romans and for *peregrini*, and in
the provinces which dated back to the days of Republic—that is
in all the public and some of the imperial provinces—it probably
survived.

Tacitus' words must then mean that in Nero's reign appeals to
the Senate (and by implication to the emperor also) were
normally made not from the magistrate *in iure* but from the *iudex*.
Suetonius' description of the way in which Augustus handled
appeals implies that this was already the rule in his reign.
Augustus, he says, regularly each year delegated the appeals of
*urbani litigatores* to the urban praetor. The term *urbani litigatores*
probably covers Italy as well as Rome itself, for Suetonius
contrasts them with provincial litigants, and all Italy fell within
the jurisdiction of the urban praetor. The appeals in question
might therefore come from municipal courts, but as they were
only competent to deal with minor cases, it is unlikely that many
did. Any major suit had to come before the praetor at Rome, and
if the appeal were made *in iure* it would be against the praetor's
own ruling. It would have been a mockery for Augustus to
delegate to the urban praetor, as a standing rule, the trial of
appeals made to him against the praetors' own decisions. Augustus'
conduct is scarcely intelligible unless the appeals which came to
him were against *privati iudices* given by the praetor, not against
the praetor himself.

If the *iudex* had been inappellable under the Republic, this was a striking innovation. Some modern authorities have taken it as such, and have sought to explain it by the power 'to judge on appeal' (ἔκκλητον δικάζειν) given to Octavian in 30 B.C.[35] This power, as will be argued later, was probably concerned with *provocatio* in capital cases. It cannot be the explanation of civil appeals from *privati iudices* to the Senate; for it was a personal grant to Octavian.

It is, however, by no means as certain as would appear from the modern legal textbooks that the judgment of a *privatus iudex* was inappellable under the Republic. No ancient author asserts that this was the case, and the doctrine is in fact based purely on an argument from silence.[36] No appeals are recorded from the judgments of *iudices* whereas we hear of several appeals from the proceedings of magistrates. This is a rather flimsy basis for what has become a central doctrine of Roman law. In so far as the argument from silence is worth anything, it applies only to trials held in Rome itself, where our evidence is relatively abundant. Here it may be argued with some plausibility that it had been possible to appeal from a *iudex* Cicero would have alluded to such appeals. For trials in the provinces, or for that matter in Italy, our information is so slight that no negative conclusions can be drawn from it.

Gaius draws a distinction between *iudicia quae legitimo iure consistunt*, for short *legitima iudicia*, and *iudicia quae imperio continentur*.[37] The former class comprise trials before a single *iudex* between Roman citizens in Rome or within one mile, the latter all other trials. It is not clear from Gaius' words, or from the examples which he gives, in which class *iudicia* held in Italy outside Rome would fall. The words he uses are 'iudicia quae in urbe Roma vel intra primum urbis Romae miliarium inter omnes cives Romanos sub uno iudice accipiuntur', which might equally well mean cases which were initiated at Rome, or were tried at Rome. On the former alternative, since the proceedings *in iure* in all cases took place before the praetor at Rome, all Italian suits

G

would be *legitima*. On the latter alternative, when the proceedings before the *iudex* took place outside Rome, as they well might when the case concerned parties domiciled in an Italian town, an Italian suit would be *imperio continens*. As examples he quotes the two extremes, Rome or the provinces, leaving Italy ambiguous, but his wording ('si . . . in provinciis agatur' or 'si Romae apud recuperatores agamus') suggests that he regards the place of the actual *iudicium* as being decisive.

Gaius cites two ways in which these two types of *iudicia* differ. In the first place *iudicia legitima* were extinguished unless brought to a conclusion within eighteen months: this time limit was imposed by the Lex Iulia iudiciaria, and it is to be inferred that there had before that law been none. *Iudicia quae imperio continentur* on the other hand were extinguished when the *imperium* of the magistrate who ordered them came to an end. The implication of this rule is that the authority of the *iudex* in this type of *iudicium* was derived from the *imperium* of the magistrate, and only lasted so long as the magistrate continued to hold his *imperium*. In a *iudicium legitimum*, on the other hand, the authority of the *iudex* was quite independent of the *imperium* of the praetor, and rested on a *lex*, presumably the Lex Aebutia, which legalised the formulary procedure. In the second place decisions of *iudicia legitima*, if the *formula* were framed according to the *ius civile*, were *ipso iure* final; the same issue could not be tried again. The decisions of *iudicia quae imperio continentur*, on the other hand, were not in strict law final: the praetor only made them so by granting an *exceptio rei iudicatae vel in iudicium deductae*, thus maintaining them by his *imperium*.

These distinctions suggest that there may have been a constitutional difference between trials at Rome and those elsewhere. At Rome the *iudex* held his authority by *lex*, his judgment was legally final. Outside Rome his authority was derived from the *imperium* of the magistrate who appointed him and his judgment was only final in so far as the magistrate maintained it. Gaius has nothing to say here or elsewhere on the subject of appeal, but it

might reasonably be conjectured that, while the *iudex* judging
between Roman citizens at Rome was inappellable, the *iudex*
elsewhere, or when a *peregrinus* was involved, seeing that he
derived his authority from a magistrate, was like the magistrate
himself subject to *appellatio*.

If this suggestion be accepted, no constitutional change need be
postulated. In Rome itself the *iudex* will have been inappellable
under the Republic, and have remained so under the Principate:
we have no evidence that he was not. Appeals from *privati iudices*
in the provinces and in Italy will have been legal under the
Republic but probably rare owing to practical difficulties. Under
the Principate they will have become commoner because Augustus
encouraged appeal in general. Appeals from *iudices* would in the
normal course go to the magistrate from whom they derived their
authority, in Italy to the praetor, in a province to the governor
or his delegates. There was however no constitutional reason
why a litigant should not appeal to another magistrate with
*maior potestas*; as Paulus says, 'iudicium solvitur vetante eo qui
iudicare iusserat vel etiam eo qui maius imperium in ea iurisdictione habeat'.[38] Later emperors discouraged provincial litigants
from by-passing the governor and appealing directly to themselves,[39] but in the early Principate, before appellate jurisdiction
became regular and systematic, they may well have been more
willing to take appeals direct from *iudices*. Indeed if their object
was, partly at any rate, to check injustice by provincial governors,
it would have been foolish to insist on all appeals coming through
them. In Italy Augustus by delegating appeals to the urban
praetor redirected them to the magistrate to whom they would
appropriately have gone in the first place: the praetor, judging at
Rome under his own eye, was unlikely to take liberties with the
law.

### The Primary Civil Jurisdiction of the Emperors and the Consuls

It has already been argued that the consuls always retained their
power of jurisdiction, though after the creation of the praetorship

they ceased to exercise it regularly, perhaps only when appealed to from the praetor. When Augustus in 19 B.C. received the *consulare imperium* he acquired a power of jurisdiction like that of the consuls.   He not only used it regularly in appellate jurisdiction, but, it would seem, occasionally in the first instance. The scanty evidence suggests that he did not take cases when the praetor could furnish a remedy by the *ordinarium ius*, but used his jurisdiction to supplement or modify the *ordinarium ius* when it seemed to him to be inequitable or contrary to public policy. Valerius Maximus cites two judgments of Augustus which appear to have been given in the first instance.[40]  In one he gave possession of his father's inheritance to a son who had been disinherited as an infant, although his father had lived in matrimony with his mother till the day of her death (presumably in childbirth).[41]  In the other a widow had married an old man when herself beyond the age of childbirth and cut her two sons by her former marriage out of her will: Augustus not only quashed the will, but compelled the second husband to refund the dowry.[42] These decisions, which go beyond the law, were evidently dictated by the same social policy which inspired the Lex Iulia de maritandis ordinibus.

Augustus also intervened to give legal sanction to *fideicommissa*, but here he seems to have made use of the dormant jurisdiction of the consuls.  The story is told in Justinian's Institutes.[43]  A certain L. Lentulus died in Africa, leaving *codicilli* in which he requested Augustus himself *per fideicommissum* to make certain dispositions of his property.   Augustus, after taking the advice of jurisconsults, decided to regard the *codicilli* as a valid will, and executed the *fideicommissa*: Lentulus' daughter, encouraged by his example, also carried out the *fideicommissa* enjoined upon her by her father. So far Augustus had been acting merely as a private citizen, though naturally his *auctoritas* carried great weight.   Later other cases arose in which Augustus, though not himself asked to execute the *fideicommissa*, was moved to intervene either out of personal regard for the injured parties, or by the fact that the testator had adjured the heir by the emperor's safety, or merely by the notorious bad faith of the heir. In these cases, according to Justinian, he ordered the consuls to interpose their authority ('iussit consulibus auctoritatem suam interponere'). Suetonius gives a slightly different picture when he states that before Claudius the jurisdiction on *fideicommissa* was normally delegated to magistrates in Rome,[44] implying that Augustus himself held the new jurisdiction but delegated its exercise to the consuls. Claudius definitely assigned it to the consuls and to two special *praetores fideicommissarii* at Rome, and extended it to the provinces, where the provincial governor exercised the jurisdiction.[45]

Another quasi-judicial function which the consuls acquired during the Julio-Claudian period was the appointment of tutors. The regular procedure under the Lex Atilia was not altogether satisfactory, and Claudius enacted that tutors might be appointed *extra ordinem* by the consuls.[46] No further specific cases are known, but in one way or another the consuls acquired considerable judicial functions. Towards the end of Augustus' reign Ovid already regards jurisdiction as one of the prominent functions of a consul, and Suetonius distinguishes Claudius' judicial work as consul and when not holding that office.[47] Much of this consular jurisdiction was no doubt appellate.

Both the emperor and the consuls exercised their primary jurisdiction only in cases which were not covered by the *ius ordinarium* or where its operation was unsatisfactory or inequitable. Seeing that their jurisdiction was thus *extraordinaria*, they were not bound to observe the cumbrous procedure of the *ordo*, but could employ the simpler and more expeditious *cognitio*. In one of the two testamentary cases which Augustus took he is said to have decreed a *missio in bona* by *decretum* as the praetor might have done if the case had been covered by the edict.[48] In the other he is by implication spoken of as holding a *cognitio*.[49] The consuls' jurisdiction on *fideicommissa* was certainly exercised by *cognitio*,[50] and in general the terms *cognoscere* and *cognitio* are always used of the emperor's jurisdiction.[51] It seems likely that *cognitio* was employed also in the appellate jurisdiction of the emperor and the consuls.

### The Capital Jurisdiction of the Emperor and the Senate

In civil jurisdiction, I would submit, there was no sharp break in theory between the later Republic and the early Principate. No new forms of jurisdiction were created by legislative enactment. A new judge did appear in the person of the emperor, but his power of jurisdiction arose out of the consular *imperium* with which he was invested. In practice Augustus did innovate, it would seem, by resuscitating the apparently dormant primary consular jurisdiction both in his own person and in that of the consuls. He also greatly extended the consular appellate jurisdiction, which was probably rarely exercised in the Republic, and here again he not only exercised this jurisdiction himself, but encouraged the consuls, using the senate as their *consilium*, to do likewise.

In capital jurisdiction on the other hand a sharp break appears between the later Republic and the Principate. Under the later Republic the only authority competent to pass a capital sentence on a Roman citizen was a *iudicium publicum*, one of the jury courts at Rome established by a series of statutes and consolidated under Leges Corneliae of Sulla.[52] The *imperium* of the magistrates was inhibited by the right of *provocatio*, which by now applied everywhere and in all circumstances, in the provinces as in Italy and Rome, in war as in peace.[53] It is difficult to conceive how the courts at Rome can have handled all criminal cases arising throughout the empire, and it has been conjectured that *de facto* many criminals must have been executed summarily, both in Rome by the magistrates and in the provinces by the governors, if their guilt was regarded as manifest or they could be induced to make a confession. But the law was explicit, and was reaffirmed in the most stringent terms by a Lex Iulia de vi publica. It is cited in slightly variant forms of Paulus[54] and by Ulpian,[55] and enacted the death penalty against anyone who, possessing any *imperium* or *potestas*, executed, flogged, tortured or put in bonds any Roman citizen 'adversus provocationem' (Ulpian) or 'antea ad populum nunc ad imperatorem appellantem' (Paulus).

In spite of the Lex Iulia de vi publica we have indubitable evidence that under the Julio-Claudians both the emperor and the Senate tried capital cases and passed and executed death sentences without any hint of *provocatio*. Both forms of trial appear in the Annals as well established at the beginning of Tiberius' reign, and it is hardly necessary to cite the abundant evidence. It may suffice to recall the preliminaries to the trial of Piso, which illustrate the relations of the imperial and senatorial courts and the *iudicia publica*.[56] One of the accusers, Fulcinius Trio, lodged a charge of murder against Piso before the consuls (who, as is generally admitted, were legally the judges, using the Senate as their *consilium*). Other accusers, including Vitellius and Veranius, objected that they had a better claim to prosecute the case, but soon joined forces with Trio. Tiberius was then asked (presumably by the combined accusers, Trio having withdrawn his charge before the consuls) to take the case. Piso for his part, according to Tacitus, did not object ('quod ne reus quidem abnuebat') as he hoped for a fairer trial from the emperor. Tiberius, however, having held an informal preliminary hearing, sent the case back to the Senate without taking any action ('integramque causam ad senatum remittit'). In the Senate he opened the proceedings by a speech in which he claimed as the only special concession ('super leges') to Germanicus' memory that his death should be investigated 'in curia potius quam in foro, apud senatum quam apud iudices', that is, in the regular *quaestio de sicariis et venificis*.

From this account it appears that the normal court for murder cases was the *iudicium publicum*, but that accusers could ask either the consuls or the emperor to take a case. The emperor—and presumably the consuls also—could either refuse or accept the charge. Tacitus' words might be taken to mean that the consent of the accused was required for trial before the emperor or the

Senate, but no such right is elsewhere mentioned, and Tacitus probably merely means that Piso was not sorry that he would be tried by Tiberius, not that he did not lodge a formal objection. The new procedure was generally employed in cases which concerned persons of high rank, especially senators, or were of political importance: charges of *maiestas* and *res repetundae* tended to come before the Senate.

There is not much evidence for the new procedure under Augustus. When in 21 A.D. Silanus, proconsul of Asia, was about to be tried before the Senate for extortion, Tiberius ordered the *libelli* of Augustus on Volesus Messala, proconsul of Africa about 12 A.D., and the *senatusconsultum* passed against him, to be read.[57] Tacitus also informs us that Augustus first employed the law of *maiestas* to punish libel in the case of Cassius Severus, who, he tells us elsewhere, was banished to Crete by the judgment of the Senate under oath.[58] Ovid's complaint to Augustus,[59]

> nec mea decreto damnasti facta senatus
> nec mea selecto iudice iussa fuga est,

implies that by A.D. 8 a trial before the Senate was a normal alternative to a *iudicium publicum*. It is usually held that the *senatusconsultum Calvisianum* of 4 B.C.,[60] whereby provincials who wished to obtain monetary compensation, without bringing a capital charge against the magistrate concerned, could prosecute by a special procedure before the Senate, proves that capital cases could not yet at this date be heard by the Senate. The argument does not appear to be conclusive, for it is possible that it was only the new simplified procedure, and not a trial in the Senate, which was excluded in capital cases. There is however no earlier evidence for senatorial trials than that of Ovid, which implies that it was well established by A.D. 8.

Trials before Augustus personally are less well attested. There are two or three undated anecdotes in Suetonius. In one Augustus, trying a man for parricide, endeavours by a leading question to induce him not to confess the crime, to avoid having to impose the penalty of the sack. In the other he is trying the case of a forged will, and to prevent all the witnesses being punished as the Lex Cornelia directed, gave out to those who were assisting in the trial ('simul cognoscentibus') not only tablets of acquittal and of condemnation but a third granting pardon to witnesses who had affixed their seals in error.[61] Suetonius' language is not very clear, but he can hardly mean that Augustus was intervening in a normal trial before a *quaestio*: he seems rather to be conducting a *cognitio* himself, with the assistance of his *consilium*, whose votes he collects. Finally there is an anecdote recorded by Dio under A.D. 10. Here a quaestor, accused of murder, persuades Germanicus to speak on his behalf: his accuser asks Augustus to take the case himself, fearing Germanicus' influence over the regular jurors in the *iudicia publica*, but Augustus refuses.[62] This evidence is not in itself impressive, but the fact that Tiberius, who clung so firmly to Augustan precedent, was prepared to take Piso's case shows that the imperial criminal jurisdiction must have been established under Augustus.

Trial of capital cases by the emperor or by the consuls was a startling innovation. In the late Republic the right of the consuls, even when supported by the *senatusconsultum ultimum* in a time of civil commotion, to execute Roman citizens without *provocatio* was hotly contested. And since the last test case in 63 B.C. the principle of *provocatio* had been emphatically reasserted by the Lex Iulia de vi publica. It is inconceivable that Augustus can have himself assumed this jurisdiction, or allowed the Senate to assume it, without statutory authority, and one must postulate a law conferring capital jurisdiction on the consuls and the emperor. This capital jurisdiction was exercised under the same statutes which governed the *quaestiones*, the *leges iudiciorum publicorum*. In all the many senatorial and the fewer imperial trials recorded by Tacitus and Pliny the offence is always one of those defined in the statutes, usually *maiestas* or *res repetundae*, but also others such as *falsum* or *adulterium* or murder. The trial is conducted according to the terms of the statutes, even if these were sometimes enlarged by interpretation, as when libel was brought within the definition of *maiestas*.[63] The penalties were also those of the laws, though the Senate claimed the right 'mitigare leges vel intendere'.[64] It certainly did not always exact the full statutory penalty, which was in most cases death: and in so far as it actually exacted the death penalty, it may be said to have made the laws more severe, in that it had under the later Republic been so long customary to allow a condemned man to go into exile that this probably was regarded as the normal 'poena legis'.[65]

The clue to the new jurisdiction of the consuls and the emperor under the *leges iudiciorum publicorum* is, I suggest, to be found in a passage of Papinian,[66] where he condemns the impropriety of 'magistratus qui cum publici iudicii habeant exercitionem lege vel senatus consulto delegatam veluti legis Iuliae de adulteriis vel quae sunt aliae similes, iurisdictionem suam mandant,' and cites as evidence for his view 'quod lege Iulia de vi nominatim cavetur ut is cui optigerit exercitio possit eam si proficiscatur mandare' (and therefore, he argues, in no other circumstances). The Lex Iulia de vi apparently laid down rules governing the conduct of magistrates to whom had been granted 'publici iudicii exercitio'. These can hardly be the praetors or *iudices quaestionum* who presided over the courts at Rome, but must be other magistrates who have obtained special authority to exercise the criminal laws. This at any rate was the interpretation put upon the law by Papinian, who is arguing 'quaecumque specialiter lege vel senatusconsulto vel constitutione tribuuntur, mandata iurisdictione non transferuntur'.

We do not know upon which magistrates the Lex Iulia conferred *exercitio iudicii publici*, but if the list opened with the consuls or those invested with consular *imperium*, the criminal jurisdiction of the emperor and the Senate would be explained. I have argued elsewhere[67] that proconsuls are attested to have possessed authority to try Roman citizens without appeal for *crimina iudiciorum publicorum* in the last decade of the first century, and it is possible that they too were granted this jurisdiction by the

Lex Iulia. There is no evidence that *legati Augusti pro praetore*, the prefect of Egypt, or procurators acquired criminal jurisdiction over Roman citizens till a much later date. It would be more in accord with constitutional propriety if the original grant had been made to the consuls and others holding a consular *imperium*, that is the emperor and proconsuls. The language of Papinian suggests that the original list, laid down by the *lex*, was extended by *senatus consulta*, and ultimately by imperial constitutions. We are told by Ulpian that Caracalla authorised even procurators who governed no province to try cases under the Lex Fabia de plagiariis and the Lex Iulia de adulteriis.[68]

It may be also that the Lex Iulia laid down rules for the conduct of trials. The consuls in fact always held trials before the Senate, whose vote seems to have been binding upon them. It is possible that proconsuls were also required to constitute a jury of Roman citizens, by whose verdict they had to abide. One of Augustus' Cyrenaean edicts reveals that in that province the proconsul might try capital charges against *peregrini* either by personal *cognitio* or by a jury court (συμβούλιον κριτῶν).[69] Another reveals that this jury court was drawn from Roman citizens possessed of 2500 denarii or more.[70] The edicts concern only the trials of *peregrini*, and it has generally been assumed that the jury court existed only for their trial and that Romans were not subject to the capital jurisdiction of the proconsul. The wording, however, might be held to support the opposite view. Augustus advises the proconsul to enrol an equal number of Greeks on the panel from which jurors are to be drawn 'in the capital cases involving Greeks' (ἐν τοῖς θανατηφόροις τῶν Ἑλλήνων κριτηρίοις), and to constitute a jury half of Romans and half of Greeks if 'a Greek accused' (Ἕλλην κρινόμενος) so desires. It would seem unnecessary to insert the word 'Greek' in these two places if the court dealt with Greeks only, and it may well be that it was empowered to try Romans also. The existence of jury courts of this type, modelled on the *iudicia publica* of Rome, is attested nowhere else in our sources. They may have been an innovation introduced by the Lex Iulia de vi intended primarily to try capital charges against Romans under the *leges iudiciorum publicorum*. They do not seem to have had a long life, being superseded by the *cognitio* of the governors.[71]

If my reconstruction be accepted, the Lex Iulia de vi publica, at the same time that it reaffirmed the Roman citizen's right of *provocatio*, greatly limited its scope by extending capital jurisdiction under the *leges iudiciorum publicorum*, against which there was no *provocatio*. Hitherto exercised only at Rome by the *quaestiones*, it was now granted to a wider group of magistrates and promagistrates both in Rome and in the provinces. The rights of Roman citizens were safeguarded by various provisions. In the first place it was only for the *crimina iudiciorum publicorum*, the offences defined by the statutes, that they could be tried; they were still protected by *provocatio* against the *coercitio* of magistrates. Secondly this right of capital jurisdiction over Roman citizens was conferred on a very select group of magistrates, and being a special grant could not, like the regular *imperium* inherent in their office, be delegated by them to others; in fact the *legati* of proconsuls never exercised this special jurisdiction.[72] Thirdly, it is at any rate possible that the magistrates to whom the jurisdiction was granted were required to try cases before some form of jury, the consuls using the Senate as such, proconsuls specially constituted courts drawn from resident Romans of a certain age and census.

One object of the law is plain. Even under the late Republic, as has already been remarked, the concentration at Rome of capital jurisdiction over all Roman citizens throughout the empire must have given rise to great delays and difficulties in so far as the law was observed, and probably led to its being frequently overridden. By the time of Augustus the situation must have become unmanageable owing to the great extension of citizenship in the provinces. Provincial governors had no longer to deal merely with *negotiatores* and such other Romans as had on their own initiative domiciled themselves in the provinces, and with the few provincials who had received personal grants of citizenship. Many provinces now contained a considerable number of Roman colonies and *municipia* whose whole population were citizens. It must have become impracticable to remit every criminal charge to Rome. The Lex Iulia de vi publica solved this problem by giving limited criminal jurisdiction to proconsuls, if not all provincial governors. If the grant was limited to proconsuls, this would not have been unreasonable on practical as well as on constitutional grounds. For it was in the public provinces—notably in Baetica, Africa, Narbonensis, Macedonia and Achaea—that the great bulk of Roman colonies and *municipia* were to be found.

This was probably the main problem which the Lex Iulia was designed to solve. Why then were the consuls and emperor included? Constitutional propriety may have had some influence here. If proconsuls were being granted a special extension of their *imperium*, it might well have been felt that a similar extension could not be denied to the consuls and the emperor, whose *imperium* was superior to theirs.

But at the same time it may have been thought useful to supplement the *quaestiones* at Rome by two more dignified courts, the consuls in the senate and the emperor in council, which would be available to deal with cases of political importance or involving persons of high degree. Augustus may well have felt the need of a court over which he could preside, or in whose deliberations he could intervene, to deal with such cases. At the trial of Primus before a *quaestio* he had, it will be remembered, been placed in an embarrassing position.[73]

There remains the problem of the change from *provocatio ad populum* to *appellatio ad Caesarem*. There was still ample scope for *provocatio* after the Lex Iulia de vi publica, and the law envisaged its continued use. One of its clauses enjoined that no one should bind an accused person or prevent him from presenting himself at Rome within a fixed time.[74] This rule implies that an accused who exercised *provocatio* was required to present himself at Rome for trial, but it leaves obscure what form this trial would take. *Provocatio* might be made if a magistrate who did not possess *exercitio iudicii publici* tried or attempted to try a citizen on a charge arising under the *leges iudiciorum publicorum*. It would seem natural that in such a case the accused should be sent for trial before the appropriate *quaestio* in Rome. No instances are known of such a case arising. *Provocatio* might also be employed against the *coercitio* of magistrates. The laws defined a limited number of crimes, and there were many other offences for which magistrates inflicted capital penalties in virtue of the general power of *coercitio* inherent in their *imperium*. *Peregrini* had no protection against this arbitrary jurisdiction, but Romans could exercise their right of *provocatio*.

*Provocatio* in the early and middle Republic gave rise to a *iudicium populi*, a trial before the *comitia centuriata*. After Sulla no such trials are recorded, save that of Rabirius, where an archaic procedure was revived for political effect, and in view of the richness of our information on this period, it is probably legitimate to deduce that they had fallen into desuetude. This may mean that offences not covered by the *leges iudiciorum publicorum* went unpunished, or that the right of *provocatio* was often ignored. Under the Principate we find that citizens are in fact protected against the *coercitio* of magistrates, but that they appeal to Caesar, as did Paul, or even if they do not appeal they are remitted to Rome for trial by the emperor, or alternatively the magistrate refers their case to the emperor for him to confirm or annul the sentence.[75]

Here the emperor seems to have taken the place of the people as the ultimate arbiter of life and death. *Provocatio ad populum* has become *appellatio ad Caesarem*, and the emperor, instead of the people, decides whether to uphold the magistrate's sentence or not. This change again can hardly have come about without legislation. Among the honours stated by Dio to have been voted to Octavian after Actium was 'to hold the *tribunicia potestas* for life and himself to give *auxilium* to those who appealed to him both within the pomerium and outside up to the first milestone . . .

and to judge on appeal and give a "vote of Athena" in all the courts' (τήν τε ἐξουσίαν τῶν δημάρχων διὰ βίου ἔχειν καὶ τοῖς ἐπιβοωμένοις αὐτὸν καὶ ἐντὸς τοῦ πωμηρίου καὶ ἔξω μέχρι ὀγδόου ἡμισταδίου ἀμύνειν . . . . ἔκκλητόν τε δικάζειν καὶ ψῆφόν τινα αὐτοῦ ἐν πᾶσιν τοῖς δικαστηρίοις ὥσπερ ᾿Αθηνᾶς φέρεσθαι).⁷⁶ Octavian, according to Dio, accepted all the honours except a few. Among those which he rejected was fairly certainly the *tribunicia potestas*, which he did not acquire till 23 B.C.⁷⁷ It does not, however, necessarily follow that he refused the special powers of *auxilium* and of jurisdiction which follow.

The first power described by Dio is that of giving *auxilium* in person like a tribune, but not only within the pomerium but for a zone of a mile outside it. The third is probably to be interpreted as the power of giving a vote of acquittal when the jury in a *quaestio* had condemned: 'a vote of Athena' (ψῆφος ᾿Αθηνᾶς) can hardly be taken in the strict sense of a casting vote when the jury was equally divided, as the right would then have been of nugatory value.⁷⁸ This grant is something quite new, for no appeal had ever been allowed from the verdicts of the *quaestiones*, and the tribunes had never been able to intervene in their proceedings. It had however been foreshadowed by the proposal of Antony 'ut et de vi et maiestatis damnati ad populum provocent si velint'.⁷⁹ Under Antony's law the people would have had the power of annulling a condemnation by a *quaestio* under two of the *leges*. In the law of 30 B.C. Octavian is given a general power of pardon in all cases under the criminal laws. Octavian, that is, as 'libertatis populi Romani vindex', to quote contemporary coinage, is not only given, in an extended form, the traditional power of the tribune to defend the liberty of the Roman citizen against the *imperium* of the magistrates, but is vested with the people's own prerogative of mercy, and that in cases where hitherto no appeal had lain to the people.

Whether Augustus accepted the first power, that of *auxilium*, we have no means of telling, for no emperor is recorded to have exercised it, though from 23 B.C. all possessed it—at any rate within the pomerium. For the third power there is evidence under Tiberius, who, when Clutorius Priscus, having been condemned to death by the Senate, was summarily executed without his being consulted, promoted a *senatusconsultum*, whereby ten days' grace should be allowed after sentence before the decree was entered in the *aerarium* for execution.[80] It appears to have later become the practice that all death sentences should be counter-signed by the emperor: Nero, Suetonius tells us, 'cum de supplicio cuiusdam capite damnati ut ex more subscriberet admoneretur' replied: 'quam vellem nescire litteras'.[81] As the anecdote is dated to Nero's early years, when Tacitus records only three capital sentences passed by the Senate, it would appear that condemna-tions by the *quaestiones* must have been regularly reviewed by the emperor. There is, it may be noted, no suggestion in our sources that the condemned man could appeal: the emperor intervened of his own motion.

It is in the light of these two powers that the third, briefly and obscurely described by Dio as ἔκκλητον δικάζειν, must be interpreted. In the context it must be a prerogative of mercy, a right to protect the liberty of the citizen against the *imperium*. It must be concerned with capital cases, and not be the ordinary right of giving *auxilium* in response to *appellatio* in civil issues which has been discussed earlier in this paper. The words strictly mean 'to try an appealed (case)', *ex appellatione cognoscere*.[82] But by Dio's time—and indeed a century earlier—the conceptions of *appellatio* and *provocatio* had become so blurred that the two words were used interchangeably,[83] and here, I suggest, ἔκκλητον δικάζειν means *ex provocatione cognoscere*. Octavian, that is, was vested with the people's own prerogative of mercy, to reverse the capital sentence of a magistrate issued in virtue of his *imperium*. This second power is parallel to the third, and is prior to it: for by the second grant Octavian was vested with a right already held constitutionally by the people, in the third with an extension of this right.

The right of granting pardon necessarily involves the right of refusing it, and Octavian was thus in effect given the power of condemning a Roman citizen to death by refusing to exercise his prerogative. When the citizen had been condemned by the *iudicia publica*, he was no worse off if the emperor refused to exercise his prerogative, seeing that hitherto he had possessed no right of appeal. When he had been condemned by a magistrate exercising his *coercitio*, he theoretically lost his right of having his case reviewed by the *comitia centuriata*. But if, as has been suggested above, this procedure had fallen into desuetude, he lost little in practice, and in fact the rights of the Roman citizen seem to have been more effectively protected by the emperor than by the people.

The criminal jurisdiction of the emperor is thus in my opinion something new, created by two separate statutory grants. One, substituting the emperor for the people as the judge in cases arising out of *provocatio*, is dated to 30 B.C. The other, the Lex Iulia de vi publica, cannot be securely dated. A Lex Iulia may belong to Caesar or to Augustus. At first sight a plausible case can be made for Caesar. He was strongly interested, as his part in the trial of Rabirius and his intervention in the Catilinarian debate show, in the right of *provocatio*. At the same time his extensive grants of citizenship must have raised the problem of criminal jurisdiction over citizens in the provinces and suggested the need for some delegation of criminal jurisdiction to provincial governors. It may also be argued that as the Lex Iulia spoke of *provocatio ad populum*, it was prior to the substitution of *appellatio ad Caesarem* for this right.

On the other hand there is no positive evidence for the capital jurisdiction of the Senate or the emperor till late in Augustus's reign, and early in the reign we find political trials, such as would later have been held before the Senate or emperor, going before an ordinary *quaestio*. In the case of Cornelius Gallus, the Senate did not act as a court, but voted that he be condemned by a court,[84] that is presumably passed a vote of censure upon him and instructed the relevant praetor to receive a charge against him.

H

Primus[85] and Caepio and Murena[86] were also tried before the regular *quaestiones*. This would suggest that the Lex Iulia was later than 23 B.C., and probably not earlier than 19 B.C. when Augustus returned to Rome. If a late date is accepted it must be presumed that the old phrase *provocatio ad populum* was used in the law from legal conservatism.

The argument for the later date is however by no means conclusive, for as the capital jurisdiction of the Senate and the emperor was voluntary, it may have long lain dormant, though on the statute book, because no accuser took the initiative of invoking it. It is even possible that the Lex Iulia, if due to Caesar, was intended only to give *exercitio iudicii publici* to proconsuls, but was sufficiently loosely drafted to be interpreted to cover the consuls or anyone holding a consular *imperium*, and that Augustus made use of this ambiguity in the latter part of his reign, when his authority was well established, to set up his own and the Senate's capital jurisdiction.

# VI

## THE AERARIUM AND THE FISCUS

# The Aerarium and the Fiscus*

EARLY imperial arrangements must have been to some extent based on late Republican practice. I will therefore first set out the financial machinery of the last half-century of the Republic, as revealed in Cicero's speeches and correspondence, supplemented by secondary sources. The aerarium at Rome was the central repository of the moneys of the Roman People. It was managed by the two urban quaestors, or rather by a body of *scribae quaestorii* under their nominal direction.[1] Normally the Polybian rule that no payment might be made save under the authority of a *senatusconsultum*[2] seems to have held: it does not appear that the old right of a consul to draw of his own initiative[3] still survived. Magistrates proceeding to a province were voted a block grant to cover their estimated expenses: *ornare provinciam* is the technical term.[4] On leaving his province a magistrate was obliged to account to the aerarium for this sum.[5] These accounts seem to have been somewhat summary. Those which Verres sent in on laying down his quaestorship were no doubt unusually brief,[6] but if it was possible for a proconsul to distribute the unexpended balance of his grant among his staff—and Cicero's refusal to follow this practice was resented by his subordinates[7]—auditing cannot have been very exact.

In some at any rate of the extraordinary commands the grant was provided by the law which conferred the command, and on a very generous scale: Cicero complains bitterly of the large *vasarium*, as he colloquially calls it, allocated to Piso to finance his Macedonian command.[8] According to Plutarch, Pompey, as proconsul of Spain, drew 1,000 talents a year from the aerarium;[9] this was no doubt a provision of the Lex Trebonia. Caelius, on the other hand, writing to Cicero, speaks of a special vote by the

Senate of funds to Pompey to pay his army;[10] this was perhaps a supplementary grant. The similar votes for Caesar's army in Gaul[11] were presumably also supplementary, for it is unlikely that Caesar would not have secured for himself a regular grant under the provisions of the Lex Vatinia and the Lex Pompeia Licinia. Most detail is given about the provisions of the Lex Gabinia. According to Plutarch,[12] Pompey was empowered to draw as much money as he liked 'from the treasuries and from the *publicani*' (ἐκ τῶν ταμιείων καὶ παρὰ τῶν τελωνῶν). This is probably an exaggeration; for Appian[13] gives a total of 6,000 talents, adding that he was authorised to collect the money. The truth would seem to be that the Lex Gabinia authorised Pompey to draw sums up to a stated total from the sources mentioned by Plutarch.

At any given time there were, of course, moneys of the Roman People elsewhere than in the aerarium, mainly in the hands of the *publicani* and of governors in the provinces. The *publicani* paid in arrear, and would therefore usually hold revenues already collected, but not yet due for payment to the Roman People. In provinces where the revenues were collected by the *publicani*, governors held only the unexpended balances of their grants. In provinces where they collected *stipendia* from the communities, they presumably also held these pending their transfer (if ever) to Rome. These moneys were said to be in the governor's 'fiscus': when Verres pocketed the sum voted to him by the Senate for purchasing corn 'cellae nomine', Cicero speaks of the transfer of the money 'in cistam . . . de fisco'.[14]

Naturally, both for the sake of economy and to avoid loss in transit, as little coin as possible was shipped from Rome to the provinces and vice versa, and most transactions were on paper. Usually the *societates publicanorum* acted as the Roman People's bankers. When the Senate allocated money to Verres for the purchase of corn in Sicily, it gave him a draft on the local *pro magistro* of the Roman company which farmed the pasture dues and customs of the island:[15] this sum would presumably be deducted from the payment due for these Sicilian taxes to the aerarium by the head office of the company. Cicero similarly, on arrival in Cilicia, drew his allowance from Laodicea by a *publica permutatio*[16] and on his return deposited the balance with the *publicani* at Ephesus.[17] But when, as in Spain, the bulk of the provincial revenues was not collected by the *publicani*, the governor presumably paid the local *stipendia* into his own 'fiscus', and paid out from it his expenditure. Any unexpended balance he would presumably leave in his 'fiscus' for his successor.

The theory and the practice of Republican finance were thus quite different. Theoretically the *publicani* paid into the aerarium the sums due in respect of the taxes they farmed, and similarly proconsuls of provinces where the communities paid *stipendia* transmitted these to Rome. From the aerarium grants were made to the provincial governors to cover their expenses. Accounts were kept on this basis, the *publicani* and such governors as collected revenue accounting to the aerarium for their receipts, and all governors accounting to the aerarium for their expenditure. In practice, on the other hand, a large proportion of the money collected in each province, whether by the governor or the *publicani*, was spent locally. Only surpluses of local revenue over local expenditure would be transmitted to Rome, and only when the expenses of a province exceeded its income would money be sent from the aerarium to a province. Thus Cicero's statement[18] that—before Pompey's eastern conquests—the revenues of the provinces except for Asia barely covered their expenses would mean that in fact little cash was shipped to Rome save from Asia.

This analysis makes intelligible Plutarch's phrase ἐκ τῶν ταμιείων καὶ παρὰ τῶν τελωνῶν. Pompey was authorised to draw money from the provincial 'fisci' and from the local agents of the *publicani* in all provinces in which he operated. It also explains the famous phrase of Suetonius[19] 'quantum pecuniae in aerario et fiscis et vectigaliorum residuis'. The document which contained this information was a 'breviarium totius imperii', drawn up by Augustus as Princeps, and not an account of the public moneys which he handled in his official capacities. The distribution of funds corresponds with Republican practice, first the amount in the aerarium, second that in the various provincial 'fisci' (in the public as in Caesar's provinces), third, the outstanding balances of the indirect taxes in the hands of the *publicani*. The main practical difference was that, since virtually all direct taxes were no longer farmed, the provincial 'fisci' would hold large sums, and the *publicani* relatively little.

Those who doubt the existence of 'fisci' in the public provinces I would refer to *Dig*. XLVIII, xiii, 11 (9), § 6, where Paulus is quoting the great Augustan lawyer, Antistius Labeo, on the subject of the Lex Iulia residuorum. 'Cum eo autem, qui, cum provincia abiret, pecuniam, quae penes se esset, ad aerarium professus retinuerit, non esse residuae pecuniae actionem, quia eam privatus fisco debeat, et ideo inter debitores eum ferri: eamque ab eo is qui hoc imperio utitur, exigeret, id est pignus capiendo, corpus retinendo, multam dicendo. sed eam quoque lex Iulia residuorum post annum residuam esse iussit.' In the situation envisaged, a proconsul (who alone would be directly accountable to the aerarium) has rendered his account to the aerarium on leaving his province, but has not lodged the balance due either in the aerarium or in the 'fiscus' (surely of his province). His successor's remedy is to sue him as a private citizen, owing money to the local 'fiscus'. Only after a year's delay does a criminal charge lie for wrongfully withholding public funds outstanding for payment into the aerarium. The suggestion implicit in this procedure is that normally a proconsul handed the balance in his 'fiscus' to his successor.

It will be simplest to state my own theory of Augustus' relation to the aerarium. I believe that Augustus, like the great Republican proconsuls, was periodically credited by votes of the Senate with such sums as would enable him to discharge his functions as proconsul; the votes would presumably have been made concurrently with the original grant and successive renewals of his province. Supplementary sums must have been voted to him to finance such *curae* as he personally undertook (i.e. those managed by his own *praefecti* and not by *curatores*). This money he was empowered to draw, like Pompey under the Lex Gabinia, from any convenient source. He would naturally draw first from the 'fisci' of his own provinces,[20] and from the *publicani* operating therein. He might find it convenient to draw from the 'fisci' and *publicani* of adjacent public provinces. Some money he must have drawn from the aerarium for expenditure in Rome and Italy, and to supplement the 'fisci' of poor but expensive provinces like Pannonia. Thus, in practice no cash would have to be moved from most of his provinces to Rome. Probably only Egypt produced a surplus over local expenditure, and this surplus was paid into the aerarium, as Velleius,[21] a contemporary, tells us. Theoretically Augustus would have been accountable for all moneys allocated to him, including the revenues accruing in his provinces, when he left his province, but since he held his command until his death he need never have rendered any account. Augustus did, according to Suetonius,[22] regularly publish the *rationes imperii*, but these were not his accounts as a magistrate but a general balance-sheet of the Empire which he drew up in virtue of his position as Princeps and published for information.

On Tiberius' accession, the vote of funds would presumably have been made without time limit, since no time limit was placed on his tenure of his powers, and this continued to be the regular practice. Tiberius omitted in his later years to publish the *rationes imperii*, and after Gaius' short-lived revival of the practice they permanently ceased to be issued. In these circumstances it would be impossible for anyone outside the imperial secretariat to check how much the emperor spent, and the vote of funds would become a formality.

There is, I admit, no evidence for this theory, but neither is there any, as far as I know, for any other theory of the public finance of the early Principate; and this theory does at least not contradict the available evidence, and falls into line with late Republican precedent. The assumption commonly made that

Augustus would naturally be entitled to use the revenues of his provinces runs counter to the whole conception of Republican finance, whereby all revenue went theoretically into the aerarium and expenditure was voted from it. Moreover, it is generally admitted, such a division could not have worked in practice, since Augustus' expenses must greatly have exceeded the resources of his provinces: a supplementary grant in some form would have been necessary. To assume, as some have done, that certain taxes or types of taxes were assigned to Augustus from the public provinces, or that he was allocated a fixed proportion of their revenue, is unwarranted by the evidence and again contrary to the principles of Republican finance.

The theory that I have outlined also explains the strong interest that the Julio-Claudian emperors showed in the efficient management of the aerarium and the measures they took to bring its management under their own control—the institution first of praetorian *praefecti aerarii* and then of *praetores aerarii* by Augustus,[23] Claudius' return to management by quaestors, who were, however, to be selected by him and to serve three years,[24] and Nero's reversion to praetorian *praefecti*, now selected by him.[25] The emperors were not in a disinterested spirit helping the Senate to manage senatorial affairs, but regulating and controlling a public treasury on which they drew from time to time.

The emperor's accounts, and also the balance-sheet of the Empire, were presumably prepared by his *a rationibus*; the office must have existed under Augustus, though it is first attested under Tiberius.[26] As early as the reign of Claudius a *procurator a patrimonio* is also attested,[27] who was responsible for the *ratio patrimonii*,[28] the accounts of the emperor's private fortune. These accounts must always have been kept separately from those of the public moneys which the emperors handled, and thus there must have been in some sense a *ratio patrimonii* from the beginning, but Claudius may have been the first to organise it as a regular department. Did the early emperors possess, in addition to their personal accounting staff, a personal treasury?

Here we are faced with a confusing ambiguity in the use of the word 'fiscus'. Its primitive meaning is a basket. Since baskets were commonly used to hold money, 'fiscus' came to be used figuratively like the English word 'pocket' to denote an individual's private fortune: thus Valerius Maximus[29] can write that Julius Caesar 'aes alienum Pompeii ex suo fisco solvi iussit'. Secondly, it came to mean a special fund, in the same way that 'the Chest' in academic language at Oxford means the funds of the University. In this sense it had, as we have seen, become under the Republic a technical term for the public funds in the hands of a provincial governor. In the early Principate it appears to be used in reference to the emperor in both these senses. First, it may denote his private fortune. Secondly, it may denote special funds under his control either of public money or of his private money. And thirdly, it early acquired a more extended meaning, analogous to our use of the word 'treasury', to denote the whole financial administration controlled by the emperor.

The early emergence of this last meaning is at first sight somewhat startling. But a new phenomenon had appeared, the huge organisation, staffed by imperial slaves, freedmen, and procurators, which exacted money due to the emperor, made payments in his name, and controlled the funds at his disposal. A word was needed to describe this new phenomenon and 'fiscus' suggested itself for a variety of reasons. The public funds handled by the imperial department of finance might be regarded as being, notionally, in the emperor's 'fiscus', in the same way that public funds in a province were said to be in the proconsul's 'fiscus'. Most of the money concerned was physically stored in sundry provincial 'fisci'. And finally the emperor made many payments for public purposes out of his own pocket, 'e fisco suo'.

In its third and most general sense 'fiscus' first appears in literature in Seneca.[30] Discussing how far a promise is binding, he writes that, if I say that I will go bail for you, this pledge does not hold in extreme cases, 'si spondere me in incertum iubebis, si fisco obligabis'. Here 'fiscus' clearly means the imperial government in

its financial aspect. Similarly, the elder Pliny, when he speaks of
Annius Plocamus 'qui Maris Rubri vectigal a fisco redemerat'[31]
and when he states that the balsam of Judaea fetched 300 *denarii* the
*sextarius* 'vendente fisco', and even more clearly when he says of
the balsam 'seritque nunc eum fiscus',[32] means by 'fiscus' the
imperial financial administration. Two Greek provincial inscriptions of the Julio-Claudian period also seem to use the word in this
sense, one from Lycosura in Achaea[33] and the other—the edict of
Tiberius Julius Alexander[34]—from Egypt, though ὁ φίσκος may
in both these cases denote the local provincial 'fiscus'.

Seneca appears to use 'fiscus' in the first sense mentioned above
in another and more famous passage of the *de beneficiis*.[35] 'Caesar
omnia habet, fiscus eius privata tantum ac sua. et universa in
imperio eius sunt, in patrimonio propria.' The obvious reading of
this passage is a rhetorical doublet, in which case it means that
'fiscus' was the bank or treasury of the *patrimonium*, the emperor's
private property. Pliny the Elder, when he relates that Augustus
leased the Collis Leucogaeus from the city of Naples for the
benefit of his new colony of Capua, 'extatque divi Augusti
decretum quo annua vicena milia Neapolitanis pro eo numerari
iussit e fisco suo',[36] seems to denote by the last words the emperor's
private fortune: unfortunately we cannot be sure that the decree
used these actual words.

The language of Tacitus and Suetonius, when speaking of the
Julio-Claudian period, obviously cannot be pressed: their use of
the term 'fiscus' is clearly at times anachronistic. It is, however,
noteworthy that they also use the word not infrequently to denote
the emperor's personal estate. Tacitus[37] states that after C. Silius'
condemnation 'liberalitas Augusti avulsa, computatis singillatim
quae fisco petebantur'. Tiberius here claims for his 'fiscus' a refund
of private presents to Silius. A similar claim seems to have been
made in respect of Sejanus' property,[38] and Aemilia Musa's
property was claimed for the 'fiscus', as she had died intestate:[39]
as the rest of the paragraph deals with property left by will to
Tiberius, it is to be presumed that in this case Tiberius claimed as

next of kin. Again, when Otho promised to compensate centurions 'e fisco suo' for the loss of their perquisites,[40] the words clearly mean 'out of his own pocket', and Vitellius' similar offer to make good their loss 'e fisco'[41] must be interpreted in the same sense. In Suetonius' anecdote of the imperial freedman who tried to defraud the 'fiscus' of his estate by changing his name, and in Juvenal's story of the great turbot, 'fiscus' must again denote the emperor's private estate.[42]

During the Julio-Claudian period there is no epigraphic record of any 'fiscus' at Rome save one, the 'fiscus libertatis et peculiorum'.[43] This fund was presumably derived from the *peculia* of deceased slaves of Caesar, from the sums with which slaves of Caesar bought their liberty, and no doubt also from the inheritances of imperial freedmen, which might be classed with *peculia*. It handled, at all events, the emperor's private profits arising from his *familia*.

Neither the literary nor the epigraphic evidence, therefore, justify the assumption that the Julio-Claudian emperors possessed a 'fiscus' in the sense of a treasury at Rome in which they kept public money. Nor, in my theory, had they any need for such a treasury. The greater part of their expenditure was in the provinces, and for this sum they drew upon the 'fisci' and *publicani* of their own and neighbouring provinces. The sums that they spent in Rome on such items as the praetorian guard, the *vigiles*, and the corn supply, they or the prefects immediately responsible drew from the aerarium as required. On the other hand there is considerable literary evidence for the existence of a 'fiscus' containing the emperor's private money and, though epigraphic evidence is lacking, such a treasury must have existed. Without it the emperors could not have maintained their expensive household establishment or have made the numerous and heavy payments which they are recorded to have made from their private estate. The private fortunes of the emperors played an important part in public finance. The State was so poor that a rich man's private resources were comparable with it, and the emperors were very rich. Augustus, as he records in the *Res Gestae*, freely subsidised the aerarium from his private funds,[44] and Nero claimed that he paid HS 60,000,000 into the aerarium annually[45] besides *ad hoc* grants like the HS 40,000,000 he subscribed to maintain public credit in 57.[46] At times, when for instance a *congiarium* was to be paid, the emperor must have had very large sums in actual cash in his 'fiscus' at Rome.

In the Flavian period new developments took place. First there appears a 'procurator fiscorum transmarinorum' at Rome.[47] Next there appear at Rome four new 'fisci'—Iudaicus, frumentarius, Asiaticus, Alexandrinus, and probably also the 'fiscus castrensis'. The first two present no great interest. The 'fiscus Iudaicus'[48] received the new Jewish poll tax. The 'fiscus frumentarius'[49] was the cash-box of the Praefectus Annonae, who presumably ceased at this time to draw *ad hoc* from the aerarium, but received a block grant. The 'fiscus castrensis',[50] with the corresponding 'ratio castrensis,'[51] was, I suspect, a special treasury created to hold the funds, drawn doubtless from the patrimonial revenue, out of which the emperor paid the expenses of his large household. The 'fiscus Alexandrinus'[52] and the 'fiscus Asiaticus'[53] have never been satisfactorily explained. The clue, I suggest, lies in the fact that Asia and Egypt were the two provinces which produced a substantial surplus over the costs of their own administration or the needs of the neighbouring provinces. Cash must have been regularly shipped from Asia and Egypt to Rome. I suggest that Vespasian (as the great financial reformer of this period) established at Rome branch offices of the provincial 'fisci' of Egypt and Asia, and drew upon them for his central expenditure, thus short-circuiting the aerarium. His motive was presumably to avoid the red tape which no doubt hampered the withdrawal of money from the aerarium, and to handle his finances through his own procurators rather than through *praetores aerarii,* whom he found in control of the treasury:[54] these, if they were chosen by lot from the praetors of the year, might be unco-operative. *Praefecti aerarii Saturni,* ex-praetors nominated by the emperor, seem to have been soon restored,[55] but these too might be less efficient, and less amenable to discipline, than imperial procurators. Vespasian would also have avoided the last vestiges of publicity for his finances, since the *rationes imperii* had long ceased to be published and now no imperial funds passed through the aerarium.

Vespasian's arrangements seem to have remained substantially unchanged till the end of the Antonine period. The aerarium, deprived of what had been its main assets, the surpluses of Asia and Egypt, could not now have contained much money, and the emperors ceased to draw on it normally. When Marcus, in the financial stress of the Marcomannic war, did draw funds from the aerarium, obtaining the Senate's authorisation to do so, the fact caused remark.[56] During all this period there was no single 'fiscus' at Rome, but such imperial funds as were kept at the capital were stored in a number of 'fisci', the Alexandrinus and the Asiaticus holding the surplus of Egypt and Asia, the Iudaicus the proceeds of the Jewish poll-tax, the 'frumentarius' the special fund of the Praefectus Annonae, the 'castrensis' the emperor's personal moneys. In popular, and indeed in semi-official, language the term 'fiscus', in the singular, denoted the imperial financial administration, but in strict official parlance, 'fisci 'in the plural was still the correct expression. When, in A.D. 118, Hadrian made his great remission of arrears, the official inscription set up by the Senate and People speaks of the money as 'debitum fiscis'.[57]

Now that imperial and public finance were completely severed, it was natural to think and speak of fiscus and aerarium as two separate and complementary organisations, one managed by the emperor and the other by the Senate, between them covering all State finance. Writers of the reign of Trajan often so use these two terms. The Younger Pliny couples the two together to denote the public finances in one sentence:[58] 'locupletabant et fiscum et aerarium non tam Voconiae et Iuliae leges quam maiestatis singulare et unicum crimen.' In another passage he contrasts them:[59] 'at fortasse non eadem severitate fiscum qua aerarium cohibes: immo tanto maiore, quanto plus tibi licere de tuo quam de publico credis.' Frontinus notes that the emoluments of the *apparitores* of the *curatores aquarum* and of the *familia publica* came from the aerarium, while those of the *familia Caesaris* came from the fiscus.[60] Tacitus and Suetonius sometimes use such phrases as 'aerario aut fisco',[61] or 'aerario vel fisco',[62] or 'aerarii fiscique',[63] in writing of earlier periods. Such phrases are probably anachronistic and cannot be used in evidence for Julio–Claudian arrangements.[64]

The terms 'fiscus' and 'fiscalis' still covered the *patrimonium*. In Africa, for instance, 'rustici tui vernulae et alumni saltum tuorum' pray Commodus that 'n(on) ultr(a) a conductorib(us) agror(um) fiscalium inquietemur'.[65] This usage continues in the Severan period and after. In Egypt the patrimonial estates (οὐσίαι) owe their rent to the fiscus (ταμιεῖον),[66] and in Asia Minor tenants of imperial lands (τὰ δεσποτικὰ χωρία) declare that their effects are pledged to the fiscus.[67] The lawyers use the same language. Callistratus[68] writes 'coloni quoque Caesaris a muneribus liberantur ut idoniores praediis fiscalibus habeantur'. In bureaucratic language the *patrimonium* was by the beginning of the third century a *ratio* of the fiscus.[69]

What happened under Severus is far from clear, and it will be best to state the evidence first. A new department, *patrimonium privatum*, or more commonly *ratio privata*, appears under a high-ranking procurator: the first procurator held office at the very beginning of Severus' reign.[70] At the same time the series of equestrian *procuratores patrimonii* ceases, the last being the first *procurator rationis privatae*: only one later *procurator patrimonii* is known, and he is a freedman.[71] But simultaneously both the *patrimonium* and the *ratio privata* produce a crop of local procurators, looking after provinces,[72] or sections or groups of provinces, and, in the case of the *ratio privata*, districts of Italy.[73] Hitherto the *patrimonium* had possessed no provincial office, save in Egypt,[74] and procurators of estates or groups of estates had apparently been subject to the procurator of the province. It

would seem, prima facie, most uneconomical to have two
procurators both engaged on estate management, merely because
the legal status of the lands differed, and in fact one procurator
sometimes doubled both jobs.[75] Finally the epigraphic evidence
for the sundry 'fisci' at Rome and their procurators fades out:
the *ratio castrensis* survives.[76]

The early third-century lawyers are rather hazy about the exact
status of the new *ratio privata*. Sometimes they seem to distinguish
it from the fiscus: Ulpian[77] writes 'quodcumque privilegii fisco
competit, hoc idem et Caesaris ratio et Augustae habere solet'.
Callistratus,[78] commenting on a constitution of the Divi Fratres,
'si in locis fiscalibus vel publicis religiosisve aut in monumentis
thensauri reperti fuerint . . . ut dimidia pars ex his fisco vindi-
caretur,' adds the words 'item si in Caesaris possessione repertus
fuerit, dimidiam aeque partem fisco vindicari': he must be
thinking of the *ratio privata*, since the ruling of the Divi Fratres
would have included patrimonial *possessiones Caesaris*, presumably
under the term 'fiscales'. What is clear from these passages is that
for all practical purposes the *ratio privata* ranked equally with the
fiscus. Fiscus seems to be equated with *ratio privata* in another
passage of Callistratus[79] where he enumerates among cases 'ex
quibus nuntiatio ad fiscum fieri solet' those in which 'princeps
heres institutus et testamentum sive codicilli subrepti esse
nuntiantur', or where it was reported 'decessisse qui in capitali
crimine esset'. The *res privata* is said to have been built out of
*bona damnatorum*,[80] and new inheritances surely went to it. The
language of the lawyers is best explained on the assumption that
'fiscus' or 'fiscalis' remained a general term embracing all imperial
finance, but that it was felt necessary to explain that the newly
created *ratio privata* had fiscal status. In Byzantine terminology
'fiscalis' or ταμειακός is one of the many synonymous terms used
to describe property of the *res privata*.[81]

This evidence suggests that Severus consolidated the numerous
existing financial departments into two principal ministries,
presided over by the *rationalis* or *a rationibus* and the *procurator*

*rationis privatae.* The division of functions between these two ministries is not clear. It is misleading to say that the *patrimonium* was merged with the fiscus under the charge of the *rationalis*, for the term 'fiscus' had always included the *patrimonium*, and as I have argued, seems to have embraced the new *res privata* as well. The distinction is not between 'fiscus' and *ratio privata*, but between *summae rationes* and *ratio privata*, both of which were comprehended within the general term 'fiscus'. The term *summae rationes* first appears in the late second century and gradually becomes standard in the third, as defining the sphere of the *a rationibus*.[82] There is no direct evidence as to what revenues or departments were included in the *summae rationes* and what in the *ratio privata*, but common sense would suggest that the first included taxation revenue, and the second revenue from estates. In the provinces, as I have shown, the two departments of the *patrimonium* and the *ratio privata* acquired under the Severi separate staffs of procurators, independent of the procurators of the provinces, and these staffs were soon merged. It seems probable that the same happened at the centre, and that the *procurator rationis privatae* had under his care two departments, the *ratio privata* proper and the *patrimonium* (under a subordinate freedman procurator). This arrangement would explain the very high rank which the *procurator rationis privatae* rapidly acquired; he was already a *trecenarius* under Severus or Caracalla,[83] equal, if not superior, to the *rationalis*. Whatever the extent of the Severan confiscations, newly acquired estates could hardly have equalled in importance the taxation revenue plus the accumulated estates of two centuries. It would also explain how, in Byzantine times, the *comes rei privatae* dealt with all landed property of the emperor, and the terms 'patrimonium (-alis)', 'fiscalis' and 'res privata' were used interchangeably.

# VII

## PROCURATORS AND PREFECTS IN THE EARLY PRINCIPATE

# Procurators and Prefects in the Early Principate

FROM the reign of Claudius 'procurator Augusti' seems to have been fairly generally accepted as the normal and appropriate title of a provincial governor of equestrian rank: the only notable exception is the prefect of Egypt. This is a startling fact, for under the Republic procurator was a term of private law, meaning the personal agent or bailiff of an individual. An attempt has been made to prove that the term was already acquiring a certain public standing from some passages of Cicero, Sallust and Caesar, where the abstract noun *procuratio* is used for offices of state.[1] But the language of these passages is figurative; and it is a very different thing to say that 'Mr. X's management of the public finances was prudent' and to style Mr. X 'Manager of the Public Finances' instead of 'Chancellor of the Exchequer' in official documents. There can be no doubt that procurator was a term of private law in the later Republic, and it always remained so except when applied to the emperor's procurators.

This being so it seems very improbable that two emperors so careful of constitutional proprieties as Augustus and Tiberius would have given the title procurator to provincial governors, and a careful examination of the evidence has made it very improbable that they did. Later historians sometimes apply the title to governors under these two emperors, as Tacitus calls Pontius Pilate procurator of Judaea.[2] But contemporary evidence, especially that of the inscriptions, shows that equestrian governors were normally styled *praefectus* or *pro legato*.

Strabo speaks of an equestrian prefect (ὕπαρχος τῶν ἱππικῶν ἀνδρῶν) governing the Maritime Alps, and the elder Pliny

mentions a prefect of an Alpine province.[3] Inscriptions record a
'praefectus civitatum in Alpibus maritumis', and two 'praefecti
civitatum' (which are listed individually) in the area later known
as the Cottian Alps;[4] these are not Roman officers, but M. Julius
Cottius, the son of King Donnus, and Albanus, son of Busallus.
Cassius Dio says that in A.D. 6 Sardinia was entrusted to 'equestrian
commanders' (στρατιάρχαις ἱππεῦσιν)'; inscriptions give the title
of *pro legato* under Augustus and *praefectus* early in Claudius'
reign.[5] Another inscription records a prefect of Corsica.[6] There
is also epigraphical evidence for a number of similar posts which
were subsequently suppressed. Between 27 and 23 B.C., when it
was surrendered to the Senate, Cyprus was governed by a *pro
legato*.[7] In Spain there were prefects of the unruly areas of
Asturia and Gallaecia,[8] probably under Augustus, and in the
newly conquered territory south of the Danube a *praefectus
civitatium Moesiae et Treballiae*, probably under Tiberius.[9] We
know also of two *praefecti* and one *praefectus pro legato* of the
Balearic Isles; two of them served under Nero.[10]

In Raetia there is an apparent conflict of evidence. Under
Tiberius there is a 'praefectus Raetis Vindolicis vallis Poeninae et
levis armaturae',[11] but another inscription records a 'procurator
Caesaris Augusti in Vindelicis et Raetis et in valle Poenina per
annos IIII, et in Hispania provincia per annos X et in Suria
biennium'.[12] This man, however, was probably a fiscal procurator
in Raetia, as he certainly was in Spain and Syria, at a time when
the province was governed by C. Vibius Pansa 'legato pro
[praet(ore) i]n Vindol(icis)'.[13] If so, the first procurator who
governed Raetia would be a 'procur. Augustor. et pro leg.
provinciai Raitiai et Vindelic. et vallis Poenin.', who probably
served under Gaius and Claudius.[14]

For Noricum there is no evidence earlier than Claudius, when
it was ruled by a procurator.[15] In Cappadocia again we have no
record of the governor's title until Claudius' reign, when it was,
if Tacitus is to be trusted, procurator.[16] Thrace, annexed by
Claudius, seems to have been ruled from the first by a procurator:

it certainly was under Nero.[17] The governor of Mauretania Tingitana, also annexed by Claudius, was already styled *procurator et pro legato* in his reign.[18]

Judaea is the only province where the evidence, all literary, is ambiguous. Philo, writing under Claudius, speaks of Pontius Pilate as 'one of the prefects appointed procurator of Judaea'.[19] Josephus in the Wars calls both Coponius, the first governor, and Pilate procurators (ἐπίτροπος), but in the Antiquities gives no title to the first three governors, calls the fourth, Gratus, a prefect (ἔπαρχος), gives Pilate the unofficial designation of governor (ἡγεμών), and styles Cuspius Fadus (under Claudius) prefect in one chapter and procurator in the next.[20] Seeing that by his time the title of the governor of Judaea had for a generation been procurator, it is likely that his use of this term is anachronistic, and that he is reproducing his sources more accurately when he uses the term prefect, which would have been strange to his ears.

In using the title of prefect for his assistants of equestrian rank Augustus was following, and, as so often, developing Republican usage. In the pages of Cicero and Caesar *praefecti* and *tribuni* (*militum*) are frequently mentioned as forming, with the quaestor and *legati*, the staff of a proconsul.[21] The *tribuni militum* were of course the officers of the legions, but might be used for special duties.[22] The *praefecti* were headed by the *praefectus fabrum*, who had ceased to have any connection with the engineers, and might be employed in any post of trust: under Augustus a *praefectus fabrum* of a proconsul of Asia was assigned 'i(uri) d(icundo) et sortiendis iudicibus'.[23] *Praefecti* were most commonly used to command units of auxiliary troops—Caesar frequently mentions his *praefecti equitum*—but they were sometimes put in charge of irregular units of citizen troops—Cicero in one of his letters mentions his *praefectus evocatorum*.[24] In the civil wars they were often put in command of towns: thus Varro, Pompey's legate in Further Spain, made C. Gallonius, a Roman knight, prefect of the town of Gades.[25] *Praefecti* might also be used for judicial purposes; Cicero sent Q. Volusius, who must have been one of his *praefecti*, to Cyprus to administer justice to the Roman citizens resident in the island.[26]

It has often been doubted whether *praefecti*, like *legati*, held an *imperium* delegated to them by their proconsul, but there is no good reason for denying it. They were assigned tasks similar in kind, and differing only in scale, from those assigned to *legati*, and the execution of these tasks required *imperium*. Jurisdiction needed *imperium*,[27] especially when exercised over Roman citizens; so also did military command,[28] certainly over citizen troops. Caesar, referring to the activities of Scipio Nasica in Asia in 49 B.C., declares:[29] 'non solum urbibus sed paene vicis castellisque singulis cum imperio praeficiebantur . . . erat plena lictorum et imperiorum provincia, differta praefectis atque exactoribus'. The language is somewhat vague and rhetorical, but it is implied that the very numerous prefects appointed by Scipio were vested with *imperium*.

Augustus therefore in appointing *praefecti* to govern a group of tribes or what amounted to a small province was merely enlarging on Republican precedent. His province was far larger than that of any Republican proconsul, his *legati* ruled areas as extensive as any proconsular province, and it was natural that his *praefecti* should rule greater areas.

The title *pro legato* appears to have been an innovation, and to have been given as an acting rank to equestrian officers[30] entrusted with unusually responsible duties. There were, it would seem, certain functions which it was felt inappropriate to entrust to a prefect, notably the command of legions. Such commands were normally given to *legati*, and *legati* had by law or constitutional convention to be senators. If therefore, Augustus wished to place legionary troops under the command of an equestrian officer, he solved the constitutional difficulty by giving him acting rank of *legatus*. The device seems to have been used only as a temporary stop-gap measure, and was rarely employed after the Julio-Claudian period.[31]

There is one prefecture which is quite exceptional, that of

Egypt. Octavian was determined, no doubt for the reasons given by Tacitus,[32] not to entrust the control of this key province to a senator, and in 30 B.C. appointed an equestrian officer, Cornelius Gallus, with the title of *praefectus Aegypti*. His functions and powers were quite abnormal for a prefect, since he not only ruled an exceptionally important province, but commanded an army of three legions besides auxiliary troops.[33]

Octavian appears to have felt that he was stretching his normal prerogative of delegating his (consular) *imperium* to equestrian prefects too far in this case. Ulpian states: 'praefectus Aegypti non prius deponit praefecturam et imperium quod ad similitudinem proconsulis lege sub Augusto ei datum est, quam Alexandriam ingressus est successor eius'.[34] This passage has been condemned as interpolated on various grounds, that the phrase 'ad similitudinem' is not found in the jurists and is late;[35] that the words 'et imperium . . . datum est' are redundant and inapposite, since on the very point on which Ulpian is commenting the position of the prefect of Egypt differed from that of a proconsul;[36] and that the passage conflicts with other statements in Tacitus and the Digest.[37] The first objection has been proved to be groundless.[38] The second is not very cogent; Ulpian may have introduced the offending words just because in this particular respect the prefect's *imperium* differed from that of a proconsul. The third is more substantial. Tacitus states: 'nam divus Augustus apud equestris qui Aegypto praesiderent lege agi decretaque eorum proinde haberi iusserat ac si magistratus Romani constituissent'.[39] Modestinus says: 'apud praefectum Aegypti possum servum manumittere ex constitutione divi Augusti'.[40] If, it is argued, there was a *lex* conferring 'imperium ad similitudinem proconsulis' on the prefect of Egypt, it would have been unnecessary for Augustus to give him the jurisdiction mentioned by a *constitutio*.

The apparent contradiction can be otherwise explained. *Legis actiones*, including *manumissio vindicta*, *adoptio* and *tutoris datio*, were not regarded as normal forms of jurisdiction, which could be exercised by any holder of *imperium*, but as peculiar to *magistratus Romani*, that is consuls and praetors and proconsuls.[41] These powers were extended to *legati Augusti*,[42] but there was some doubt whether, for instance, *legati* of proconsuls possessed them. Paulus declared that they could manumit,[43] and Ulpian that, by a ruling of Marcus, they could appoint *tutores*.[44] But Marcianus says 'apud legatum vero proconsulis nemo manumittere potest quia non habet jurisdictionem talem', and in another passage Ulpian adds: 'nec adoptare potest: omnino enim non est apud eum legis actio'.[45] Doubt might well have arisen whether the prefect of Egypt, to whom a special *imperium* like that of a proconsul had been granted by law, was a *magistratus Romanus* capable of *legis actiones*, and it was on this subsidiary issue that Augustus gave a ruling.

I would maintain therefore that Ulpian's statement on the *imperium* of the prefect of Egypt is genuine, and I would add that those who doubt it must explain for what motive the compilers of the Digest should have inserted the alleged interpolation. They manipulated the texts of the ancient jurists in order to bring them into conformity with the law as it stood in Justinian's day, but this passage of Ulpian was a matter of purely antiquarian interest, which had no bearing on current law.

Octavian then regularised the abnormal position of the prefect whom he had appointed to govern Egypt by a special law. He must have felt that an equestrian prefect in command of an important province and three legions was too glaring an anomaly to be accepted on the strength of his consular *imperium*. The fact that he caused the prefect's *imperium* to be assimilated to that of a proconsul suggests that the law was passed before 27 B.C., at a time when all provincial governors were proconsuls. After the settlement of 27 B.C., when the districts of Augustus' province were governed by his *legati pro praetore*, it would have been more natural to assign the prefect of Egypt an *imperium* of like rank. As it was the curious anomaly resulted that Augustus and his prefect after 23 B.C. both enjoyed *imperium proconsulare*, and

Augustus was superior to him only in that his *imperium* was *maius*.

The procurators of Augustus and Tiberius, on the other hand, were officially only their private agents. They fall into two classes, the procurators of provinces, who handled all the emperor's financial affairs within each, and the lesser procurators who were bailiffs of individual estates which the emperor owned in a private capacity. That provincial procurators were regarded as private agents is strongly suggested by Augustus' action in appointing his freedman Licinus to be procurator of Gaul,[46] and was explicitly affirmed by Tiberius, as quoted by Tacitus in reference to his procurator of Asia: 'non se ius nisi in servitia et pecunias familiares dedisse: quod si vim praetoris usurpasset manibusque militum usus foret, spreta in eo mandata sua'.[47] In the imperial provinces these procurators, it is true, performed functions which to modern ideas were inappropriate to private agents. In Spain, Strabo tells us, they paid the troops,[48] and Licinus, according to Seneca and Cassius Dio, collected the tribute of the Gauls.[49] In the public provinces their main business was the management of the emperor's private property, but they seem also to have made compulsory purchases of supplies for the troops.[50] Finance, however, was not in the view of the Romans a magisterial function: they were after all used to the taxes being collected by private contractors. And the procurators possessed no more than did the *publicani* any powers of coercion or jurisdiction. As Cassius Dio explains: 'In those days those who managed the imperial finances were not allowed to do more than collect the customary revenues, and in case of disputes to accept judgment in court by the laws on an equality with private citizens'.[51] The procurators of estates were probably mere bailiffs. Herennius Capito, procurator of Jamnia, which had been bequeathed by Herod's sister Salome to Livia, and had passed from her to Tiberius, is called by Philo a mere revenue collector (φόρων ἐκλογεύς).[52]

Procuratorships and prefectures may nevertheless not always

have been kept strictly apart. Under the Republic it was apparently not unusual for proconsuls to grant prefectures (including command of troops) to the procurators of important persons, in order to give them power to collect their principals' debts.[53] Cicero rightly objected to this practice as an abuse, but complacent proconsuls may have thought it proper thus to assist the procurators of Augustus. This may explain how Lucilius Capito, Tiberius' procurator of Asia, apparently had troops at his disposal despite Tiberius' orders.[54] A century later we find Pliny, on the emperor's instructions, assigning troops to the procurator of the province and his assistant procurator; and in so doing he seems to have been following the precedent of his predecessors, the proconsuls of Bithynia.[55] In his own provinces it would have been even more natural for the emperor to instruct his legates to put small bodies of troops at his procurators' disposal; Catus, the procurator of Britain, had a few men, including centurions, under his command when he took possession of Pratusagus' property in the emperor's name.[56] Even Herennius Capito, the humble procurator of Jamnia, sent soldiers to assist Agrippa for debt:[57] they were presumably lent to him by the prefect of Judaea or the legate of Syria.

Conversely prefects of provinces may have been concurrently procurators of Augustus. The prefect of Egypt was, we are told by Philo, intimately concerned with finance,[58] and we know from the case of Pilate that the prefects of Judaea, besides their military and judicial functions, handled the finances of the province.[59] The same was probably true of all prefects of provinces. It was not customary for military officers, as the *praefecti* essentially were, to deal with public finance; imperial *legati* never did so. It may be therefore that for financial purposes a prefect of a province was deemed to be acting as a procurator of Augustus, and he may even have held two posts, a military command and a private agency, concurrently. This is suggested by a number of cases in which a governor is styled *procurator et praefectus* or *pro legato*. Two cases of the latter combination occur under Claudius, in Raetia and in Mauretania Tingitana:[60] in the latter province it recurs in Trajan's reign and later.[61] In Sardinia we find a *procurator et praefectus* under Vespasian, and here again the combination of titles recurs in later reigns.[62] It may be that Philo was being not muddleheaded but strictly accurate in describing Pilate as 'one of the prefects appointed procurator of Judaea'.[63]

If this is so, the change under Claudius will have been one of nomenclature rather than of substance. Claudius, with typical lack of tact, preferred to stress that equestrian governors of provinces were his procurators rather than that they were his prefects, just as he openly secured judicial powers for his financial procurators as such instead of giving them prefectures when required.[64] Both changes were no doubt made easier by the fact that by now the term *procurator Augusti* had come to have an official ring, but both were very sudden and the former like the latter seems to have been due to the personal initiative of Claudius. Not only were the governors of the newly annexed provinces of Thrace and Mauretania apparently from the first styled procurators, but those of Raetia and Noricum were so styled in Claudius' reign.[65] It would even appear that the prefect of Egypt was sometimes called a procurator under Claudius. Philo in two passages gives this title to Flaccus, the elder Pliny states that statues of porphyry were first brought from Egypt to Rome for Claudius by Vitrasius Pollio, 'procurator eius'.[66] An embassy from Alexandria, probably to Claudius, alludes to the prefect as 'your procurator' (τὸν σὸν ἐπίτροπον), and finally Claudius himself in his letter to the Alexandrians calls Vitrasius Pollio his procurator (τοῦ ἐμοῦ ἐπιτρόπου). In Egypt the old title of prefect prevailed, and in some other provinces, such as Sardinia and Tingitana, the procurator continued to add the title *praefectus* or *pro legato* to his style, no doubt because his military functions were prominent. Elsewhere procurator became the regular title of an equestrian governor until Severus revived the title *praefectus* in Mesopotamia.

# VIII

## THE DEDITICII AND THE CONSTITUTIO ANTONINIANA

# The Dediticii and the Constitutio Antoniniana

IT is generally agreed that *P. Giessen* 40 includes a copy of the Greek version of the Constitutio Antoniniana, which in A.D. 212 granted the Roman citizenship to all (or nearly all) the free inhabitants of the Empire.[1] The papyrus is unfortunately badly damaged and there are two large lacunae in the operative sentence of the edict. The text runs: δίδωμι τοί[ν]υν ἅπα (c. 28 letters) ν οἰκουμένην π[ολιτ]είαν Ῥωμαίων [μ]ένοντος (c. 28 letters) ἅτων χωρ[ὶς] τῶν [δε]δειτικίων. Such a large lacuna cannot be filled except by guesswork, but the general sense required in the first is indicated by Ulpian's statement (*Dig.* I. v. 17): 'in orbe qui sunt ex constitutione imperatoris Antonini cives Romani effecti sunt'. The gap has accordingly been filled in various ways, such as ἅπα[σιν τοῖς κατοικοῦσιν τὴ]ν οἰκουμένην or ἅπα[σιν ὅσοι ἐὰν ὦσι κατὰ τὴ]ν οἰκουμένην.

The second lacuna presents much greater difficulty, for it introduces a new element unknown to our other authorities. Grammatically, it would appear, the main clause is followed by a genitive absolute beginning μένοντος (representing an ablative absolute beginning *manente*) and this is followed by the phrase *praeter dediticios*. The run of the sentence suggests that the exception applies to the genitive absolute clause. It might however be possible so to fill the gap as to attach the exception to the verb. The words [μ]ένοντος οὐδενὸς ἐκτὸς τῶν ἐμῶν δωρημ]άτων have been suggested,[2] and though this particular supplement is not very convincing Greek (δώρημα is an odd word, and why the plural?) and is almost certainly too long for the space, it would be rash to say that the missing words might not have been something to this effect.[3] Again the missing clause may have been some purely formal saving clause qualifying πολιτείαν ʿΡωμαίων: [μ]ένοντος [τῷ φίσκῳ τοῦ λόγου ἀπαραβ]άτως— 'saving the rights of the fiscus'—has been proposed.[4] In such a case, though the sentence would be inelegant, it would be possible—and indeed in this particular case necessary—to attach the exception to the main verb.

We may clear the ground by endeavouring to discover the meaning of the term *dediticii*. They are defined by Gaius[5] thus: 'vocantur autem peregrini dediticii hi qui quondam adversus populum Romanum armis susceptis pugnaverunt, deinde victi se dediderunt'. *Deditio* was unconditional surrender and left the members of the community which made it without rights at the mercy of the Roman people.[6] Mommsen has shown that in her earlier career (the conquest of Italy) Rome very rarely left her defeated enemies in the condition of *dediticii* other than momentarily, either granting them her citizenship, full or *sine suffragio*, or reconstituting them as an independent allied community. Mommsen held, however, that later in her career, when she began to acquire provinces, Rome omitted to regulate definitively the status of their inhabitants, who thus remained permanently in a position which could in strict legal language be only described as that of *dediticii*, though he admitted that this term was never applied to them, and that they in practice enjoyed the right of self government. But, Mommsen held, the 'tolerated autonomy' which the provincial communities enjoyed was precarious and therefore legally null, and the provincials were in strict law all *dediticii*.[7]

This view is still accepted by many scholars, but it seems excessively formalistic. The autonomy of the provincial communities was not merely tolerated. It was regulated by the *lex provinciae*: the *lex Pompeia quae Bithynis data est* laid down to whom the *civitates* of Bithynia and Pontus might or might not grant their citizenship, fixed age limits for their magistracies and defined how their councils were to be filled up.[8] In these circumstances it is difficult to believe that the provincial *civitates* had no legal existence. In one case, that of Thermae, which was an ordinary stipendiary city of Sicily, Cicero expressly says, 'cum . . . senatus et populus Romanus Thermitanis . . . urbem agros legesque suas reddidisset'.[9] Moreover in strictly legal language—in that of the military diplomas, for instance—provincials are consistently styled not *dediticii* or *peregrini dediticii*, but simply *peregrini*.

On these grounds I would maintain that the provincial communities were formally recognised as *civitates* of *peregrini*; Trajan defines Nicomedia as a *peregrina civitas* in a strictly legal context.[10]

Who then were the *dediticii* of the Constitutio Antoniniana? The word was still used more or less in its literal meaning in the fourth century to denote barbarians from without the empire who surrendered themselves: Ammianus Marcellinus speaks of 'Laetos quosdam, cis Rhenum editam barbarorum progeniem, vel certe ex dediticiis qui ad nostra desciscunt', and tells how Julian, in a raid beyond the Rhine, 'quosdam occidit, orantes alios praedamque offerentes dediticios cepit'.[11] An inscription dated A.D. 232 records a body of troops styled 'Brittones dediticii Alexandriani', which was presumably embodied from such barbarians.[12]

In the second place there were the freedmen of whom the Lex Aelia Sentia enacted that 'eiusdem condicionis liberi fiant cuius condicionis sunt peregrini dediticii',[13] and of whom the lawyers always speak as *dediticiorum numero*. The little that we know about the status of *dediticii* refers to this class, but it is difficult to disentangle which of their disabilities were peculiar to freedmen of this status, and which were common to all *peregrini dediticii*. The prohibition against residence within a hundred miles of Rome was enacted in the Lex Aelia Sentia,[14] and therefore peculiar to *liberti dediticiorum numero*. The rules governing the disposition of the property of deceased members of the class were modelled on the rules applicable to other freedmen,[15] and were therefore peculiar to freedmen. Incapacity to inherit (from a Roman) was common to all *peregrini*.[16] Incapacity to make a will was inferred by Gaius from the intentions of the legislator of the Lex Aelia Sentia,[17] by Ulpian 'quoniam nec quasi civis Romanus testari potest cum sit peregrinus, nec quasi peregrinus quoniam nullius certae civitatis civis est ut secundum leges civitatis suae testetur'.[18] It has been inferred from the second clause that *nullius certae civitatis civem esse* was a general mark of *peregrini dediticii*. But in fact Ulpian is merely saying that *liberti dediticiorum numero* belonged to no *civitas*.

There remains the principal disability of *liberti dediticiorum numero*, incapacity to obtain the Roman citizenship. As Gaius states, 'nec ulla lege aut senatus consulto aut constitutione principis aditus illis ad civitatem Romanam datur'.[19] That is, no such avenues to citizenship were open to them as to freedmen of Latin status. Furthermore, even under the rules of *erroris probatio*, whereby when a Roman man or woman married a Latin or peregrine in ignorance of his or her true status, the spouse and the children were accorded the Roman citizenship, a special exception was made if the spouse were *dediticiorum numero*: the children were given the citizenship, but the spouse remained in his or her old status.[20] It was according to Suetonius the principal object of the Lex Aelia Sentia that criminous slaves should be excluded from the citizenship: 'ne vinctus unquam tortusve quis ullo libertatis genere civitatem adipisceretur'.[21] The basic provision of the Lex Aelia Sentia was 'ut qui servi a dominis poenae nomine vincti sint, deve quibus ob noxam quaestio tormentis habita sit . . . et postea vel ab eodem domino vel ab alio manumissi, eiusdem condicionis liberi fiant cuius condicionis sunt peregrini dediticii'.[22] It would seem to be a legitimate inference that the draftsmen of the Lex Aelia Sentia so defined the status of criminous freedmen in order to exclude them from the citizenship, and that therefore incapacity to obtain the Roman citizenship was a disability attaching to all *peregrini dediticii*.[23]

If this argument is sound, it clinches the case that provincials in general were not *dediticii*; for they were freely granted the Roman citizenship. It appears, however, from a letter of Pliny that Egyptians differed from other provincials in that they were not eligible for the Roman citizenship.[24] Josephus states that 'the present masters of the world, the Romans, have forbidden to the Egyptians alone participation in any kind of citizenship.'[25] A clause in the Gnomon of the Idios Logos, which not only debars Egyptians from service in the legions but enacts that an Egyptian who serves surreptitiously does not gain any change of status thereby, confirms these statements.[26] It is tempting to infer that Egyptians were classified as *peregrini dediticii*, and this was the reason for this rather arbitrary rule, which was in fact circumvented by granting first the Alexandrian and then the Roman citizenship.[27] The term Egyptian, it has been established, denoted all inhabitants of Egypt (or rather persons whose *origo* was Egypt) except citizens of Alexandria, and presumably the other Greek cities, Naucratis, Ptolemais and later Antinoopolis.[28] If the view enunciated above is correct, the reason why the Egyptians permanently remained *dediticii* was that there were no *civitates* in Egypt, except for the few Greek cities. The Egyptians could not thus become ordinary *peregrini*, citizens of foreign cities recognised by Rome, but remained surrendered enemies, *peregrini dediticii*, directly subject to Rome. If this is so the inhabitants of certain other provinces, such as Cappadocia, which had few cities and were for the most part directly administered by Roman officials, must also have been *dediticii*.

To return to the Constitutio Antoniniana and *P. Giessen* 40, it is now fairly generally accepted that in 212 all free inhabitants of the empire became Roman citizens, or at any rate that any exceptions were negligible. This is the unanimous statement of the ancient authors,[29] and it has been demonstrated that the Egyptians, who were if not *dediticii* certainly very low grade *peregrini*, did receive the citizenship.[30] This of course does not mean that from 212 onwards all free inhabitants of the empire continued to be Roman citizens. The Lex Junia and the Lex Aelia Sentia continued in force, and under them some freedmen became Latins and others *dediticiorum numero*, until these two statuses were abolished by Justinian.[31] Barbarians continued from time to time to surrender themselves and settle in the empire, becoming *dediticii*: others entered under treaty and became *foederati*.[32]

It follows that if the words χωρ[ὶς] τῶν [δε]δειτικίων are to be construed with the main verb δίδωμι . . . π[ολιτ]είαν ῾Ρωμαίων, the term *dediticii* cannot in the Constitutio Antoniniana denote the Egyptians—and other similar categories of provincials. This is possible. The term *dediticius*, though it apparently conveyed some exact meaning to the draftsmen of the Lex Aelia Sentia, seems to have been unfamiliar and somewhat puzzling to the lawyers of the second and third centuries. Gaius can only give a text book explanation of it, and none of the legal writers can explain what its significance was in the Lex Aelia Sentia.[33] In their writings it survives only as the name of the status given to freedmen with a criminal record, and it is elsewhere known only as a description of surrendered barbarians. In the early third century it may well have been forgotten that it was the status of certain categories of provincials, and the rule debarring Egyptians (and possibly other provincials) from the citizenship may have come to be regarded as a peculiar disability of Egyptians as such; Pliny seems to take this view of the matter.

It may be then that the Constitutio Antoniniana did except from the general grant of the citizenship freedmen *dediciorum numero* and barbarian *dediticii*. These would have been very reasonable exceptions. Freedmen with a criminal record would not be desirable citizens, and there was a strong legal tradition debarring them absolutely from the citizenship. Barbarian immigrants were unassimilated and unreliable. These classes would have been very small, and it is thus understandable that the literary sources should have ignored their exclusion, and that it should have left no trace on our record.

Grammatically, however, it is more probable that the exception χωρ[ὶς] τῶν δεδειτικίων applies to the genitive absolute clause beginning [μ]ένοντος and ending –άτων. In that case there would have been no exceptions to the grant of citizenship, which accords with the other evidence available, but those who were at the time of the grant *dediticii* were exempted for some subsidiary provision. It is impossible to determine what the subsidiary provision was, but it may be profitable to enquire what consequential changes were demanded by the universal grant of citizenship, and whether in any of them a distinction might have been drawn between those who before the grant had been *peregrini* and those who had been *dediticii*.

The Constitutio Antoniniana would naturally have involved the consequence that Roman law became the sole law of the empire. Here no distinction between *peregrini* and *dediticii* would be expected, and none was to the best of our knowledge made. A theory has been advanced that *peregrini* were allowed the option of using either Roman law or that of their city, and that this concession was necessarily denied to *dediticii*, who had no cities. It is difficult to disprove this theory. Non-Roman legal practices and doctrines certainly did survive for some time, and some of them eventually found their way into Roman law. But this was probably due to the conservatism of lawyers and notaries, who could not easily adjust themselves to the new system. The papyri show that some attempt was made by Egyptians to conform to Roman rules, and their evidence suggests that Roman law was officially obligatory, but imperfectly understood and applied. Elsewhere evidence of actual legal practice is so scanty that no firm conclusions are possible, but it seems very improbable that any law but that of Rome was officially recognised.[34]

The Constitutio Antoniniana might also have had repercussions on the status and constitution of the hitherto peregrine cities of the empire. Logically it might have been expected that they would all have become *municipia*, and that their internal institutions would have been remodelled to conform with the standard Roman pattern. In fact this does not seem to have happened. The old local magistracies survived,[35] and so did the old titles of the cities, the general term *civitas* being used except for the old *municipia* and *coloniae*. The saving clause may therefore have specified that the existing status of the cities should remain unaffected by the fact that all their members had become Roman citizens.[36] *Dediticii* may have been excepted from this clause, which did not affect them, since they had no cities, but it would for the same reason seem otiose to mention them.

Another question which would have required regulation as a result of the Constitutio Antoniniana was the local citizenship, or, to use the technical term of the Roman lawyers, the *origo*, of the newly enfranchised citizens. Most existing Roman citizens (if not domiciled at Rome itself) were *municipes* or *coloni* of some *municipium* or *colonia*. Those who had received individual grants of citizenship, and their descendants, remained concurrently citizens of their city of origin.[37] For the bulk of the new citizens this rule would have naturally applied: they would have retained their previous local citizenship. But there would have been a substantial number of anomalous cases. A number of western cities ruled subject populations, *attributi* or *contributi*.[38] In the East also some cities had subject populations. The Mariandyni were subject to Heraclea Pontica: at Cyrene Strabo distinguishes the citizens (πολῖται) from the peasants (γεωργοί): at Prusias ad Hypium an inscription contrasts 'those on the register' (οἱ ἐγκεκριμένοι) with 'the inhabitants of the rural area' (οἱ τὴν ἀγροικίαν κατοικοῦντες).[39] In the Greek East it would moreover seem to have been usual to exclude freedmen and their descendants from the citizenship. At Pergamun in 133 B.C. descendants of freedmen were ranked below resident aliens, and at Ephesus in 85 B.C. freedmen were treated likewise.[40] Under the principate the same practice prevailed at Sillyum, where freedmen were ranked with resident aliens below citizens,[41] and at Alexandria, where the Gnomon of the Idios Logos treats freedmen of Alexandrians as a separate class.[42] At Alexandria, and doubtless in other Greek cities, bastard sons of citizens were excluded from the citizenship.[43]

There must therefore have been a considerable number of persons, apart from the *dediticii*, who in 212 were not citizens of any city. When all alike became Roman citizens, it may well have appeared anomalous that they should remain excluded from their local citizen registers. There were moreover cogent practical reasons for enrolling them. This was a period when the cities of the empire were finding it increasingly difficult to fill their magistracies and to keep their councils up to strength. It must have seemed unreasonable that residents in the city or its territory who were otherwise suitable should be ineligible merely because they were not citizens.[44] As early as the reign of Antoninus Pius the city of Tergeste petitioned the emperor that suitably qualified members of the tribes of the Carni and Catali, which had been attributed to the city by Augustus, should (though *peregrini*) be allowed to hold the aedileship and thus become decurions of Tergeste, and thereby acquire the Roman citizenship.[45]

We have no direct evidence that this anomaly was rectified by the Constitutio Antoniniana[46] or by consequential edicts, but it is assumed in the extracts from the third-century jurists preserved in the title 'ad municipalem et de incolis' of the Digest (L. i) that all Roman citizens are *municipes* of some *municipium*: *incolae* are *municipes* of one *municipium* resident in another. Under the rules which they enunciate freedmen acquire the *origo* of their patrons, legitimate sons that of their fathers, bastards that of their mothers.[47] No one can escape being enrolled on the register of some city. One extract from the *Ad Edictum* of Ulpian, which he wrote in the reign of Caracalla and in which he mentions the Constitutio Antoniniana, suggests that new members from the country districts were being enrolled on the citizen register of the cities.[48] It runs: 'qui ex vico ortus est eam patriam intelligitur habere cui reipublicae vicus ille respondet'. No doubt can have arisen in normal times about the *origo* of the inhabitants of a city's territory: if a man's father was a *municeps*, so was he, wherever he lived. The question can only have been asked when villagers who had not hitherto been *municipes* were being enrolled and neighbouring cities put forward rival claims.

The *dediticii* would naturally be excluded from enrolment, since they belonged to no *civitas*. It may well have been considered desirable, moreover, to stress their exclusion explicitly, for there was a potential clash of interests between the Roman State and the cities. The Roman government had financial and other claims on the *dediticii*; Egyptians were, for instance, liable to State liturgies, and very many of them were tenants of State land, and similar conditions probably prevailed in other directly administered provinces like Cappadocia. Their obligations to the State might be endangered if the cities claimed them and imposed their liturgies upon them. There was a similar clash of interests in the case of *conductores vectigalium fisci* and *coloni Caesaris*, and the imperial government had long ruled that members of these classes were exempt from civic *munera* and *honores*.[49] None the less we find the inhabitants of an imperial estate in Lydia complaining in the early third century of 'those who harry and oppress your tenants on the score of magistracies and liturgies', despite the fact that 'all our property has been for generations under a prior obligation to the fiscus by the rule of our tenancy'.[50]

Such a conflict of interests would have been particularly liable to arise in Egypt. Here Septimius Severus had given civic status to the metropoleis of the nomes by giving them councils (βουλαί) and enrolling their inhabitants in tribes (φυλαί). But the citizen bodies of the metropoleis comprised only those registered as urban residents (οἱ ἀπὸ μητροπόλεως); this is demonstrated by the fact that the tribes in which they were grouped were merely the old wards of the towns (ἄμφοδα) renamed.[51] The townsmen presumably now ceased to be *dediticii*: the villagers of the surrounding nome remained excluded, and Severus expressly ruled that villagers must not be pressed into the liturgies of the metropoleis (μὴ δεῖν ἀπὸ τῶν ⟨κωμῶν⟩ κωμ[ητῶν εἰς τὰ]ς μητροπολειτικὰς ἄγεσθαι λειτουργίας). From the record of a judicial hearing we learn that none the less the city of the Arsinoites was still in the middle of the third century endeavouring to impose its liturgies on villagers, alleging that this had always been customary.[52] By this date both townsmen and villagers were alike Roman citizens, but the old distinction between them was maintained; the city's claim was disallowed by the prefect. It may have lasted into the fifth century. Isidore of Pelusium in one of his letters states that Egyptians and Cappadocians were legally excluded from magistracies (ἀρχαί).[53] He is, as the context shows, alluding to imperial offices, such as provincial governorships, but his statement is, if magistracy be taken in that sense, demonstrably untrue; Egyptians and Cappadocians were freely employed in the imperial service. May it not be that Isidore is—perhaps tendentiously—misinterpreting a rule which excepted the bulk of Egyptians and Cappadocians from civic magistracies? It is suggestive that the two provinces to which he says the rule applied should be those in which, if my argument is sound, the bulk of the inhabitants would before the Constitutio Antoniniana have been *dediticii*.

To sum up my argument, I would maintain that in the reign of Augustus the status of *peregrini dediticii* was attributed not only to barbarians from beyond the frontiers who surrendered themselves, but to those provincials who, like the Egyptians, were not organised in *civitates* but were direct subjects of Rome. It was held to be inherent in the status of a *dediticius* that he could not acquire the Roman citizenship, and freedmen with a criminal record were for that reason assimilated to *dediticii* by the Lex Aelia Sentia. The Constitutio Antoniniana excepted *dediticii* either from the grant of the citizenship or from some subsidiary provision. If the former alternative is correct, the original significance of *dediticii* must by then have been forgotten, and the term applied only to surrendered barbarians and freedmen with criminal records; for the Egyptians undoubtedly received the citizenship. If the *dediticii* were excepted from some subsidiary provision, that provision probably related to the local citizenship of the new citizens. There is some evidence that certain categories of residents hitherto excluded from the local citizenship were now enrolled, and also some evidence that persons hitherto *dediticii* remained excluded from the local citizenship.

It seems very unlikely that the Constitutio Antoniniana was the fruit of any idealistic motives. Caracalla's main objective was probably, as Cassius Dio asserts, fiscal—to make all the inhabitants of the empire liable to the *vicesima hereditatum* and the *vicesima libertatis*. He was, as the sharp debasement of the denarius during his reign shows, extremely hard-pressed financially, and it is significant that he simultaneously doubled the rates of both these taxes and abolished the various exemptions enjoyed by near kinsmen in respect of the inheritance tax.[54] At the same time the Constitutio simplified the law and the administration in certain ways. It substituted one code of private law for the innumerable local laws which had hitherto prevailed, and put an end to the many conflicts of law which the former state of affairs had involved, and their resultant anomalies and injustices. It replaced the multitudinous and divergent laws of local citizenship, which often left a man without any city, by the simple rules of *origo*, which assigned everyone, legitimate or bastard, freeborn or freedman, to his appropriate city. But in the main the *Constitutio* acknowledged a fait accompli, abolishing a legal distinction which had ceased to correspond with the actual situation. In the matter of military recruitment the old distinction between the legions and the *auxilia* had long become purely nominal: Roman citizens frequently preferred to serve in the *auxilia*, and *peregrini* were freely admitted to the legions. In the matter of appeal to Caesar and immunity from flogging the old distinction between *cives Romani* and *peregrini* had already been replaced by the social distinction between *honestiores* and *humiliores*.[55] But though it made little practical difference it may by formally admitting all its inhabitants to the citizenship of Rome have done something to promote the unity of the empire.

# IX

## 'IN EO SOLO DOMINIVM POPVLI ROMANI EST VEL CAESARIS'

# 'In eo solo dominium Populi Romani
est vel Caesaris'

THE doctrine that *dominium* in provincial soil was vested in the Roman people or in Caesar has been taken far more seriously in modern, than it ever was in ancient, times. There is no evidence, as the late Professor Tenney Frank argued,[1] that the doctrine had any effect on the policy of the Roman government under the Republic or in the early years of the Principate. It may be added that there is equally little evidence that it was put to any practical use at any later period. At no time did the Roman government treat provincial landholders as tenants at will, or assume the right of arbitrarily dispossessing them: confiscation always remained a penal measure. Julius Frontinus,[2] writing under Domitian, does, it is true, use the doctrine to explain why provincial landholders pay tribute: 'possidere enim illis quasi fructus tollendi causa et praestandi tributi condicione concessum est.' But it may be questioned how seriously Frontinus intended these words to be taken: the 'quasi' suggests that he is speaking figuratively. And in any case the theory had no effect on administrative practice. A tenant could be evicted for failing to pay his rent:[3] a landowner who did not pay his tribute remained, despite the theory, liable only for the amount of his debt to the State.[4]

Even in the Byzantine period the distinction between private land and land belonging to the State, or rather to the emperor, remained perfectly unequivocal. If Justinian was conscious that the *dominium* in provincial soil was vested in himself, he parted with his rights in a singularly light-hearted manner. So far as legal procedure went he assimilated Italian to provincial soil, abolishing such peculiarly Italian concepts as *nudum ex iure Quiritium dominium*[5] and *usucapio* by two years' possession, and applying to Italian soil the provincial rule of *longi temporis praescriptio*.[6] The result of his reforms, he nevertheless states, is that 'his modis non solum in Italia sed in omni terra quae nostro imperio gubernatur *dominium* rerum, iusta causa possessionis praecedente, adquiratur'.[7] The italics are mine: Justinian lays no stress on the change, and it is only the commentator Theophilus who at this point recalls the doctrine of Gaius, and underlines the emperor's beneficence in surrendering his rights.[8]

The doctrine does not seem, in fact, to have interested constitutional lawyers. It is to explain problems of private law that it is invoked by Gaius. It is enunciated in so many words to account for the fact that *solum Italicum*, when a corpse was lawfully buried in it, became *religiosum*, whereas *solum provinciale* in similar circumstances became *pro religioso* only. The answer is that we make land *religiosum* 'mortuum inferentes in locum nostrum', and the land in the provinces is not ours.[9] The doctrine also clearly in Gaius' mind underlies the other differences between Italian and provincial soil. The former is *res mancipi*, can be conveyed by *mancipatio* and *in iure cessio*, and is capable of *usucapio*. The latter is *nec mancipi*, can be conveyed by *traditio* only, and is incapable of *usucapio*.[10]

Gaius' treatment of *loca sacra* and *religiosa* is not altogether satisfying. The distinction between the two is, he says, that land becomes *sacer* only by authority of the Roman People, whereas a private citizen can make his land *religiosus*.[11] He goes on to explain why provincial land cannot become properly speaking *religiosus*. He then adds: 'item quod in provinciis non ex auctoritate populi Romani consecratum est proprie sacrum non est.'[12] Now we know from a letter of Trajan to Pliny[13] that provincial soil could not become *sacer*. It would appear therefore that in this awkward sentence Gaius is shuffling. He knows that in the provinces the soil is incapable of becoming either *religiosus* or *sacer*. His theory accounts satisfactorily for the former fact. The latter is left unexplained and Gaius glosses over the difficulty by restating the unexceptionable principle that land can be rendered *sacer* only by authority of the Roman People and inconsequently adding 'in provinciis'.

Trajan not only states that provincial soil is incapable of being *sacer*, but gives an explanation which is more satisfying than that of Gaius: 'cum solum peregrinae civitatis capax non sit dedicationis quae fit nostro iure.' The explanation will cover all the facts. *Sacer, religiosus, res mancipi, mancipatio, in iure cessio* and *usucapio* are concepts and processes of the *ius civile* and therefore applicable to *ager Romanus* only. *Traditio*, being *iuris gentium*, is applicable to all negotiable objects, including provincial soil.

Trajan's viewpoint seems to be shared by Cicero. When Decianus entered in the Roman census estates that he had acquired at Apollonis, a free city of Asia, Cicero asked: 'sintne ista praedia censui censendo, habeant ius civile, sint necne sint mancipi, subsignari apud aerarium aut apud censorem possint?'[14] Most of these questions would have to be answered in the negative if the land were, as in Gaius' theory, *ager publicus populi Romani*, but the second, 'habeant ius civile,' surely implies that Cicero regarded land in the territory of Apollonis as *iuris peregrini*.

Trajan's theory is not only authoritative as that of an emperor; it also seems to have the support of a great constitutional theorist of the Republic; and finally it explains the facts. I venture to suggest that it is correct. What then is the origin of Gaius' doctrine? Since it was never taken up by the government, despite its obvious usefulness as a constitutional principle, but is known only as an explanation of problems of private law, it was in all probability evolved in order to explain such problems. It will therefore be useful to trace the development of Roman land law.

Under Roman law *ager privatus* could be conveyed either by the formal processes of *mancipatio* or *in iure cessio* or by the informal process of *traditio*. The two former transferred the *dominium* from seller to buyer. The last transferred *possessio* only, but this flaw in the transaction was automatically remedied by the lapse of

L

time, since *possessio* in good faith for two years conferred *dominium* by *usucapio*.[15] These rules naturally applied to Roman citizens (or *peregrini* possessing *commercium*) and to *ager Romanus*.

Under the Republic it was apparently assumed that the territory of any community which accepted the Roman citizenship became part of the *ager Romanus*, and thus after the enfranchisement of the Italian allies the *ager Romanus* became to all intents and purposes coincident with Italy. Hence the concept of *solum Italicum*. Nevertheless there was *ager Romanus* outside Italy. Most of it was *ager publicus*, so that questions of conveyancing did not arise. But when the Roman People founded transmarine colonies, the parts of its *ager publicus* thus converted into *ager privatus* seem to have been regarded as possessing the same rights as Italian soil: at any rate the allotments at Carthage under the Lex Rubria do not appear, so far as can be judged from the fragmentary text of the Lex Agraria, to be differentiated from *ager privatus* in Italy.[16]

It seems to me probable that Caesar and Augustus continued to regard it as normal that Roman colonies planted in the provinces should form part of the *ager Romanus*. We know at any rate that a large number of their colonies possessed what Pliny and later authors call the *ius Italicum*,[17] whereby their soil had the same legal quality as that of Italy. Provincial *municipia* seem, on the other hand, to have been treated differently: we know of very few which possessed the *ius Italicum*, and these are of late origin.[18] The reason for this change of policy was probably fiscal. *Ager Romanus* was theoretically subject to the Roman *tributum*, but, as this was never levied, it was practically tax-free. This had not mattered so long as the communities enfranchised were Italian, since the Italian allies had never paid taxes to Rome. But when Caesar introducèd the practice of granting the citizenship freely to provincial communities, the financial consequences would have been serious had their territories according to custom become *ager Romanus*. The same considerations of course applied to transmarine colonies, and ultimately led to the same change of policy, but at first their condition was not altered, partly perhaps because they were felt to be more intimately a part of the Roman State, partly because they consisted of men who were already Roman citizens, and most of them veterans, and who therefore had special claim to consideration, partly, no doubt, because they were relatively few in number.

How the change in policy was effected we do not know, but the most plausible hypothesis is that a clause was inserted in the charters of newly created *municipia*, stating that the quality of the soil was unaffected by the enfranchisement of the community. If this was so a novel situation would have arisen. Hitherto individual Romans had bought and sold provincial land. What forms of law they used we do not know. It seems most probable that, as later in imperial Egypt,[19] they employed the legal procedure of the place, though they may have had recourse to *traditio*, which being *iuris gentium* was universally applicable. But now there were whole communities of Roman citizens, who could use no other law but Roman, buying and selling land which was not Roman. *Traditio* was the only procedure available to them.

Lawyers would naturally have compared the processes applicable on Italian and on provincial soil. On provincial soil there was no *mancipatio* or *in iure cessio*, but only *traditio*. On Italian soil *traditio* was also common, perhaps indeed the normal procedure, but it conveyed *possessio* only: *dominium* followed by *usucapio*. On provincial soil, the lawyers argued, *traditio* similarly transferred *possessio*—but there was no *usucapio*. Where then had the *dominium* vanished?

At this stage it will be profitable to examine with greater care the doctrine enunciated by Gaius. In the first place he states that the *dominium* in provincial soil 'populi Romani est vel Caesaris'. Caesar's appearance is unexpected and, on any sound constitutional doctrine, inexplicable. In the second place he divides provincial soil into two categories, *praedia stipendiaria* and *tributaria*, and explains that 'stipendiaria sunt ea quae in his provinciis sunt quae propriae populi Romani esse intelleguntur, tributaria sunt ea

quae in his provinciis sunt quae propriae Caesaris esse creduntur'.[20]
It would seem that in their search for a *dominus* of provincial land
the lawyers seized on the phrases *provinciae publicae* and *provinciae Caesaris* and interpreted them as meaning owned by the
Roman People and Caesar respectively.

If provincial land was in reality *solum peregrinarum civitatium*
and the theory that 'in eo solo dominium populi Romani est vel
Caesaris' is a conveyancer's phantasy, Mommsen's view of the
juristic status of the provinces must be abandoned. He held that
provincial communities made or were deemed to have made a
*deditio* on annexation, and that their juristic position remained
unchanged thereafter. Thus the inhabitants of the provinces were
in strict law *dediticii*, and their land *ager publicus populi Romani*.
I have already argued that the evidence does not seem to tally
with Mommsen's view of the personal status of provincials, the
majority of whom appear to have been not *dediticii* but *peregrini*,
that is, members of *civitates peregrinae*. I suggested that, though
a *deditio* was made or deemed to have been made on annexation,
its effects were undone in so far as the *lex provinciae* reconstituted
(or in some cases constituted) *civitates*.[21] The members of these
became *peregrini*, and their territories, I would now add, became
*solum peregrinarum civitatium*: to quote Cicero:[22] 'cum . . . senatus
et populus Romanus Thermitanis . . . urbem agros legesque suas
reddidisset.'

I further suggested that where no *civitates* were constituted, as
in Egypt, the inhabitants remained *dediticii*. It should follow that
the land in such areas remained *ager publicus populi Romani*. This
in Egypt was substantially true, but on this point the Romans
seem to have tempered legal logic with expediency. They kept
the land of the conquered government, but allowed private land-
owners in most cases to retain their title. Nevertheless the principle that the land of a conquered people belonged to the Roman
government unless and until a city was constituted on it would
seem to have still prevailed in the Flavian period. Josephus[23] says
that on the conclusion of the Jewish war Vespasian ordered 'all

the land of the Jews to be sold; for he did not found a city there, keeping the land in his own possession' (πᾶσαν χώραν ἀποδόσθαι τῶν Ἰουδαίων· οὐ γὰρ κατῴκισεν ἐκεῖ πόλιν, ἰδίαν ἑαυτῷ τὴν χώραν φυλάττων). If one allows for the confusion between the emperor and the Roman People, already at this period common in ordinary and especially provincial minds, these words seem to express correctly the official attitude to provincial soil.

# X

## *THE ROMAN CIVIL SERVICE*
## *(CLERICAL AND SUB-CLERICAL GRADES)*

# The Roman Civil Service
## (Clerical and Sub-Clerical Grades)

THE first and indeed the only Roman clerical officer to achieve historic fame was Gnaeus Flavius, a *scriba* of the aediles, who published the secrets of the *ius civile* and of the calendar and was himself elected aedile in 304 B.C.[1] From this incident some interesting facts emerge on the status and organisation of the early Roman civil service. *Scribae*, if one may generalise from Gnaeus Flavius' case, were, unlike the public γραμματεῖς of the Greek cities, professional clerks who normally made the civil service their life's career,[2] and were therefore experts at their job—sometimes considerably more expert than their annually changing masters. On the other hand, they were not, like the δημόσιοι who often performed similar work in Greek cities, public slaves, but citizens,[3] though of rather humble standing. Flavius was the son of a freedman and, when he stood as aedile, the returning officer refused to accept his name until he formally renounced his profession. *Servi publici* were not unknown at Rome, particularly in the service of the priestly colleges, but the greater and more important part of the civil service consisted of salaried citizens.[4]

We know very little more about the Roman civil service till we get down to the last fifty years of the Republic, when Cicero, particularly in the *Verrines* and in a letter to Quintus, gives us some interesting information, and the epigraphic evidence begins with a fragment of Sulla's law on the twenty quaestors, dealing with their *scribae*, *viatores* and *praecones*. With this evidence may be conveniently combined the many inscriptions of the Principate which illustrate the survival of the Republican civil service under the empire.

We hear at this period of many sub-clerical grades, doctors (*medici*), surveyors (*architecti*), *haruspices* to interpret omens, *pullarii* to keep the chickens needed for divination, but we know little of the organisation and terms of service of these technical officers.[5] In what follows I shall be speaking of the less specialised grades, the messengers (*viatores*),[6] the heralds (*praecones*),[7] and the lictors, who had not only the ceremonial duty of constituting a guard of honour to the magistrates they served,[8] but, in the provinces at any rate, acted as gaolers and executioners. In a province the post of chief lictor might be both influential and lucrative; Cicero gives a lurid but not necessarily untrue picture of how Sextus, Verres' principal lictor, amassed a small fortune by exacting douceurs from the friends and relations of prisoners in return for allowing them amenities in prison or a painless execution.[9] These were all what might be called established officers, permanently registered at the aerarium. One officer, the *accensus*, was exceptional in that he was a personal appointment by the magistrate concerned, who normally nominated a freed-man of his own.[10]

A cut above all these minor fry were the clerical grade—the *scribae*.[11] Even when he is denouncing the iniquities of Verres' *scriba*, Cicero is careful to state that his remarks do not apply to the *ordo scribarum* as a whole, which is a highly respectable body,[12] and he proudly records the *scribae* among the sound elements in the body politic who welcomed his return from exile.[13] It appears from the *Verrines* that it was customary for a magistrate to reward his *scriba* on the conclusion of his service with a gold ring,[14] and that *scribae* claimed to belong to the equestrian order.[15]

The organisation of the service was complicated, and is in some points obscure: the evidence comes mainly from Imperial inscriptions. The officers of each grade attached to each magistracy normally formed a separate panel (*decuria*) or group of panels: for instance, the *scribae* of the quaestors were organised in three *decuriae*, which apparently served in the aerarium annually in rotation, and so also were their *viatores* and *praecones*.[16]   The consuls and praetors counted for this purpose as one college, and the lictors, the *praecones*, and probably also the *viatores* serving them each formed a group of three *decuriae*;[17] but these do not seem to have served in rotation, for one of them was allocated to the consuls.[18]   Other magistracies were served by single *decuriae* of *apparitores*, but the sub-division of magistracies was sometimes carried very far; the curule, plebeian, and cereal aediles, for instance, had each their separate staff of *scribae*.   Most colleges seem to have had their own *viatores* and *praecones*; lictors, of course, were confined to those possessing *imperium*; *decuriae scribarum*, though recorded for practically all of the lesser colleges, are curiously lacking for consuls and praetors.[19]   The *decuriae* were all attached to actual magistrates, no provision being made for pro-magistrates.   There is, however, absolute evidence that pro-consuls and propraetors were served by *apparitores* of all grades,[20] and that praetors and censors (and presumably therefore consuls) had their *scribae*.[21]

The *decuriae* are apparently to be regarded as pools from which the magistrates drew their staffs.   We know from a letter of Pliny that in his day a quaestor of a province drew his *scriba* by lot, and this arrangement is so typical of Republican usage that it is probably general and primitive.[22]   On the other hand, from the mock testimonial which Cicero writes for Verres' *scriba*, it appears that he had served Verres in his successive offices of legate, praetor, and propraetor,[23] and must therefore have been chosen by his employer and not allotted to him.   At the same time Cicero makes it abundantly clear that Verres' *scriba* was a member of the *ordo scribarum* and enrolled in a *decuria*.[24]

The working of the system is a little difficult to visualise, but it would appear that *apparitores*, though drawing a continuous salary from the aerarium as members of the *decuriae*, were not continuously employed, but only as allotted to the magistrates of the college to which they were attached or as selected by pro-magistrates—and, in the case of *scribae*, by consuls and praetors.

A provincial staff would thus consist of several *scribae*—the *scriba quaestorius* proper officially allotted to the quaestor and others employed by the proconsul or propraetor and his *legati*[25]— and lictors, *viatores* and *praecones* employed by the governor, quaestor and *legati*, all drawn from the *decuriae* at Rome.[26]

The most interesting point which emerges from Cicero is that a place on the panels of the *scribae* was obtained by purchase.[27] Cicero waxes rather sarcastic over this method of appointment, whereby, as he says, any scallywag may rise, if he can scrape together the necessary cash, 'ex primo ordine explosorum in secundum ordinem civitatis', but it does not seem generally to have reflected any discredit on the *ordo scribarum*. The precise working of the system is, like most corrupt practices, rather obscure. *Scribae* and other *apparitores* were nominated, it would appear, by the magistrates of the college which they served[28] but once nominated they were irremovable save for misconduct. Plutarch tells of the difficulty which Cato as quaestor had in sacking two dishonest clerks at the treasury. One he succeeded in convicting of a private delict, but the other was acquitted by a tie of votes in the court of discipline, which consisted of the quaestors; Cato nevertheless refused to employ him or pay him his salary.[29] And not only had the *apparitor* a freehold in his office, but he could perform the services by deputy; the Lex Cornelia de XX quaestoribus expressly allows the *viatores* and *praecones* of the quaestors *vicarium dare subdere* and orders the quaestors to accept these *vicarii*.[30] Purchase presumably came in at this stage: Roman magistrates did not sell the original nominations, but the original nominees sold their practices to *vicarii*. The growth of a system of purchase implies that the service was lucrative, and if so the official salary, which Cicero says was small,[31] must have been regularly supplemented by perquisites in some form. I suspect that Cicero is somewhat disingenuous when he raises his hands with holy horror at the 4 per cent rake-off on the price of *frumentum emptum* which Verres entered *scribae nomine*.[32] This form of perquisite must have been fairly regular, if strictly illegal, for Verres to enter it openly on his accounts; there were no doubt many others less reputable.

The picture which I have endeavoured to draw of the Republican civil service will, I hope, correct the impression still too commonly given in textbooks that a Roman magistrate struggled single-handed with his official duties without any staff worthy of the name. Plutarch in a too little quoted passage of the *Cato minor*, draws a very different picture. In the aerarium the *scribae quaestorii* were accustomed to have it all their own way, until the conscientious Cato, having carefully read up the regulations, created consternation among them by telling them what to do instead of signing on the dotted line like the average quaestor.[33] The *scribae*, at any rate, were men of a certain standing, as well as experience, and magistrates must have leaned a good deal on them, both on the accounting and judicial side of their work.[34] The sub-clerical grades were of a lower social status, but even among them lictors must have acquired considerable experience in court procedure. Cicero is very sarcastic about Verres' use of his sub-clerical officers as *iudices* and on his *consilium*,[35] but when we find a highly respectable proconsul of Africa under the Principate recording as members of his *consilium* not only his own and his quaestor's *scribae* but his *haruspex*,[36] one wonders whether Verres' conduct was so exceptional or so scandalous.

These grades of clerical and sub-clerical officers survived under the Principate in the service of the old Republican magistrates, including the proconsuls, legates and quaestors of the provinces, and officers of similar grades were attached to the new magistracies and quasi-magistracies which were created in the early Principate: the *praefecti frumenti dandi*, for instance, and the *curatores aquarum* had their staff of *scribae librarii*, *accensi* and *praecones*, and the latter lictors and architects as well.[37] It is indeed during the Imperial period that we have most epigraphic evidence on these grades, by way of inscriptions either recording the careers of individuals or the corporate activities of the *decuriae*.

These inscriptions show that much the same conditions prevailed as under the late Republic. Incidentally, we hear for the first time of another grade, the porters (*geruli*).[38] *Accensi* continued to be freedmen of the magistrates whom they served.[39] The other sub-clerical grades are of humble status, often freedmen.[40] *Scribae* continued to be of rather superior standing. A certain number proceeded to equestrian military posts;[41] others record with conscious pride the grant of a public horse;[42] many are honoured in their municipalities.[43] They evidently, as in Cicero's day, still clung to the lower fringe of the equestrian order. The inscriptions frequently record a man holding a large number of posts under different colleges of magistrates and often in different grades, but do not make it plain whether these posts were held successively or if the men concerned were pluralists holding places in a number of *decuriae* simultaneously. With the active officers are often associated the *munere functi*, or *honore usi*, presumably those who had sold out.[44]

The service survived at least until the sixth century,[45] and in the fourth and early fifth the *decuriales urbis Romae* were still vigorously maintaining their right to assist at certain legal processes and, what was more important in their eyes, to collect the fees.[46] Even at this late period they seem still to have served in the provinces,[47] and they were now recruited in the provinces.[48] But long before this time their duties seem to have become purely formal and their posts had in many cases become sinecures: even in Trajan's reign Frontinus complains that the *apparitores* of the *curatores aquarum*, though they still drew their salaries from the aerarium, had ceased to function.[49] Meanwhile, to cope with the increasing mass of clerical work which the higher administrative standards of the Principate demanded, two new types of civil servant were evolving, the imperial slaves and freedmen who assisted the secretaries and procurators, and the military clerks who formed the *officia* of provincial governors.

Under the first heading I do not intend to speak of such important functionaries as *a rationibus*, *ab epistulis*, or the provincial procurators, who fall rather in the administrative grade. My concern is with the *proximi*, *melloproximi* and *adiutores* of the imperial secretariats, and the cashiers and accountants—*dispensatores*, *arcarii*, *tabularii* and the like—who served in the financial offices. These remained imperial slaves or freedmen to the end of the Principate, when the heads of their departments had long become *equites*.[50] There are two principal points which I want to make about these lower grades. One is how remarkably economical the service was, for the emperor's purse at any rate, if not for the public. I do not claim to have looked more than cursorily through the immense mass of inscriptions, mainly tombstones, in which are recorded the family relationships and the careers of these humble folk, but I gained a strong impression that the emperors were very rarely reduced to buying slaves. Under the early Principate in particular the second names, such as Pallantianus or Agrippianus, which many bear, show that they accrued by inheritance to the emperor from friends or members of his family, client kings, and not least from the great imperial freedmen; many more must have begun their career as *vicarii* of imperial slaves, and been added to the *familia* on their master's death. In the later centuries one is struck by the number who were born in the emperor's service. Since most of the records are tombstones, and an imperial slave was normally manumitted while still in the prime of life, the number of records of imperial slaves is relatively small. But of them a high proportion record themselves as *Caesaris vernae*, and a number who do not call themselves *vernae* can be proved to have been such. There are countless inscriptions of a freedman father and his children, who are still *Caesaris nostri servi*, or must have been so originally, since they are by now *Augusti liberti*. More exceptionally a son who is *Augusti libertus* records aged parents still slaves of Caesar. It would almost seem that the imperial government deliberately postponed the manumission of an imperial slave until he had produced a sufficient number of children born in servitude to carry on the service. As a result the service must in the second and third centuries have been almost entirely hereditary.[51]

The emperor thus incurred no capital expense in recruiting his service. On the other hand, that the emperor drew considerable profits from his *familia* is, I think, proved by the existence, from as early as the time of Claudius, of a *fiscus libertatis et peculiorum* to collect them.[52] How considerable the *peculia* of imperial slaves might be is indicated by the inscription set up to Musicus, a slave of Tiberius, who occupied the not very elevated position of a *dispensator* in the *fiscus Gallicus provinciae Lugdunensis*, by his domestic staff: they numbered sixteen, and included a *negotiator* to manage his business affairs, a *sumptuarius* to control his household expenditure, two cooks, two footmen (*pedisequi*), a valet (*a veste*), two chamberlains (*a cubiculo*), two butlers (*ab argento*), three secretaries (*a manu*), a doctor, and a lady whose functions are discreetly veiled. The emperor certainly secured this little group of slaves, as well as the silver plate and the wardrobe they looked after, for Musicus died still a slave.[53]

The term *libertatis* has puzzled commentators, who have generally rather reluctantly concluded that it must refer to the *vicesima libertatis*,[54] and expressed justifiable surprise that the *fiscus libertatis et peculiorum* should have dealt with matters so disparate as a public tax which flowed into the aerarium, and the property of the emperor's defunct slaves. I should like to suggest that *libertatis* in this context meant the sums paid for their freedom by imperial slaves. It was normal in the ancient world for slaves to purchase manumission, and in the huge imperial *familia* these payments must have been a regular and sizeable source of income. Even when an imperial slave had won his freedom the emperor had, like any other patron, certain claims on his services (*operae*) and, when he died, on his inheritance, which no doubt swelled the takings of the *fiscus libertatis et peculiorum*.

The second point which I wish to make is that even slaves of Caesar enjoyed a relatively high social station and an adequate income. Some married female imperial slaves or freedwomen, but the majority seem to have contracted unions with freed-women outside the imperial *familia*, or with women of free birth; these by a special dispensation from the *SC Claudianum* became imperial freedwomen, the children of the marriage being claimed as slaves of the emperor. Imperial slaves were able to rear families, and to acquire their own domestic slaves; bachelors, like Musicus, could maintain a considerable household of slaves. One may reasonably ask whether the *commoda* furnished by the fiscus were calculated on so generous a scale as to allow for these luxuries. It seems improbable, and the conclusion is, I think, that imperial slaves must have regularly made a good deal on the side by way of fees and perquisites from the public.[55]

The other form in which a civil service developed was by seconding soldiers for staff duties.[56] The system had its roots in the practice of the late Republic, when we find picked soldiers, styled *beneficiarii*, attached to the person of a commander.[57] The earliest allusion to it under the Principate is the statement of Tacitus that when Gaius withdrew Legion III Augusta from the command of the proconsul of Africa, the legate of the legion and the proconsul shared the *beneficia*.[58] Later, as higher grades were created, the term *beneficiarii* came to be limited to the lower grades.[59] As reconstructed by Domaszewski from the inscriptions the standard form of what came to be called the *officium* of a *legatus Augusti pro praetore* was a centurion as *princeps praetorii*,[60] three *cornicularii*,[61] three *commentarienses*,[62] ten *speculatores* per legion he commanded,[63] and a large number of plain *beneficiarii* —thirty are recorded on an inscription of a legate of Numidia who shared his staff equally with the proconsul of Africa: so sixty would be the norm.[64] The higher grade officers, the *princeps*, *cornicularii* and *commentarienses* were assisted by *adiutores*.[65] Little is known of the functions attaching to the various grades, except that *speculatores* and perhaps *commentarienses* were concerned with the custody of prisoners and the execution of the condemned.[66] There were, in addition, numerous minor grades, such as *quaestionarii* (torturers),[67] and various types of clerks,

M

*exceptores, exacti, librarii,*[68] as well as equerries (*stratores*)[69] and a numerous bodyguard of *equites* and *pedites singulares.*[70]

The staffs of this type were allocated to all *legati Augusti pro praetore*, and also, it would seem, though there is no epigraphic evidence, to proconsuls. It is certain, despite the lack of inscriptions, that the proconsul of Africa had a military *officium*, drawn from the Legio III Augusta, as well as a civilian staff of *scribae*, etc., both from Tacitus' remarks and from the fact that the legate of Numidia had an *officium* of half the normal size.[71] The ruling of Ulpian that proconsuls cannot have their own *stratores*, but in their place soldiers perform the duty in the provinces, shows that proconsuls were allocated some military personnel to attend them,[72] and a *commentariensis* is attested for the proconsul of Asia in A.D. 250.[73] The prefects of the City, of the *praetorium*, of the *annona* and of the *vigiles*,[74] and procurators, both praesidial and financial, had smaller staffs on a similar model; it will be remembered that Pliny as legate of Bithynia allocated ten *beneficiarii* to the procurator of the province and a centurion, two *equites* and ten *beneficiarii* to the prefect of the Pontic shore.[75] When the officer concerned had troops under his command the men were taken from these troops; the *officia* of the prefects of the City, the *praetorium* and the *vigiles* came from the urban and praetorian cohorts and the *vigiles* respectively, and the legates of the military provinces drew from their own legions. Legates of provinces which had no legions drew their staffs from any unit stationed in their area—the legate of Gallia Lugdunensis, for instance, from the urban cohort stationed in Lugdunum[76]—or failing that, from the legions of a neighbouring province.[77]

Service on the staff was a considerable promotion for the legionary private, and the inscriptions suggest that once on the staff a soldier stayed there, unless as not infrequently happened he obtained a commission as a centurion. Inscriptions record promotion from *beneficiarius* or *speculator* to the higher grades of *commentariensis* and *cornicularius.*[78] An interesting case is a soldier of the first urban cohort at Lugdunum, who joined up in 73, was promoted *beneficiarius* in or before 79, and *commentariensis* in 84, serving on the staff of three successive legates. On completing his service in 88 he was *evocatus* and two years later promoted centurion of his original cohort.[79] Another inscription, probably of the third century, from Arabia, shows a man starting as *beneficiarius* and being promoted successively to *commentariensis, cornicularius,* and finally centurion of the *officium*.[80] Other inscriptions show that some men were selected for staff duties immediately upon enlistment; M. Aur. Augustianus first served for four years as *exceptor* of the governor of Moesia Superior, then was transferred to the praetorian guard, where he served for five years in another clerical post as *eques sive tabularius,* after which he was promoted centurion.[81] By the third century at any rate a separate cadre of *officiales* was already forming which had very little connection with the fighting troops.

*Officiales,* being of the rank of N.C.O.s, received quite good pay, which they could supplement with sundry perquisites. Ulpian in his book *de officio proconsulis* mentions one of these, *panniculariae,* or the personal effects of executed prisoners. The *speculatores, optiones* or *commentariensis,* he rules, should not be allowed to seize them, nor should a governor pocket them for himself. The best plan is to build up from them a fund for supplying paper to the officials, or rewards of bravery to the troops, or presents to barbarian envoys. Some scrupulous governors transmitted these paltry sums to the fiscus, but this, in Ulpian's view, 'perquam diligentiae est'.[82] This new type of civil service, it may be noted, differed from the old Republican service in that its members did not go out with the governor from Rome to his province but were permanently attached to a particular province, serving a succession of governors. This distinction is noted by Paulus, who rules that 'praesidis provinciae officiales, quia perpetui sunt', are allowed to lend money at interest, contrary to the usual rule which forbade governors and their staffs to have business dealings with the provincials.[83] Such officials, who not only knew the ropes of procedure, but were also familiar with local conditions, must have had a great advantage over a governor new both to the routine of administration and to the district he had to administer.

During the first two centuries of the Principate the *officia* seem to have been mainly concerned with judicial and police duties. Most of the officers whom they served—the three great prefects at Rome, and legates and proconsuls in the provinces—had little or no financial work. Procurators had two separate staffs, a military *officium* to assist them in their judicial duties and a *familia* of slaves and freedmen to deal with accounts. During the third century, however, the praetorian prefects and the provincial governors began, owing to the growing importance of the *annona militaris*, to require accounting staff, and there is some evidence in the inscriptions that they satisfied this demand by adding military accountants to their staff. I have already mentioned Aurelius Augustianus, who served as 'eques sive tabularius' in the praetorian prefecture—evidently an important post as he was promoted direct to centurion from it.[84] In the provinces also we meet with soldiers who served as *librarii* or *adiutores* in the *officium rationum*.[85]

The common statement, based on the words of Lactantius, 'officiorum omnium milites',[86] that Diocletian militarised the civil service, needs considerable qualification. On the one hand, the larger and more important half of it was already military— the *officia* of the praetorian prefects and of all provincial governors: and the *officia* of the deputies or *vicarii* of the praetorian prefects were naturally formed on the same model. On the other hand, there is good evidence that there was still a substantial freedman element in the civil service at the end of Diocletian's reign. In the persecution edict which he issued in 303 not only were Christians possessed of any dignity, that is senators and equestrians, deprived of it, but οἱ ἐν οἰκετίαις were reduced to slavery.[87] Οἱ ἐν οἰκετίαις is an odd phrase, but evidently denotes government employees of some kind, and the penalty of enslavement seems appropriate for freedmen; it certainly cannot mean military *officiales*, who, incidentally, would by 303 have already been purged when Christians were expelled from the army in 298. *Augusti liberti* are then probably meant—the Latin original may have been something like *in familiis Caesaris*. This interpretation is confirmed by a comparison of Diocletian's edict with that of Valerian in 257, which deprived Christian senators and equites of their rank, and ordered *Caesariani* to be sent in chains to imperial estates.[88]

Even in the highly favoured palatine offices, the *sacra scrinia* or secretariats and the financial departments of the *res summa* (*largitiones*) and *res privata*, the transition from freedman to military status seems to have been gradual, by the grant of successive privileges, and not yet to have been complete in Constantine's reign. In a constitution dated 319,[89] Constantine, after granting certain immunities to retired *palatini*, adds *agentes in rebus* to the list of beneficiaries 'licet meritis militaribus videantur esse subnixi'. It would seem then that the *palatini* were not by this date *milites*. Again in 326 he grants the right of *castrense peculium* to all *palatini*, which would not have been necessary had they been already *milites*, and moreover justifies the innovation by a long rhetorical argument.[90] Nor were military ranks ever introduced. The chief clerks of the *sacra scrinia* were still graded as *proximi* and *melloproximi*.[91] The *palatini* of the finance offices had a peculiar system of grading of which I can find no trace under the Principate, but which is clearly not military. The higher officials had by the mid-fourth century achieved equestrian status, and were graded *perfectissimi*, class I, II, or III, *ducenarii* and *centenarii*. Below these come *epistulares*, who seem to represent the lowest equestrian grade, the *sexagenarii*, and at the bottom of the scale the remainder of the clerks are graded as *formae primae*, *secundae* and *tertiae*.[92] A similar classification into three *formae* is found among the *castrensiani* or personal household, and this suggests that it was the mark of originally servile establishments.[93]

In the provinces part of the slave or freedman element appears to survive during the fourth century under the style of *Caesariani*, who formed the staffs of the *rationales rei privatae*, the successors of the provincial *procuratores rationis privatae* and *patrimonii* of the third century.[94] They are always spoken of in the Codes in terms of the most violent obloquy, and the story which Ammianus tells, that a band of brigands in Syria successfully impersonated the *officium* of the *rationalis*, and carried off all the chattels of the leading citizens of a town on the pretence that they had been confiscated, suggests that the evil reputation of the *Caesariani* was not undeserved.[95] Whether there were also *Caesariani* on the staffs of the *rationales summarum*, who took the place of the provincial procurators, does not appear.[96]

The majority, however, of the provincial procurators developed into *praesides*. In Diocletian's day *praesides* seem still to have possessed a freedman *familia* besides their military *officium*, for Eusebius records among the martyrs of Palestine, one Theodulos τῆς ἡγεμονικῆς τυγχάνων οἰκετίας.[97] By 319 the freedmen *tabularii* had acquired military status and were absorbed into the *officium*.[98] The process of fusion was no doubt facilitated by the fact that in the offices of the praetorian prefects and the *consulares* of provinces, who had possessed no slave or freedman *familia*, military *officiales* already existed to deal with the finance. *Tabularii*, or as they preferred to be called in the Byzantine period *numerarii*,[99] continued, perhaps as a result of their mixed origin, to hover on the borderline of military or servile officials. Constantine towards the end of his reign made the provincial *numerarii* liable to torture,[100] and Julian definitely deprived of their military status not only those in the provinces but even those in the praetorian prefecture, making them *condicionales*.[101] This measure was revoked by Valentinian and Valens in respect of the *numerarii* of the prefects,[102] and apparently provincial *tabularii* and *numerarii* later re-acquired their military status. But even in the sixth century the judicial grades affected to despise the finance officials as outsiders.[103]

The *officia* of the praetorian and urban prefects, vicars and provincial governors, as recorded in the fifth century by the

*Notitia Dignitatum,* still show obvious affinities with the *officia* of the Principate.[104] All are headed by a *princeps*[105] and a *cornicularius*[106] and contain a *commentariensis*:[107] by this date this last officer certainly handled criminal cases and had custody of prisoners.[108] The lower grades of *speculator*[109] and *beneficiarius*[110] have by now disappeared, but both are occasionally mentioned in the constitutions and authors of the fourth century. Various other grades have appeared. I have already discussed the financial officers, the *numerarii* or *tabularii,* under whom were a host of *scriniarii,* from whom they selected their *adiutores* and *chartularii.*[111] Prefects and vicars have also *curae epistularum* to conduct their correspondences on financial matters,[112] and the praetorian prefects *regendarii* to control the public post.[113] On the judicial side the *adiutor*[114] of the *princeps* achieves independent rank, and an *ab actis*[115] and in some offices an *a libellis*[116] appear. Below them come a greatly increased number of *exceptores,* or shorthand writers, from whom were drawn the *adiutores* and *chartularii* of the higher officers.[117] None of the new judicial offices was created before 331 when a constitution envisages direct promotion from *exceptor* to *commentariensis.*[118] None (except a *libellensis,* and he does not seem to be an established officer) appears in the *ordo salutationis* of the province of Numidia in Julian's reign.[119] The *Notitia* with a few exceptions records only clerical officers and ignores the rich profusion of sub-clerical grades—*singulares, mittendarii, cursores, nomenclatores, stratores, praecones* and *draconarii* —which form the tail of the *officium.*[120]

The military *officia* of the *magistri militum, comites rei militaris* and *duces* also show a clear affinity with those of the Principate. They are all headed by a *princeps* and include a *commentariensis.* The great majority have no *cornicularius,* perhaps because the military officers had little civil jurisdiction: where there is a *cornicularius* he does not usually come in his traditional place immediately below the *princeps,* which suggests that even in these cases the post had been abolished and restored later with lower seniority.[121] The military like the civil *officia* have their *numerarii*, after whom the *primiscrinii*, *qui numerarii fiunt*, and the other *scriniarii* are sometimes recorded.[122] As in the civil offices the *adiutor* (*principis*) has achieved independent status.[123] The *officia* of eastern *comites* and *duces* have as the lowest post before the *exceptores* an *a libellis sive subscribendarius*, and the western military *officia* in the corresponding position a *regerendarius*, who perhaps performed the same duties. *Comites* and *duces* in the East mention their *singulares*.

On the status and emoluments of civil servants in the Byzantine period we have abundant evidence in the Codes. With the exceptions noted above, all were technically soldiers; officials in the praetorian prefecture were, we happen to know, on the strength of Legio I Adiutrix.[124] They wore military uniform[125] and received rations (*annona*), and in some cases fodder (*capitum*), which were, or could be, issued in kind down to A.D. 423, when they were compulsorily commuted at rates fixed by the praetorian prefecture.[126] But their military status was purely nominal and their form of *militia* is from the first clearly distinguished from the *armata militia* of real soldiers.[127] In status a sharp line must be drawn between the provincial officials, the *cohortales*, as they are generally called, and those of the centre, the *palatini*, with whom may be classed the *vicariani* and *praefectiani*.[128] Constantine made service in all the *officia* a hereditary obligation,[129] but it was only necessary to enforce this rule in the provincial *officia* where service was unpopular.[130] The contempt in which *cohortales* were held is demonstrated by Julian's action in enrolling the clergy of Cappadocian Caesarea in the *officium* of the provincial governor.[131] Similarly the rule forbidding officials to aspire to any other, and higher, *militia*, which in the fourth century was applied even to *praefectiani*,[132] was by the fifth only imposed on *cohortales*, and on them it was enforced with ever increasing rigour: in the early fifth century a *cohortalis* could be promoted outside his own *officium* only by a personal grant of the emperor,[133] but in 442 even such special grants were declared null and void.[134] In the fifth and sixth century laws *cohortales* and *curiales* are regularly classed together as the two hereditary castes to whom any kind of promotion was forbidden.[135]

By contrast a post in the palatine ministries or the praetorian prefecture was a coveted prize. Substantial fees were paid for enrolment—the admission fee to the prefecture had risen from 5 to 20 *solidi* in Justinian's reign,[136] and that to the *sacra scrinia* was 15 or 20[137]—but despite this staffs tended continually to swell and the constant effort of the emperors was to cut them down.[138] Their efforts were in general unavailing, for so soon as an establishment of so many *statuti* was laid down, a huge mass of *supernumerarii* accumulated and the emperor had to lay down a maximum establishment of supernumeraries; in 399 the *officium largitionum* was limited to 610 supernumeraries in addition to its establishment of 224 *statuti*.[139] Supernumeraries were not entitled to *annonae* or other official emoluments.[140] Some worked in the offices, presumably picking up a living from fees or being paid for their services by the *statuti*, others merely waited for a vacancy. In some offices the former class received preference when vacancies arose.[141]

As promotion was, for those at any rate who commanded no interest in high quarters, by strict seniority,[142] this inflation of numbers meant that it took years to climb to the top of an office, and the emperors displayed great anxiety to keep the procession moving, by insisting that heads of offices retire after a fixed short term—usually a year or two.[143] Despite their efforts, officials were often senile—for there was no age limit—before they reached the coveted senior posts, in which case they were sometimes allowed to perform their duties by deputy.[144]

So great was the competition for places in some offices that vacancies were bought from retiring officials, and by the early sixth century some classes of posts were officially saleable.[145] We know most about the *sacra scrinia*. Here, a vacancy on the establishment of each *scrinium* was caused every other year by the compulsory retirement of its head, the *proximus*. This vacancy was offered to the senior supernumerary at a fixed tariff

of 250 *solidi*, payable to the retiring *proximus*. If he could not
afford it, it went to the next senior, and so on, till a willing pur-
chaser was found. When a vacancy arose by the death of an
established officer (*statutus*) it was similarly offered to the senior
supernumerary but in this case the 250 *solidi* went to the heirs or
assigns of the deceased *statutus*.[146] Officials of the *sacra scrinia* who
aspired to a place among the *adiutores* of the *quaestor sacri palatii*
had to purchase their promotion from the retiring *adiutores*.
There was apparently no tariff here till Justinian fixed it at 100
*solidi*, except for the three senior officials, the *laterculensis* and the
two *melloproximi*, who could still sell their jobs for what they
would fetch.[147]

It is evident from a number of laws in the Code that many
aspirants did not possess the ready cash to pay for their *militia* on
the nail, and borrowed money on mortgage for the purpose. In
this case the creditor had a lien on the post, and should his debtor
die prematurely could claim repayment from the purchase price
paid by whoever succeeded to the vacancy.[148] In this milieu it is
not surprising to find that the other usual abuses of an over-
ripe bureaucracy flourished. Absenteeism was rife: we have
regulations prescribing mild penalties for officials who have not
been seen at their office for one, two, three, or more years.[149]
Pluralities were common. Justin endeavoured to suppress them,
but excepted cases where two posts were by long custom held
concurrently.[150]

It was not the pay which made the civil service attractive. In
the reign of Justinian the great majority of the clerks in the
praetorian prefecture were graded as cavalry troopers, receiving
only one ration allowance (*annona*) and one fodder allowance
(*capitum*), the whole being commuted for 9 *solidi* per annum, and
even the highest officials on the judicial side reached only three
ration allowances and two fodder allowances totalling 23 *solidi*.[151]
Byzantine officials lived not on their pay, but on fees—*sportulae*
—collected in part from each other, but in the main from the
general public. Fees were payable for every transaction—for

letters of appointment to every post from the highest down to
*defensor* of a city,[152] for all judicial processes,[153] and for the collec-
tion of taxes; for by the general practice of antiquity the taxpayer
paid a gratuity to the collector for his trouble in collecting the
money from him—the sum was fixed by Majorian at 2½ *solidi*
for each *iugum*, divisible between the officials of the various
finance departments, the *palatini*, the *praefectiani*, the *exactor*, the
provincial officials and also the *curiales*.[154]

*Sportulae* were in origin illicit tips, and Constantine still so
regarded them. In one of his more hysterical constitutions he
strives by severe penalties to eradicate the system root and
branch. 'Let the grasping hands of the officials forthwith refrain,
let them refrain I say, for unless after this warning they do refrain
they will be cut off by the sword. Let not the *velum* of the judge
be for sale, admission purchased, the *secretarium* infamous with
rival bids, the very sight of the governor at a price. . . . Let the
depredations of him who is called *princeps* of the *officium* be
removed from the opening of the case. Let the *adiutores* of the
same *princeps* of the *officium* make no extortion from the litigants.
Let the intolerable assaults of centurions and other officials demanding small sums and great be repulsed. Let the insatiable
greed of those who give back the record of the case to the litigants
be moderated.'[155] By Julian's reign the imperial government had
resigned itself to the inevitable, and *sportulae* were no longer prohibited but regulated. The *ordo salutationis* of the province of
Numidia gives a detailed schedule. For the *princeps* for granting
an official—to enforce judgment—within the town, five Italian
bushels of wheat or the price thereof; within a mile seven bushels,
for every additional ten miles two bushels, for overseas a hundred
bushels. For the *cornicularius* and *commentariensis* half of the above
sums each. For the official granted two bushels. For *exceptores*
for a *postulatio simplex* five bushels, for a *contradictio* twelve
bushels, for a *definita causa* twenty bushels. For the *libellensis* for
every petition two bushels. Besides which the litigants had to
provide paper for the necessary records: one large tome was to

suffice for a *postulatio simplex* and four for a *contradictio*, not more than six for a *definita causa*. It is clear that there is nothing 'under the counter' about *sportulae* by this time; even two bushels of wheat could hardly be unobtrusively slipped into the palm of an expectant-looking official.[156]

I opened this paper with an allusion to the first and only Roman clerical officer who played a part in history. I cannot end better than by paying a tribute to the last and only Roman clerical officer who achieved literary fame. I allude of course to the poet and antiquary John the Lydian. His poetical works have, alas, perished; personally I particularly deplore the loss of his little panegyric on Zoticus, the praetorian prefect under whose auspices he started his official career, a tribute so greatly appreciated by its subject that he rewarded the author with a *solidus* for every line, payable out of public funds.[157] But we are fortunate in still possessing three prose works, one of which, 'On the magistracies of the Roman constitution', is of greater interest, since the bulk of it deals with the office of the praetorian prefect, in which John himself served for many years. It is a testimony both to John's antiquarian learning and to his loyalty to his department that he is able to trace the origins of the praetorian prefecture to the *magister equitum* of the regal period—the change from ἵππαρχος to ὕπαρχος or ἔπαρχος is, as he repeatedly remarks, trifling[158]—and can moreover demonstrate that the post of *cornicularius* of the praetorian prefect—which he himself held—goes back to the foundation of Rome.[159]

John is an appropriate figure with whom to conclude, since he is in his own person the complete bureaucrat. He is a lover of forms for their own sake, the longer and more complicated the better, and delights in the intricacies of official procedure; one of his great sorrows is that proceedings in the praetorian prefecture were no longer conducted in Latin,[160] which no one, with the doubtful exception of the officials, understood, and he takes every opportunity to air his own scholarship in that language, giving the meaning and derivation of the Latin terms in which the official jargon of the prefecture abounded, and citing some of the old Latin formulae in extenso—in vain, alas, for generations of Greek copyists have reduced his Latin to gibberish.[161] His major passion is departmental loyalty. His book is a lament for the fallen greatness of the praetorian prefecture, and he hates with all a civil servant's bitterness the upstart department of the Magister Officiorum, which had robbed the prefecture of its control of the post and of the arms factories, and, worst insult of all, had introduced one of its staff into the post of *princeps* of the praetorian *officium*, thus robbing the *praefectiani* of the crown of their career.[162]

Within the department John is a stout protagonist of the judicial side as against the financial. The financial officials, he repeatedly asserts, were properly speaking hardly members of the *officium*; they had only achieved the grant of *probatoriae* by the injudicious generosity of Theodosius the Great, they did not figure on the old *matrices* of the *officium*, and they still were excluded from the procession which, on ceremonial occasions, attended the prefect.[163] John's feelings may be imagined when, instead of men of letters or barristers, vulgar finance clerks, like Marinus the Syrian[164] or John the Cappadocian,[165] were promoted praetorian prefects. Not that he leaves his feelings to be imagined; pages of passionate declamation lament the depth of degradation to which such prefects have brought the once glorious office. His archvillain is John, whose financial exactions, he alleges, so impoverished the provincials that they could not afford to litigate, with the deplorable result that the fees payable to the judicial side of the prefecture sank to a mere pittance.

He recounts his own career as a melancholy example of the decline of the prefecture. He made a brilliant start, owing to the fortunate circumstance that the prefect of the time, Zoticus, was a fellow-townsman and friend. Zoticus not only pressed upon him a place among the *exceptores*, but showed him the ropes to such good effect that in his first year he netted not less than 1,000 *solidi*—and this with moderation (σωφρόνως). The *adiutores* of the *ab actis*, he explains, selected him as one of their three chartularies, not only demanding no fee for the appointment but actually paying him a stipend of 24 *solidi* a year; the other two chartularies, he notes with a certain pride, were aged seniors who had paid for their posts. In this position he reaped a rich, though unspecified, harvest of fees from compiling the *personale* and the *cottidianum* and concurrently he drew up *suggestiones* and practised as an *exceptor* in the *secretum*. Zoticus' good offices did not end here. Not only did he, as I have mentioned already, show his appreciation of John's poetic talent in a tangible form, but he also found him a wife who brought him 100 pounds of gold in dowry.[166]

John sadly contrasts with the bright promise of his youth the bitter disappointment of his declining years. At length, after 39 years of service, he reached the highest post in the *officium* accessible to a *praefectianus* now that the position of *princeps* had been usurped by a *magistrianus*—the ancient and honourable dignity of *cornicularius*. But what did he find? When a *magistrianus* had first been introduced into the *officium*, an arrangement had been reached between him and the *cornicularius* for the partition of fees: the *cornicularius* had retained the *completiones*, which brought on an average not less than 1,000 *solidi* a year, and the *princeps* had undertaken, in order to square the account, to pay the *cornicularius* a pound of gold per month. 'But', says John, 'I do not blush to call justice to witness that I speak truth, not a penny did I receive from the *princeps* nor from the *completiones*.'[167] To such a depth had John of Cappadocia reduced the empire.

It is easy to poke fun at the Byzantine bureaucracy, but cumbersome and corrupt though it was, it served some useful purposes. The emperors relied on the clerical grades, perhaps not altogether in vain, as a check against the far more arbitrary extortions and illegalities of the administrative officers, the provincial governors in particular. The permanent clerks of the *officia* not only knew the regulations better than the governors, who served only for a year or two; they also had a less pressing need to get rich quickly and could content themselves with more or less regular perquisites, hallowed by custom; and being permanent residents they could not but have had some fellow feeling for the ordinary provincials. Many imperial constitutions make the *officium* equally responsible with the governor for obeying the law, and indeed impose upon it the duty, enforced by the threat of a corporate fine, of resisting illegal action by the governor.[168]

I would go further than this. One of the complex of causes which kept the eastern half of the empire a going concern while the western fell to pieces was the fact that the eastern emperors usually had large financial resources at their command, while the western were bankrupt, and could levy troops from their own provinces while in the West the only resource was barbarian mercenaries. This is partly due to the greater wealth and higher population of the eastern provinces; but it is also due to the more effective administrative control exercised by the East, which enabled it to mobilise for the defence of the empire a larger proportion of the wealth and manpower available. And the principal reason for this was that in the West the great offices of state were the perquisite of the wealthy land-owning class who used their powers to protect their own interests, but in the East the powers of the state were, from the fifth century at any rate, wielded by bureaucrats, men like Marinus the Syrian and John the Cappadocian, who, it is true, lined their own pockets liberally, but did also fill the treasury.[169]

# NOTES

## I. THE IMPERIUM OF AUGUSTUS

[1] Cassius Dio, LIII. 12-13. Strabo (p. 840) gives a truer picture of the division of the provinces, when he enumerates the separate public provinces, and treats Caesar's share as one area which he subdivided as convenient into districts under *legati*, consular or praetorian, or equestrian governors.

[2] Cic. *ad Fam.* 1. 9. 25. Dio's words in LIII. 12. 1, may imply that the Senate's decree was confirmed by a law; the late Republican precedents are not decisive, particularly as Caesar held Transalpine Gaul by virtue of a *senatus consultum* only.

[3] Cassius Dio, LIII. 14. 2; cf. XL. 56. 1.

[4] Strabo, p. 840 (peace and war and control over kings); *ILS*, 244 (treaties).

[5] Appian, *Mith.* 97; Cassius Dio, XXXIX. 33. 2.

[6] Cassius Dio, LIII. 11.

[7] Cic. *Phil.* IV. 9; *ad Att.* VIII. 15. 3. Mr. C. E. Stevens has pointed out to me that Republican consuls might on occasion exercise this *maius imperium* in a small way. Cicero writes to a proconsul (*ad Fam.* XIII. 26.3), 'quod quo minore dubitatione facere posses, litteras ad te a M. Lepido consule, non quae te aliquid iuberent (neque enim id tuae dignitatis esse arbitrabamur), sed quodam modo quasi commendaticias sumpsimus', which implies that a consul could issue commands to a proconsul by letter.

[8] H. W. Pleket, *The Greek Inscriptions in the Rijksmuseum Van Oudheden at Leyden*, pp. 49 ff. The letter of Octavian to Norbanus Flaccus, proconsul of Asia (Jos. *Ant. Jud.* XVI. 166, cf. 171 and Philo, *Leg. ad Gaium*, 40, § 315), must be dated between Actium and the restoration of the Republic and therefore cannot be used as evidence of normal consular prerogative.

[9] Cassius Dio, LIV. 3. 1-3. For the date see note 11 (Murena was alive at the time).

[10] Cassius Dio, LIII. 31.1.

[11] Cassius Dio, LIV. 3. 4; Vell. Pat. II. 91; Suet. *Aug.* 19. 1, 56. 4, 66. 3, *Tib.* 8; for the date, the *Fasti Capitolini*.

[12] Cassius Dio, LIII. 30. 1-2; Suet. *Aug.* 28. 1.

[13] Cassius Dio, LIII. 32. 5.

[14] Cassius Dio, LIII. 13. 1, 16. 2, LIV. 12. 4-5.

[15] *SEG*, IX. 8, especially the use of κελεύω in III and ἀρέσκει in IV; Jos. *Ant. Jud.* XVI. 162-5 (κελεύω is used in the last clause ordering publication in Asia); cf. also Pliny, *Ep.* X. 99, for an *edictum divi Augusti* regulating Bithynian

cities, and a letter of Agrippa to Cyrene (Jos. *Ant. Jud.* XVI. 169-70), also using κελεύω and citing a letter of Augustus to the governor of Cyrenaica.

[16] Cic. *ad Fam.* I. 9. 25.

[17] *Dig.* I. xvi. 1; cf. 4, § 6: 'post haec ingressus provinciam mandare iurisdictionem legato suo debet: nec hoc ante facere quam fuerit provinciam ingressus. est enim perquam absurdum, antequam ipse iurisdictionem nanciscatur (nec enim prius competit quam in eam provinciam venerit) alii eam mandare quam non habet'.

[18] Cic. *In Pis.* 50.

[19] *Dig.* I. xvi. 2; cf. Pliny, *Ep.* VII. 16, 32.

[20] Cic. II *Verr.* V. 39-41; *ad Att.* VII. 7. 4.

[21] *Res Gestae*, 10.

[22] Appian, *BC*, V. 132; Orosius, VI. 18. 34; Cassius Dio, XLIX. 15. 5-6.

[23] Cassius Dio, LI. 19.6, 20. 4. See below p. 95.

[24] Tac. *Ann.* III. 70; XIV. 48; XVI. 11.

[25] *Res Gestae*, 6.

[26] Ehrenberg and Jones, *Documents*[2], 94a.

[27] Op. cit. 279.

[28] Op. cit. 30 (*ludi saeculares*), 278 (aqueducts), 307 (Mitylene), 311 (*repetundae*).

[29] Cassius Dio, LIII. 32. 5; LIV. 3. 3; *ILS*, 244.

[30] Tac. *Ann.* I. 7.

[31] Tac. *Ann.* III. 56.

[32] Contrast *de lege agr.* I. 21, with II. 10.

[33] Caesar, *BC*, I. 7.

[34] Tac. *Ann.* I. 2.

[35] *Res Gestae*, 5; Cassius Dio, LIV. 1. 3-5, 2. 1.

[36] Cassius Dio, LIV. 6. 1-2.

[37] Cassius Dio, LIV. 10. 1-3; *Res Gestae*, 11, 12.

[38] Cassius Dio, LIV. 10. 5. It has been suggested to me that it was at this date that Augustus toyed with the idea of being third consul (Suet. *Aug.* 37).

[39] Suet. *Aug.* 49. 1; *Tib.* 37. 1; Cassius Dio, LV. 26. 4; Tac. *Ann.* I. 7. The mere command of troops in Italy is not perhaps decisive, for the law evidently allowed proconsuls to muster their troops and march them to the frontier or port of embarkation, and Augustus must presumably have used this loophole to keep the praetorians in being between 1st July, 23, and the spring of 22, when he remained in Rome as proconsul. But it would have been stretching the law very far to keep troops permanently in arms, and illegal to use them, as Augustus and Tiberius did (see Suet. *Aug.* 32. 1; *Tib.* 37. 1; Tac. *Ann.* IV. 27), to maintain order in Italy.

[40] Cassius Dio, LIII. 17. 5-6. See below, pp. 83ff.

[41] Suet. *Aug.* 45. 4.

[42] Ovid, *Tristia*, II. 135. Ovid's use of formal terms (*edictum, poena, relegatus*) shows that his exile was legal *relegatio*. The power of *relegatio* was dependent on the *imperium*, as is shown by the rulings of the Digest (XLVIII. xxii. 7, §§ 1, 6-17), which lay down that a *praeses* can relegate to an island only if he has one in his

province, and can interdict from his own province only; his writ ran only where his *imperium* was operative. Augustus could have claimed as a precedent the *relegatio* of a Roman knight by Gabinius as consul in 58 B.C. (Cic. *pro Sestio*, 29-30).

⁴³ Cassius Dio, LVI. 23. 2-3; Suet. *Aug.* 24. 1; Tac. *Ann.* I. 31. If the anecdote in Suetonius is true and belongs to this period, it would prove that Augustus himself enforced the levy.

⁴⁴ Tac. *Ann.* VI. 11.

⁴⁵ *Dig.* V. i. 12: 'item hi quibus id concessum est propter vim imperii, sicut praefectus urbi, ceterique Romae magistratus.'

⁴⁶ The date is given by Jerome's Chronicle.

⁴⁷ Cassius Dio, LIV. 6. 4-5; Tacitus' omission of his name proves that he was not formally *praefectus urbi*.

⁴⁸ Cassius Dio, LIV. 6.6.

⁴⁹ The date is given by Cassius Dio, LIV. 19. 6.

⁵⁰ Tac. *Ann.* I. 14, 81 (Tiberius was of course following Augustus' precedent).

⁵¹ *Res Gestae*, 8.

⁵² *Essays*, pp. 65 ff.

⁵³ Tac. *Ann.* XII. 41.

⁵⁴ Cassius Dio, LX. 23. 4.

⁵⁵ Cassius Dio, LIV. 28. 1.

⁵⁶ Suet. *Tib.* 21. 1; Vell. Pat. II. 121.

⁵⁷ Tac. *Ann.* VI. 11, contrast I. 7. By this theory Piso would have been appointed in A.D. 12 or 13 when Augustus was getting beyond active work (see Cassius Dio, LVI. 26. 2, 28. 2) and reappointed early in Tiberius' reign, thus providing some nucleus of fact for the scandalous anecdote recorded in Pliny, *NH*, XIV. 145, and Suet. *Tib.* 42. 1; cf. Seneca, *Ep.* 83. 14.

## II. THE CENSORIAL POWERS OF AUGUSTUS

¹ Tac. *Ann.* XI. 25.

² Suet. *Aug.* 27.

³ Ib. 35, cf. 54.

⁴ Ib. 34.

⁵ Ib. 38.3-40. 1.

⁶ Cassius Dio, LII. 42.

⁷ Id. LIV. 13-14.

⁸ Id. LIV. 26, 35, LV. 13.

⁹ Also mentioned in Suet. *Aug.* 37. 1.

¹⁰ Suet. *Aug.* 38. 3.

¹¹ Cassius Dio, LIII. 1.

¹² Suet. *Aug.* 97, *Tib.* 21.

¹³ Cassius Dio, LIV. 35.

¹⁴ Cassius Dio, LV. 13.

[15] See below p. 41.
[16] Cassius Dio, LII. 42.
[17] *ILS*, 6123.
[18] Cassius Dio, LIV. 1.
[19] Vell. Pat. II. 95.
[20] Cassius Dio, LIV. 10.
[21] Id. LIV. 28.
[22] Cf. Seneca, *Consol. ad Marciam*, 15, for a similar incident under Tiberius.
[23] Cassius Dio, LIV. 30.
[24] Id. LV. 13.
[25] *ILS*, 9483, 'III. vir centur. equit. recognosc. censoria potestat.', Tac. *Ann.*
III. 30, 'censoria potestate legendis equitum decuriis functus'.
[26] Suet. *Aug.* 35.


## III. THE ELECTIONS UNDER AUGUSTUS

[1] G. Tibiletti, *Principe e magistrati repubblicani* (Rome, 1953), 283-9.
[2] Suet. *Aug.* 41. 1.
[3] Cassius Dio, LIV. 17.
[4] Cassius Dio, LIV. 26; cf. 30.
[5] Cassius Dio, LV. 13.
[6] Tac. *Ann.* I. 75, II. 37.
[7] *ILS*, 212, col. II, 3 ff.
[8] Cassius Dio, LIV. 26.
[9] See above, pp. 22-3.
[10] Suet. *Vesp.* 4. 3.
[11] Suet. *Aug.* 38. 2.
[12] Cassius Dio, LIX. 9.
[13] Ovid, *Tristia*, IV. x. 29-37.
[14] Suet. *Aug.* 94. 10.
[15] The *Thesaurus* yields few examples of *latus clavus* in its technical sense, and these in Flavian or later authors (e.g. Tacitus, *Dial.* 7; Pliny, *Ep.* II. 9, VIII. 23). Usually—and always in Augustan authors—it means either the actual dress or senatorial rank. Seneca, *Ep.* 98. 13: 'honores reppulit frater Sextius, qui ita natus ut rem publicam deberet capessere latum clavum divo Iulio dante non recepit,' looks at first sight like a formal grant in the technical sense under Caesar, and Seneca may have meant this. But he or his authority more probably meant 'senatorial rank' or 'a seat in the Senate'.
[16] Cassius Dio, LIV. 26, cf. *ILS*, 914-5.
[17] Cassius Dio, LIV. 26, 30, LVI. 27.
[18] Cassius Dio, LV. 24.
[19] Tac. *Ann.* III. 29.
[20] Mommsen, *Staatsrecht*[3], I, 554-7. The only evidence is Cassius Dio, LII. 20

(in the speech of Maecenas), and the inscriptions, which show that most senators, other than patricians, did hold the aedileship or tribunate (a few very early ones hold both). Velleius, who is not backward in recording his offices, mentions nothing between his quaestorship and praetorship (II. 111, 124).

21 Cassius Dio, LIV. 2.

22 Vell. Pat. II. 91-2; Cassius Dio, LIII. 24. The fire brigades were taken from the aediles in 7 B.C. (Cassius Dio, LV. 1; cf. Suet. *Aug.* 30. 1).

23 Cassius Dio, LIII. 28.

24 Vell. Pat. II. 89; Cassius Dio, LIII. 32.

25 Cassius Dio, LVI. 25.

26 Tac. *Ann.* I. 14.

27 Cassius Dio, LVI. 25.

28 See the *fasti* (Ehrenburg and Jones, *Documents*², pp. 32-43).

29 Tac. *Ann.* I. 14, 81.

30 Vell. Pat. II. 92.

31 Tac. *Ann.* I. 15.

32 E.g. *ILS*, 1043, 1051, 1056, 1068, 1086, etc. (quaestors), 1022, 1039, 1045, 1051, 1061-2, etc. (tribunes), 1096 (one aedile).

33 *ILS*, 944.

34 Suet. *Aug.* 56. 1.

35 Cassius Dio, LV. 34.

36 *ILS*, 244.

37 Cassius Dio, LIV. 10.

38 Cassius Dio, LV. 34.

39 Cassius Dio, LIII. 2.

40 Suet. *Aug.* 40. 2.

41 Cassius Dio, LIII. 21.

42 Syme, *The Roman Revolution*, 370-1.

43 *Res Gestae*, 5; Cassius Dio, LIV. 1 and 2.

44 Cassius Dio, LIV. 6 and 10.

45 Vell. Pat. II. 92.

46 Cassius Dio, LIV. 16; cf. Suet. *Aug.* 40. 1, and *Dig.* XLVIII, xiv.

47 Cassius Dio, LV. 5.

48 Suet. *Aug.* 40. 2.

49 Cassius Dio, LV. 34.

50 Tibiletti, *Principe e magistrati Repubblicani*, 17 ff.

51 Op. cit. 28 ff.

52 Op. cit. 75 ff.

53 Cap. xiv. Tibiletti also cites Cassius Dio, XLVI. 44-5 (Octavian's first consulate). But here also the Senate's part must have been to release him from the Lex annalis.

54 Cassius Dio, LV. 34.

55 Suet. *Aug.* 38. 3; see above, pp. 22-3.

56 Pliny, *NH*, XXXIII. 30.

57 Lines 55-7. Since I wrote the above, James H. Oliver and Robert E. A.

Palmer (*AJPhil.* LXXV (1954), 231, 246-7) have proposed another restoration which would eliminate the two classes of equites in this passage. I am not convinced by their restoration, but it makes it impossible to use this passage as evidence for my thesis, which will, I hope, stand without it.

⁵⁸ *ILS,* 6747.

⁵⁹ Pliny, *NH,* XXXIII. 32; cf. 29, and Horace, *Sat.* II. vii. 53.

⁶⁰ Horace, *Epod.* IV. 15-16.

⁶¹ Suet. *Aug.* 40. 1.

⁶² Strabo, III, 169; V, 213.

⁶³ Asconius, *in Pis.* 94.

⁶⁴ Suet. *Iulius,* 41. 2.

⁶⁵ Suet. *Aug.* 32. 3.

⁶⁶ Cassius Dio, LV. 13.

⁶⁷ Suet. *Aug.* 32. 3.

⁶⁸ Pliny, *NH,* XXXIII. 29-31.

⁶⁹ Mommsen, *Staatsrecht,*³ III. 406, n. 2; 553, n. 3; now they are known also from the *Tabula Hebana,* ll. 13-16.

⁷⁰ Cic. *pro Cluentio,* 121; cf. Horace, *Sat.* I. iv. 121-3.

⁷¹ Ovid, *Tristia,* II. 132, 'nec mea selecto iudice iussa fuga est'.

⁷² Suet. *Calig.* 16. 2.

⁷³ *ILS,* 6572-3; cf. 5006.

⁷⁴ Ib. 6744, cf. 7122.

⁷⁵ Ib. 6862.

⁷⁶ Ib. 5016.

⁷⁷ Ib. 6523.

⁷⁸ Ib. 6772.

⁷⁹ Ib. 4093.

⁸⁰ Seneca, *de Benef.* III. 7.

⁸¹ In an able article (*Rhein. Mus.* 1953, 201-13, 'iudex selectus'), which I only saw after mine was written, Mr. Staveley has upheld the continued existence of the *tribuni aerarii* as a decury. Like myself, he holds that the *iudices selecti* were the *decuriae equitum* (whom he takes to be *equo publico*), but he argues that the fifth decury which Gaius added probably was a *decuria equitum,* and that there were therefore under Augustus two *decuriae* of *selecti* (*equites*), one of *tribuni aerarii,* and (later) one of *ducenarii.* I would reply that the *iudices selecti* seem to be identical with the whole panel which provided jurors in criminal trials both in the late Republic (when therefore *selecti* included senators, equites, and *tribuni aerarii*), and in the Augustan age: the term is unlikely to have changed its meaning, apart from Ovid's words, cited in n. 70. The title *tribuni aerarii* may have survived, but if so, the jurors so called were in my view among the *selecti,* and held the equestrian census, and might therefore be also called equites, as Cicero frequently calls them in the late Republic: the meaning of the term, as Mr. Staveley agrees, remains a mystery.

⁸² Mommsen, *Staatsrecht*³, III. 535, n. 3.

⁸³ Tac. *Ann.* III. 30; Suet. *Tib.* 41.

84 Suet. *Aug.* 32. 3.

85 Cassius Dio, LIV. 18, 35, LV. 3.

86 *Dig.* XLVIII. xiv. 1 § 4; *SEG*, IX. 8, l. 117.

87 *Fr. Vat.* 197-8; cf. Gaius, IV. 30.

88 Suet. *Aug.* 32. 3.

89 Suet. *Aug.* 29. 3, 32. 3, *Tib.* 41.

90 Tac. *Ann.* III. 30.

91 Pliny, *NH*, XXXIII. 30, 'nondum provinciis ad hoc munus admissis'; cf. n. 66.

92 Suet. *Aug.* 32. 3.

93 The proconsuls, quaestors, and legates of the public provinces (c. 35), *legati pro praetore* (c. 12), *legati legionis* (c. 25), other judicial *legati*, not to speak of *comites* of governors and special *legati* for the *census* and *dilectus*.

94 See n. 7.

95 Vell. Pat. II. 124.

96 Suet. *Aug.* 46.

97 Marsh, *The Reign of Tiberius*, 63; Syme, *The Roman Revolution*, 362, 372-3.

98 Marsh, op. cit. 43 and 67; Syme, op. cit. 362, 434-5.

99 Tac. *Ann.* I. 15.

100 *AE*, 1952, 80.

101 'Longum illud carmen comitiorum', or 'solemnia comitiorum' still went on in Pliny's day (*Pan.* 63. 2, 64. 1) and indeed in Dio's (LVIII. 20).

102 Tibiletti, op. cit. 166 ff.

103 Tac. *Ann.* I. 15, clearly all belongs to the same sitting.

104 Tac. *Ann.* I. 14. The chief objection to this view is that in *Ann.* II. 36, Asinius Gallus 'censuit in quinquennium magistratuum comitia habenda . . . princeps duodecim candidatos in annos singulos nominaret': here it must be meant that Tiberius was to draw up a list of twelve candidates per annum for the next five years. Tiberius is represented as objecting to this suggestion as unduly extending his powers, but only on the grounds that nominating twelve candidates for one year involved him in odium enough, to do so for years in advance would be intolerable. I think that Tacitus has misunderstood or misrepresented Tiberius' speech.

105 Tac. *Ann.* XIV. 28.

106 Suet. *Vesp.* 2. 3.

107 Pliny, *Ep.* II. 9, VI. 6, cf. VIII. 23.

108 Pliny, *Ep.* VI. 19.

109 Pliny, *Ep.* III. 20.

110 Pliny, *Ep.* III. 20, IV. 25.

111 Tac. *Hist.* I. 77.

112 Tac. *Ann.* I. 81.

113 Cassius Dio, LVIII, 20.

114 Cassius Dio, LIX. 9 and 20.

115 Tibiletti, op. cit. 239 ff.

## IV. I APPEAL UNTO CAESAR

[1] Val. Max. IX. v. 1.

[2] Plut. *Gaius Gracchus*, 9.

[3] Bruns, *Fontes*[7], 10, ll. 76-9.

[4] Gellius, X. iii. 3.

[5] Sallust, *Bell. Iug.* 69. The various versions of the incident are fully discussed by Reid in *JRS*, I (1911), 77 ff.

[6] Such a view is not only absurd but is contradicted by the story of Marcellus and the Comensis (also discussed at length by Reid, loc. cit.). The one point that does emerge clearly from this story is that Marcellus flogged the man to demonstrate that he was in his opinion a Latin and not a Roman. Reid also cites Livy, *Epit.* 57 (Scipio at the siege of Numantia), as evidence that Romans on active service were not liable to regular flogging (*virgis*) but only to chastisement with the *vitis*.

[7] E.g. Crassus in 71 B.C., Plut. *Crassus*, 10. An alternative explanation is that decimation, like the *fustuarium*, was, as appears from Polybius, VI. 37-8, carried out by the men themselves, and might therefore be regarded as technically not an act of the commander's *imperium*.

[8] Cic. *II Verr.* V. 139-73.

[9] As does Greenidge, *Class. Rev.* 1896, 226-7.

[10] This point is made by Strachan Davidson, *Problems of the Roman Criminal Law*, 118-19.

[11] *II Verr.* V. 146, 161, 165.

[12] *Dig.* XLVIII. vi. 7 (Ulpian), 'lege Iulia de vi publica tenetur qui, cum imperium potestatemve haberet, civem Romanum adversus provocationem necaverit, verberaverit, iusseritve quid fieri aut quid in collum iniecerit ut torqueatur, 8 (Maecianus), 'lege Iulia de vi publica cavetur ne quis reum vinciat impediatve, quominus Romae intra certum tempus adsit,' Paulus, *Sent.* V. XXVI. 1, 'lege Iulia de vi publica damnatur qui aliqua potestate praeditus civem Romanum antea ad populum nunc ad imperatorem appellantem necavit necarive iusserit, torserit, verberaverit, condamnaverit inve publica vincula duci iusserit.'

[13] Cassius Dio, LI. 19. See below, pp. 94ff.

[14] *Acts*, xvi. 37.

[15] *Acts*, xxii. 25.

[16] *Acts*, xxv. 9-12, xxvi. 32, xxvii. 1, xxviii. 16.

[17] Pliny, *Ep.* X. 96. 4.

[18] Eusebius, *HE*, V. 1.

[19] Jos. *Bell. Jud.* II. 308.

[20] Suet. *Galba*, 9.

[21] Cassius Dio, LXIV. 2.

[22] Pliny, *Ep.* II. 11.

[23] Pliny, *Ep.* X. 58. Flavius Archippus must have been a citizen at the time of his conviction, or he would have cited the grant of citizenship as evidence that Domitian had pardoned him.

²⁴ *ILS*, 2927.

²⁵ *Dig.* XXVIII. iii. 6 § 9, XLIX. i. 16.

²⁶ The rules of appeal, whether in capital or in civil cases, are treated together in the lawyers, e.g. *Dig.* XLIX. ix. 1 (*divi fratres*); v. 2 (Scaevola); iv. 2; xiii. 1 (Macer).

²⁷ This rule applied to both civil and capital appeals, see *Dig.* XLIX. iv. 1 § 5-15, 2 (especially § 3). A capital sentence was suspended while the appeal was pending. *Dig.* XXVIII. iii. 6 § 8 and 9; XLVIII. xix. 2 § 2, xx. 2; XLIX. vii. 1 § 3.

²⁸ *Dig.* XXVIII. iii. 6 § 7; XLVIII. viii. 16, xix. 27 §§ 1-2, xxi. 2 § 1; XLIX. iv. 1.

²⁹ *Dig.* XXVIII. iii. 6 § 7; XLVIII. xix. 2 § 1, xxi. 2 § 1, xxii. 6 § 1; XLIX. iv. 1.

³⁰ XLVIII. ii. 6, xix. 10 § 2, 28 §§ 2-5; L. ii. 2 § 2. Paulus, *Sent.* V. xxi. 1.

³¹ *Dig.* I. xvi. 6 (Ulpian, *de officio proconsulis*) 'solent etiam custodiarum cognitionem mandare legatis, scilicet ut praeauditas custodias ad se remittant, ut innocentem ipse liberet. sed hoc genus mandati extraordinarium est: nec enim potest quis gladii potestatem sibi datam vel cuius alterius coercitionis ad alium transferre'; 11 (Venuleius Saturninus, *de officio proconsulis*), 'si quid erit quod maiorem animadversionem exigat, reicere legatus apud proconsulem debet: neque enim animadvertendi coercendi vel atrociter verberandi ius habet'; xxi. 1 (Papinian), 'quaecumque specialiter lege senatus consulto vel constitutione principum tribuuntur, mandata iurisdictione non transferuntur: quae vero iure magistratus competunt, mandari possunt'; § 1 'verius est enim more maiorum iurisdictionem quidem transferri, sed merum imperium, quod lege datur, non posse transire: quare nemo dicit animadversionem legatum proconsulis habere mandata iurisdictione. Paulus notat: et imperium quod iurisdictioni cohaeret, mandata iurisdictione transire verius est'; 5 §1 (Paulus), 'mandata iurisdictione privato etiam imperium quod non est merum videtur mandari, quia iurisdictio sine modica coercitione nulla est'.

³² *Dig.* II. i. 3 (Ulpian): 'imperium aut merum aut mixtum est, merum est imperium habere gladii potestatem ad animadvertendum facinorosos homines, quod etiam potestas appellatur.' Cf. note 31.

³³ See note 31.

³⁴ *Dig.* I. xviii. 6 § 8 (Ulpian), 'qui universas provincias regunt, ius gladii habent et in metallum dandi potestas eis permissa est'. Cf. notes 31 and 32.

³⁵ *Dig.* I. xxi. 1 (Papinian), 'et ideo videntur errare magistratus qui, cum publici iudicii habeant exercitionem lege vel senatus consulto delegatam, veluti legis Iuliae de adulteriis et si quae sunt aliae similes, iurisdictionem suam mandant. huius rei fortissimum argumentum, quod lege Iulia de vi nominatim cavetur, ut is cui optigerit exercitio possit eam si proficiscatur mandare: non aliter itaque mandare poterit quam si abesse coeperit, cum alias iurisdictio etiam a praesente mandetur.'

³⁶ A definition and list of *publica iudicia* is given by Macer in *Dig.* XLVIII. i. 1. In support of my thesis I may point out that jurisdiction under specific *leges* was granted in the early third century to procurators acting temporarily *vice praesidis*: see *Collatio*, XIV. iii. 2-3. The passage is corrupt, but apparently means that

procurators in this position did not possess general capital jurisdiction but only in cases falling under the lex Fabia de plagiariis and the lex Iulia de adulteriis, and this by special grant of Caracalla.

[37] The *poena legis* was in strict law death, in practice under the Republic *aquae et ignis interdictio* (see p. 191, n. 65). This penalty is rarely cited by the Severan lawyers (*Dig.* XLVIII. vi. 10 § 2; x. 33; *Collatio*, XII. v. 1), more often translated into its imperial equivalent of *deportatio* (*Dig.* XLVIII. viii. 3 § 5, x. 1 § 13, Paulus, *Sent.* IV. vii. 1; V. xxiii. 1). The actual penalties imposed were various (e.g. *Dig.* XLVIII. viii. 3 § 5, 'legis Corneliae de sicariis et veneficis poena insulae deportatio est et omnium bonorum ademptio, sed solent hodie capite puniri nisi honestiore loco positi fuerint, ut poenam legis sustineant: humiliores enim solent vel bestiis subici; altiores vero deportantur in insulam'; also *Dig.* XLVIII. viii. 16; xix. 38 § 7-9; Paulus, *Sent.* V. xxiii. 1, 13, 14, 16, xxv. 1-2, 7-13). The power of varying the penalty goes back to the end of the first century at least; for Flavius Archippus and the victim of Marius Priscus were condemned *in metallum*, a penalty unknown to the *leges*.

[38] It was probably for the same reason that Pliny was instructed by Trajan to send up in chains to the praetorian prefects a man who had been relegated and had returned to his home without permission (Pliny, *Ep.* X. 56-7). Trajan gives as his reason that it was not enough, in view of his contumacy, to enforce the original penalty. The implication is that the man was a Roman citizen and the appropriate punishment was one which Pliny could not inflict on a citizen, that is, a capital penalty, such as *deportatio*. (Cf. *Dig.* XLVIII. xix. 28 § 13, for a ruling of Hadrian on similar cases.) Here again we find a provincial governor having to refer to the emperor a case which did not come under the *leges publicorum iudiciorum*, but where a capital penalty was appropriate.

[39] It is perhaps a slight confirmation of this view that Paulus in Dig. XLVIII. ii. 3, cites the standard form of *libellus* under the lex Iulia de adulteriis as beginning 'Apud illum praetorem vel proconsulem', i.e. accusations were received by the praetor of the court of adultery at Rome, or proconsuls (but not legates). Cf. also Pliny, *Ep.* X. 72, where it appears that proconsuls (but not *legati Augusti*) had been granted jurisdiction 'de agnoscendis liberis restituendisque natalibus'.

[40] See note 34.

[41] See notes 31 and 32.

[42] Cassius Dio, LIII. 13.

[43] Paulus, *Sent.* V. xxvi. 2: 'hac lege excipiuntur, qui artem ludicram faciunt, iudicati etiam et confessi, et qui ideo in carcerem duci iubentur quod ius dicenti non obtemperaverint, quidve contra disciplinam publicam fecerint: tribuni etiam militum et praefecti classium alarumve ut sine aliquo impedimento legis Iuliae per eos militare delictum coerceri possit.'

[44] Cassius Dio, LII. 22 (from the speech of Maecenas), confirmed by *Dig.* XLVIII. iii. 9 (see note 52).

[45] Suet. *Aug.* 45, Tac. *Ann.* I. 77.

[46] *ILS*, 9200.

[47] *ILS*, 1368, 1372, 9200, *CIL*, III. 1919.

[48] *ILS*, 1111.

[49] Jos. *Bell. Jud.* II. 117.

[50] *Acts*, x. 1: cf. *PW*, IV. 304.

[51] Cassius Dio, LII. 22 (again from the speech of Maecenas), confirmed by *Dig.* XLVIII. iii. 9 (see note 52).

[52] *Dig.* XLVIII. iii. 9 (Venuleius Saturninus, *de officio proconsulis*), 'de militibus ita servatur, ut ad eum remittantur, si quid deliquerint, sub quo militabunt: is autem, qui exercitum accipit, etiam ius animadvertendi in milites caligatos habet.'

[53] *Passio S. Perpetuae*, 6. It is possible that the proconsul of Africa possessed *ius gladii* in the military sense, since he commanded a cohort of III Augusta (*ILS*, 2487) and an urban cohort (*ILS*, 2120-3). But this is irrelevant to my present point, which is that *ius gladii* is used here of a power of *coercitio* over civilians.

[54] *IGR*, IV. 1057.

[55] *CIL*, VIII. 9367 (= 20995), 20996 (= *ILS*, 1356).

[56] Since all regular troops were by this date Roman citizens, any governor with troops under his command would require *ius gladii*, not merely those with legions. But of the few praesidial procurators who existed at this time, most, e.g. those of the Alpine districts and Epirus, probably had no troops.

[57] *Passio S. Perpetuae*, 6. Vibia Perpetua and her father (who was flogged) were presumably Romans.

[58] *Dig.* XLIX. i. 10 § 1.

[59] Paulus, *Sent.* V. xxxiii.

[60] *Dig.* XLIX. i. 6.

[61] Paulus, *Sent.* V. xxxv.

[62] *Dig.* XXVIII. iii. 6 § 9; XLIX. i. 16.

[63] *Dig.* XXVIII. iii. 6 § 8-9; XLIX. ix. 1.

[64] *Dig.* XXVIII. iii. 6 § 10; XLVIII. xix. 9 § 11-15, 43 § 1; L. ii. 2 § 2.

[65] See above notes 28 and 29.

[66] *Dig.* XLVIII. xix. 15.

[67] *Dig.* XLVIII. v. 38 § 8; viii. 1 § 5.

[68] *Dig.* XLVIII. xxii. 6 § 2.

[69] *Collatio*, XIII. iii; *Dig.* XLVII. xxi. 2.


# V. IMPERIAL AND SENATORIAL JURISDICTION IN THE EARLY PRINCIPATE

[1] Lest my language here and elsewhere should offend those who hold that the *formula* was a statement freely agreed between the parties and the *iudex* an arbitrator as freely accepted, I would explain that by using such words as 'determine' and 'appoint' I mean only that in the final resort it was the magistrate who decided under what *formula* the case should be heard and by what *iudex*, and that he could overrule objections by the parties. Otherwise justice could not have been done, for a defendant with a weak case could have held up the trial indefinitely.

Nor would the parties have taken resort to *appellatio* in order to try to get the *formula* changed, as they did. A plaintiff clearly had to accept the magistrate's rulings, as the latter could refuse to proceed unless he did. Against a recalcitrant defendant the magistrate could presumably bring pressure by threatening a *decretum* in the plaintiff's favour. Cicero's statement (*pro Cluentio*, 120) 'neminem voluerunt maiores nostri non modo de existimatione cuiusquam sed ne pecuniaria quidem de re minima esse iudicem nisi qui inter adversarios convenisset' may represent the theory of Roman law, but surely not the practical reality.

² Gaius, IV. 9, 'rem vero et poenam persequimur velut ex his causis ex quibus adversus infitiantem in duplum agimus; quod accidit per actionem iudicati . . .': cf. IV. 102 (*satisdatio* required in this action). Cf. Cic. *pro Flacco*, 49. There was also an obscure process known as 'revocare in duplum': Paulus, *Sent.* V. va. 6a, 7, 8, *App. leg. Rom. Visig.* II. 6, 9, 10.

³ Cic. *pro Flacco*, 49 apparently alludes to a *restitutio* on the plea of *metus*: it was perhaps on these grounds that many of Verres' *iudicia* were *restituta* by his successor (Cic. II *Verr.* II. 62–3).

⁴ Rescript of Hadrian, *Dig.* XLII. i. 33.

⁵ Gaius, IV. 53, 57, cf. Suet. *Claud.* 14. Persons under twenty-five could claim *restitutio in integrum* from the *sententia* of a *iudex* without any specific cause (Ulpian, *Dig.* IV. iv. 7 § 4) but this was merely a part of the general protection given to minors.

⁶ Cic. *pro Flacco*, 49.

⁷ Gaius, IV. 52, *Dig.* XLIV. vii. 5 § 4, L. xiii. 6; Ulpian, *Dig.* V. i. 15, 16.

⁸ The *actio iudicati* could, it seems, be contested only if the *iudex* had committed some manifest and flagrant error in fact or law (*Dig.* XLIX. viii. 1).

⁹ It is true that *restitutio in integrum* might involve *appellatio*. For when the defeated party applied for *restitutio* the other litigant might object and appeal to another magistrate to veto the decree whereby it was to be granted, or alternatively a litigant who was refused *restitutio* by the magistrate under whom the case had been initiated might appeal to another to grant it to him. Neither of these procedures is attested until the Principate (*Dig.* IV. iv. 38, 39) but there seems no reason why they should not have been possible under the Republic. But in such cases *appellatio* was not made from the sentence of the *iudex*, but from a magisterial act.

¹⁰ Cic. *pro Quinctio*, 29, 63, 65.

¹¹ Cic. *pro Tullio*, 38–9.

¹² Caesar, *BC*, III. 20.

¹³ Cic. II *Verr.* I. 119.

¹⁴ Val. Max. VII. vii. 6.

¹⁵ Ulpian, *Reg.* I. 7; *Dig.* I. x.

¹⁶ Cic. *Acad. Prior.* II. 97.

¹⁷ Auct. ad Herenn. II. 19.

¹⁸ Pomponius (*Dig.* I. ii. 2 § 34) states that the tribunes of the plebs, as well as the consuls, praetors and aediles, 'in civitate iura reddebant'. But he also is probably only speaking of their indirect influence. When the tribunes were

appealed to they might hold an enquiry (*cognoscere*) on the issue to determine whether to receive the appeal (see Asconius, *in Mil.* 41), and such *cognitiones*, which were put on record, might be cited as legal precedents. Such tribunician *cognitiones*, which might in effect decide a case, are mentioned under the Principate in Juvenal, VII. 228, Aulus Gellius XIII. xii, and apparently Tac. *Ann.* XIII. 28.

[19] Lex Rubria (Bruns, *Fontes*[7], 16), cap. xxi, xxii.

[20] Bruns, *Fontes*[7], 17.

[21] Cic. II *Verr.* II. 30.

[22] Cic. II *Verr.* III. 138.

[23] Cic. *ad Fam.* XIII. 26. Cicero would surely not have so elaborately explained that the consul's letter was not in this case a command unless consular commands to proconsuls had been normal practice in such circumstances. Proconsuls no doubt often resented such interventions, which might be regarded as reflections on their probity; hence Cicero's laboured apology to his honoured—and perhaps touchy—friend.

[24] Cic. *Phil.* IV. 9.

[25] Suet. *Aug.* 33. 3.

[26] Tac. *Ann.* XIV. 28.

[27] Paulus, *Sent.* V. xxxv.

[28] Even if Augustus received no formal grant of consular *imperium*, it is abundantly clear that he exercised an *imperium* indistinguishable from that of the consuls in Rome and Italy (see above, pp. 13ff.).

[29] Tac. *Ann.* XIII. 4, Suet. *Nero*, 17.

[30] Though the formulary procedure was normal in Sicily for all civil cases, whether between Romans or *peregrini*, Verres tried two inheritance cases himself by *cognitio* (Cic. II *Verr.* II. 19-20, 25-6), and since Cicero does not protest, he was evidently within his rights as far as procedure went. Both cases concerned *peregrini*, but there is no reason to think that a governor could not exercise *cognitio* in cases between Romans.

[31] Gaius, II. 278.

[32] Gaius, IV. 109.

[33] It may be noted that in this work he alludes to appeals from *iudices* (*Dig.* II. viii. 9).

[34] Tac. *Ann.* XII. 60, 'nam divus Augustus apud equestris qui Aegypto praesiderent lege agi decretaque eorum proinde haberi iusserat ac si magistratus Romani constituissent': their jurisdiction even included manumission (*Dig.* XL. ii. 21, 'apud praefectum Aegypti possum servum manumittere ex constitutione divi Augusti'). I do not fully understand why *P. Mich.* III. 159 (= Riccobono, *Fontes*[2], III. 64) should not be regarded as a trial under the formulary procedure; and in *BGU*. 114 (= Riccobono, *Fontes*[2], III. 19) the prefect in saying ἐκ τῶν τοιούτων αἰτιῶν κριτὴν οὐ δίδωμι, appears to be acting under the same procedure.

[35] This is apparently the view advanced by Perrot, *L'appel dans la procédure de l'ordo iudiciorum*, Paris, 1907 (not accessible to me), cited by Jolowicz, *Historical Introduction to Roman Law*[2], 576.

[36] I have found no reference given for the doctrine in any textbook of Roman law. Mommsen (*Staatsrecht*[3], I. 272, note 2) can argue only from silence.

[37] Gaius, IV. 103-9.

[38] *Dig.* V. i. 58.

[39] Rescript of Marcus and Verus, *Dig.* XLIX. i. 21. pr. and § 1.

[40] Valerius Maximus does not suggest that these cases arose by appeal from the praetor's decision, and indeed it is difficult to believe that the injured parties would have approached the praetor, as under the *ius ordinarium* they had no possible claim. Augustus' decisions may well have formed precedents for the later *querela inofficiosi testamenti*. Claims under this heading were not decided *extra ordinem*, but by the centumviral court (Pliny, *Ep.* V. 1, *Dig.* V. ii. 13, 17) under the fiction that the testator was not of sound mind (*Dig.* V. ii. 2, 5).

[41] Val. Max. VII. vii. 3.

[42] Val. Max. VII. vii. 4.

[43] Just. *Inst.* II. 23. § 1 and 25. pr.

[44] Suet. *Claud.* 23. 1.

[45] For the special praetors see Pomponius in *Dig.* I. ii. 2 § 32; for the jurisdiction of the consuls and provincial governors, Gaius, II. 278, Ulpian, *Reg.* XXV. 12. Quintilian (III. vi. 70) shows that application was made directly to the consul or praetor at Rome.

[46] Suet. *Claud.* 23. 2, cf. Just. *Inst.* I. 20. § 3.

[47] Ovid, *ex Ponto*, IV. v. 17, ix. 43, Suet. *Claud.* 14.

[48] Val. Max. VII. vii. 3, 'Divus Augustus in bona paterna ire decreto suo iussit'.

[49] Val. Max. VII. vii. 4, 'si ipsa aequitas hac de re cognosceret, possetne iustius aut gravius pronuntiare'.

[50] Ulpian, *Reg.* XXV. 12, *Dig.* L. xvi. 178; Quintilian, III. vi. 70.

[51] Suet. *Aug.* 93, *Claud.* 15, *Nero*, 15, *Dom.* 8. 1. The anecdote told in *Claud.* 15 is particularly interesting. Claudius proposes to try a case, the defendant objects that it is not 'cognitionis rem sed ordinarii iuris', thus implying that the imperial jurisdiction always takes the form of *cognitio*, and furthermore that such *cognitio* is improper in cases where the *ius ordinarium* is applicable.

[52] There is a mysterious allusion in the Lex Iulia Municipalis (Bruns, *Fontes*[7], 18, l. 119) to municipal *iudicia publica* ('queive in eo municipio colonia praefectura foro conciliabulo quoius erit iudicio publico condemnatus est erit'), but it is scarcely possible to believe that a municipal court had capital jurisdiction.

[53] See above, pp. 53-4.

[54] Paulus, *Sent.* V. xxi. 1.

[55] *Dig.* XLVIII. vi. 7.

[56] Tac. *Ann.* III. 10 and 12, cf. also II. 79.

[57] Ib. III. 68.

[58] Ib. I. 72 and IV. 21.

[59] Ovid, *Tristia*, II. 131-2.

[60] *SEG*, IX. 8. v.

[61] Suet. *Aug.* 33, 51.

[62] Cassius Dio, LVI. 26.

[63] Tac. *Ann.* I. 72.

[64] Pliny, *Ep.* IV. 9. 17. cf. II. 11. 2.

[65] Levy (*Sb. Ak. Heidelberg, Phil. Hist. Kl.*, 1930-1, *Abh.* 5) has demonstrated that in the leges Corneliae the penalty remained technically death, and it may well be doubted whether, despite Cic. *Phil.* I. 23, Caesar's laws on *vis* and *maiestas* made any formal change. The occasional attempts to justify the milder penalty of *aquae et ignis interdictio* as being that of the laws (Tac. *Ann.* III. 50, XIV. 48) were probably based rather on the invariable Republican interpretation of the laws than on their text.

[66] *Dig.* I. xxi. 1.

[67] See above, pp. 56ff.

[68] *Collatio*, XIV. iii. 2-3.

[69] *SEG*, IX. 8. iv.

[70] *SEG*, IX. 8. i.

[71] It is fairly obvious that there was no jury in the capital cases judged by Marius Priscus (Pliny, *Ep.* II. 11).

[72] *Dig.* I. xvi. 6 pr., 11, xxi, 1 § 1, Cassius Dio, LIII. 14.

[73] Cassius Dio, LIV. 3.

[74] *Dig.* XLVII. vi. 8, 'lege Iulia de vi publica cavetur ne quis reum vinciat, impediative quominus Romae intra certum tempus adsit'.

[75] See above, pp. 54-6

[76] Cassius Dio, LI. 19.

[77] See Last, 'On the tribunicia potestas of Augustus', *Rend. Ist. Lomb.* LXXXIV (1951), pp. 93-110.

[78] The phrase seems to be used in one other passage only (Philostratus, *Vit. Soph.* 568) and there appears merely to mean a decisive favourable judgment.

[79] Cic. *Phil.* I. 21.

[80] Tac. *Ann.* III. 51, Suet. *Tib.* 75, Cassius Dio, LVII. 20.

[81] Suet. *Nero*, 10. 2.

[82] From Dio himself we have LII. 22, τὰς δίκας τάς τε ἐκκλήτους καὶ τὰς ἀναπομπίμους (*ex appellatione* and *ex relatione*), LIX. 8, ὥστε μήτε ἔκκλητόν ποτε ἀπ' αὐτοῦ δικάσαι, LXXVII, 8, ἐξ ἐκκλήτου δίκης κρινόμενον. Aelius Aristides (XXVI. 37, L. 74, ed. Keil) uses ἔκκλητος similarly. Ἐκκαλοῦμαι is the normal translation of *appello*, e.g. *IG*, II-III². 1100, l. 49 (under Hadrian), Riccobono, *Fontes²*, III. 101 (A.D. 340). Ἐπικαλοῦμαι is also used for *appello*, e.g. Plutarch, *Marcellus*, 2, *IG*, V. 21 (second century), and ἐπίκλησις for *appellatio* (*OGI*, 458, l. 82, under Augustus).

[83] Pliny (*NH*, VI. 90) can say 'appellationem esse ad populum' and Tacitus (*Ann.* XIV. 28) 'qui a privatis iudicibus ad senatum provocavissent'. Examples are frequent in the Severan jurists as cited in the Digest. In Greek Dionysius of Halicarnassus (*Ant. Rom.* V. 19. 4, 70. 2, VII. 41. 1 as against IX. 39. 2) carefully distinguishes προκαλοῦμαι (*provoco*) from ἐπικαλοῦμαι (*appello*). Ἐπικαλοῦμαι is used for Paul's appeal to Caesar (*Acts*, xxv. 11-12).

[84] Cassius Dio, LIII. 23, cf. Suet. *Aug.* 66. 2.

[85] Cassius Dio, LIV. 3.
[86] Cassius Dio, LIV. 3, Suet. *Tib.* 8.


## VI. THE AERARIUM AND THE FISCUS

* This article is an attempt to develop in greater detail the ideas set forth in two earlier contributions to the *Journal of Roman Studies* by Professor Tenney Frank ('On Augustus and the Aerarium', XXIII (1933), 143) and by Professor Last ('The Fiscus: a Note', XXXIV (1944), 51), and owes much to them. My thanks are also due to Mr. G. R. C. Davis, who has kindly allowed me to use much material from his unpublished thesis (D.Phil. Oxford) on 'The Administrative Staff of the Roman Emperors at Rome from Augustus to Alexander Severus', and to my pupil, G. E. M. de Ste. Croix, who furnished me with a number of useful references and acute criticisms.

[1] Plut. *Cato minor*, 16.
[2] Polyb. VI. 13.
[3] Polyb. VI. 12, 13.
[4] Cic. *ad Att.* III. 24. 1; *ad Q.f.* II. 3. 1; *in Pis.* 5; Suet. *Iul.* 18.
[5] Cic. *ad fam.* II. 17, V. 20; *ad Att.* VI. 7.
[6] Cic. II *Verr.* I. 36.
[7] Cic. *ad Att.* VII. 1. 6.
[8] Cic. *in Pis.* 86.
[9] Plut. *Caesar*, 28.
[10] Cic. *ad fam.* VIII. 4. 4.
[11] Cic. *de prov. cons.* 28; *pro Balbo*, 61.
[12] Plut. *Pompey*, 25.
[13] Appian, *Mith.* 94.
[14] Cic. II. *Verr.* III. 197.
[15] Cic. II. *Verr.* III. 163 *seqq.*
[16] Cic. *ad fam.* III. 5.
[17] Cic. *ad fam.* V. 20. 9; cf. II. 17. 4.
[18] Cic. *de imp. Cn. Pompei*, 14.
[19] Suet. *Aug.* 101; cf. Tac. *Ann.* 1. 11; Cassius Dio, LVI. 33; and also Suet. *Aug.* 28; Cassius Dio, LIII. 30, for a similar document drawn up in 23 B.C.
[20] E.g. the 'fiscus Gallicus provinciae Lugdunensis' of *ILS*, 1514.
[21] Vell. Pat. II. 39. 2.
[22] Suet. *Calig.* 16; also Cassius Dio, LIX. 9. The fact that Tiberius, who in general kept rigidly to constitutional forms, omitted in the later years of his reign to publish the *rationes imperii* supports the view that they were not legally required of him.
[23] Cassius Dio, LIII. 2 and 32; Tac. *Ann.* XIII. 28-9.
[24] Cassius Dio, LX. 24. 1-3; Suet. *Claud.* 24; Tac. *Ann.* XIII. 28-9; *ILS*, 966-7.

[25] Tac. *Ann.* XIII. 28-9.

[26] *CIL*, VI. 8409.

[27] *ILS*, 1487.

[28] *ILS*, 1643, *CIL*, VI. 3962, 8506.

[29] Val. Max. VI. ii. 11.

[30] Seneca, *de beneficiis*, IV. 39. 3.

[31] Pliny, *NH*, VI. 84.

[32] Pliny, *NH*, XII. 113, 123.

[33] *SIG*³, 800.

[34] *OGIS*, 669.

[35] Seneca, *de beneficiis*, VII. 6. 3.

[36] Pliny, *NH*, XVIII. 114.

[37] Tac. *Ann.* IV. 20.

[38] Tac. *Ann.* VI. 2.

[39] Tac. *Ann.* II. 48.

[40] Tac. *Hist.* I. 46.

[41] Tac. *Hist.* I. 58.

[42] Suet. *Vesp.* 23; Juv. IV. 55.

[43] *CIL*, VI. 8540a, in the reign of Claudius, is the earliest mention.

[44] See Tenney Frank, *JRS*, XXIII (1933), 143 ff.

[45] Tac. *Ann.* XV. 18.

[46] Tac. *Ann.* XIII. 31.

[47] *AE*, 1932, 58. The inscription is not accurately dateable and might be late Julio-Claudian. This official was in my view the forerunner of the procurators of the 'fisci Asiaticus' and 'Alexandrinus', which are discussed below.

[48] Suet. *Dom.* 12; coins of Nerva; cf. *ILS*, 1519.

[49] *ILS*, 1540-4.

[50] *ILS*, 1570, 1651, 1660.

[51] *ILS*, 1648, 1650; *CIL*, VI. 8519, 8521-2, 37744, VIII. 2702, 18250.

[52] *ILS*, 1518; *N. d. Scavi*, 1901, 20; *CIL*, VI. 5744, 8573, XV. 7974 a, b, ranging from the Flavian dynasty to Antoninus Pius.

[53] *ILS*, 1507, 1515-17; *CIL*, XIII. 1800, ranging from Domitian to Commodus.

[54] Tac. *Hist.* IV. 9.

[55] Funisulanus Vettonianus (*ILS*, 1005) and Pompusius Mettius, 'praefectus aerarii Saturni annos IIII' (*CIL*, VI. 1495), may fall under Vespasian's reign, but might have held the office late in Nero's reign. The first certain Flavian *praefectus aerarii Saturni* is Antistius Rusticus (*JRS*, XIV (1924), 180) under Domitian.

[56] Cassius Dio, LXXII. 33.

[57] *ILS*, 309.

[58] Pliny, *Pan.* 42.

[59] Pliny, *Pan.* 36.

[60] Frontinus, *de aqu.* 118. Here, it may be added, the distinction goes back to Claudius, but then meant something different. The emperor's slaves were his private property and would naturally be maintained out of his private funds, his 'fiscus' in the Julio-Claudian sense. Frontinus no doubt means no more than

O

that the funds were in the one case issued by the *praefecti aerarii Saturni*, and in the other by the *a rationibus*.

[61] Tac. *Ann.* II. 47. As much has been built on this passage, which deals with the remission for five years to Sardis of 'quantum aerario aut fisco pendebant', I should like to stress the extreme improbability on any theory that the tribute arising from each individual city was divided between two treasuries at Rome: surely, if there was at that date an imperial treasury at Rome which drew moneys from Asia, such moneys would have been a block grant from the 'fiscus Asiaticus'.

[62] Tac. *Ann.* VI. 17.

[63] Suet. *Vesp.* 16.

[64] In one passage (*Ann.* VI. 2) Tacitus contrasts 'aerarium' and 'fiscus': 'bona Seiani ablata aerario ut in fiscum cogerentur, tamquam referret.' By comparison with *Ann.* IV. 20, it would appear that Tiberius claimed the estate of Sejanus for himself, as being the product of his gifts, instead of allowing it to go as *bona damnatorum* into the aerarium. 'Fiscus' thus here means the emperor's private estate.

[65] *ILS*, 6870, III.

[66] Wilcken, *Chr.* I. 174, of A.D. 199.

[67] Keil and Premerstein, *Denkschr. Ak. Wien*, LVII, 55.

[68] *Dig.* L. vi. 6 (5) § 9.

[69] *CIL*, XV. 4102, 4111, 4114, etc. 'fisci rationis patrimonii provinciae Baeticae,' etc.

[70] *ILS*, 1387; *AE*, 1945, 80; cf. *ILS*, 5920 for the date.

[71] *ILS*, 1738, under Caracalla.

[72] *ILS*, 1330, 1371, 1439.

[73] *ILS*, 1347, 1370, 1422, 8852.

[74] *ILS*, 1491. 'qui proc. Alexandriae ad rat. patrimonii' under Hadrian; this may be a Latin version of the often attested *procurator usiacus*.

[75] *ILS*, 1330 and, if *item* means concurrently, 1439.

[76] *CIL*, VIII. 2702, 18250; VI. 2104, b, 40.

[77] *Dig.* XLIX. xiv. 6 § 1.

[78] *Dig.* XLIX. xiv. 3 § 10.

[79] *Dig.* XLIX. vi. l. pr.

[80] SHA, *Vita Severi*, 12.

[81] E.g. *Cod. Just.* XI, lxviii (title), lxix (title and laws 1 and 2), lxxi-lxxiv (titles); Marcian, *Nov.* 2; Just. *Nov.* 2; Theodoret, *Ep.* 42.

[82] *ILS*, 1452, 1740, 6333; cf. 1347, 2942.

[83] *ILS*, 478.

## VII. PROCURATORS AND PREFECTS IN THE EARLY PRINCIPATE

[1] By H. G. Pflaum, *Les Procurateurs équestres*, p. 14-15, citing Cic. *ad Att.* IV. i. 6, *ad Fam.* IV. 6. 2, XII. 14.5, *ad Q.f.* III. 9. 3, *Acad.* I. 11, *de Off.* I. 85, *de Rep.* II. 51, Caesar, *BC*, III. 108. 1, Sallust, *Bell. Jug.* 14. 1.

[2] Tac. *Ann.* XV. 44.

[3] Strabo, IV. p. 203, Pliny, *NH*, X. 134.

[4] *ILS*, 1349, 94, *CIL*, XII. 80. The first two are nos. 243 and 166 in Ehrenberg and Jones, *Documents*[2], henceforth cited as *EJ*.

[5] Cassius Dio, LV. 28, *ILS*, 105 (*EJ*, 232a), *Eph. Epigr.* VIII. 744, *Not. Scav.* 1892, 289; cf. *ILS*, 2684 (*EJ*, 249), 'praefectus cohortis Corsorum et civitatum Barbariae in Sardinia'.

[6] *CIL*, XII. 2455.

[7] *CIL*, X. 7351.

[8] *ILS*, 6948, *CIL*, II. 3271.

[9] *ILS*, 1349 (*EJ*, 243).

[10] *ILS*, 235, 8902, 9196. Numerous other *praefecti civitatum* of minor importance, and often of later date (especially in Africa), are listed in *PW*, XXII. 1290-4.

[11] *ILS*, 2689 (*EJ*, 244).

[12] *ILS*, 9007 (*EJ*, 224).

[13] *ILS*, 847 (corrected text in *PW*, s.v. 'legio', XII, 1226).

[14] *ILS*, 1348.

[15] *ILS*, 1349 (*EJ*, 243): *AE*, 1936, 83, which is undated, seems to be early.

[16] Tac. *Ann.* XII. 49; Cassius Dio in his account of the annexation (LVII. 17) gives no title to the equestrian governor.

[17] *ILS*, 231.

[18] *AE*, 1924, 66.

[19] Philo, *Leg. ad Gaium*, 38.

[20] Jos. *Bell. Jud.* II. 117, 169, *Ant. Jud.* XVIII. 2, 31-3, 55, XIX. 363, XX. 2. In XVIII. 237 the title ἱππάρχην given to Marullus must surely be an error for ὕπαρχον or ἔπαρχον.

[21] Cic. II *Verr.* I. 73, III. 134, *pro Cluentio*, 99, *pro Rab. Post.* 13, 19, *ad Att.* V. 17. 2, VI. 1. 2, *ad Fam.* III. 8. 7, V. 20. 7, VII. v. 3; Caesar, *BG*, I. 39, III. 7, *BC*, I. 21.

[22] As in Caesar, *BG*, III. 7.

[23] *ILS*, 6286.

[24] Cic. *ad Fam.* III. 6. 5.

[25] Caesar, *BG*, II. 18; cf. *BC*, III. 12, *Afr.* 68. 4, 76. 1, *ILS*, 5319 and many other instances where the precise title is not given collected by Broughton, *Magistrates of the Roman Republic*, II, pp. 232, 284, 303, 312-3, 356, 367-8.

[26] Cic. *ad Att.* V. 21.

[27] *Dig.* I. xxi. 1 § 1, 'imperium quod iurisdictioni cohaeret mandata iurisdictione transire verius est', 5 § 1, 'mandata iurisdictione privato etiam imperium, quod non est merum, videtur mandari, quia iurisdictio sine modica coercitione nulla est'.

²⁸ Cic. *Phil.* V. 45, 'demus igitur imperium Caesari, sine quo res militaris administrari, teneri exercitus, bellum geri non potest'.

²⁹ Caesar, *BC*, III. 32.

³⁰ All persons bearing the title *pro legato* are of equestrian rank; besides the instances cited above in notes 10, 14 and 18, see *ILS*, 2677, 2678 (*EJ*, 234), *AE*, 1938, 173 (*EJ*, 233).

³¹ Only in Mauretania Tingitana, see below, note 61.

³² Tac. *Ann.* II. 59, *Hist.* I. 11.

³³ Strabo, XVII. p. 797.

³⁴ *Dig.* I. xvii. 1.

³⁵ W. Kalb, *Juristenlatein²*, 82, *Roms Juristen*, 145, note 3.

³⁶ H. M. Last, *JEA*, XL (1954), 68–73.

³⁷ S. Solazzi, *Aegyptus*, IX (1928), 296–301.

³⁸ See Solazzi, loc. cit., p. 299, note 3.

³⁹ Tac. *Ann.* XII. 60.

⁴⁰ *Dig.* XL. ii. 21.

⁴¹ *Dig.* XL. i. 14, ii. 1, 8, 18 § 1, 20 § 4, Ulpian, *Reg.* i. 7, viii. 2-5, xi. 18-20.

⁴² *Dig.* XL. ii. 5, 7: Ulpian in *Reg.* viii. 2-5 and xi. 18-20 speaks of *praesides* in general (including proconsuls and *legati Augusti*) as capable of acting in the provinces: similarly in *Dig.* XXVI. v. 1 he mentions proconsuls, *praesides* and the prefect of Egypt.

⁴³ *Dig.* XL. ii. 17.

⁴⁴ *Dig.* XXVI. v. 1 § 1.

⁴⁵ *Dig.* I. xvi. 2, 3.

⁴⁶ Cassius Dio, LIV. 21, Suet. *Aug.* 67. 1 , Seneca, *Apocolocyntosis*, 6.

⁴⁷ Tac. *Ann.* IV. 15.

⁴⁸ Strabo, III. p. 167.

⁴⁹ See above, note 46.

⁵⁰ This is suggested by the rather mysterious misdeeds of Tiberius Nicephorus at Cibyra in Claudius' reign (*IGR*, IV. 914); see D. Magie in *Studies in Roman Social and Economic History* (ed. P. R. Coleman-Norton), pp. 152-4). For a later example see Pliny, *Ep.* X. 27.

⁵¹ Cassius Dio, LVII. 23; cf. Tacitus' more epigrammatic statement in *Ann.* IV. 6

⁵² Philo, *Leg. ad Gaium*, 30. He is styled 'procurator' in *AE*, 1941, 105 (*EJ*, 225) and ὁ τῆς Ἰαμνείας ἐπίτροπος in Jos. *Ant. Jud.* XVIII. 158: for the history of Jamnia see Jos. *Ant. Jud.* XVIII. 31, *Bell. Jud.* II. 167.

⁵³ Cic. *ad Att.* V. 21. 10, VI. 1. 4-6, 2. 8, 3. 5-6: cf. II *Verr.* III. 75, for the grant of a *praefectura* to a *publicanus*.

⁵⁴ As Capito was condemned he evidently had somehow usurped *imperium* and the use of troops (Tac. *Ann.* IV. 15).

⁵⁵ Pliny, *Ep.* X. 27; Maximus already had three soldiers before Pliny arrived.

⁵⁶ Tac. *Ann.* XIV. 31-2.

⁵⁷ Jos. *Ant. Jud.* XVIII. 158.

⁵⁸ Philo, *in Flaccum*, 3-4.

⁵⁹ Jos. *Ant. Jud.* XVIII. 60, *Bell. Jud.* II. 175.
⁶⁰ *ILS*, 1348, *AE*, 1924, 66.
⁶¹ *ILS*, 1352, 1353.
⁶² *CIL*, X. 8023-4, *ILS*, 5350 (Domitian), 530, 1358-60, 5526. See also *ILS*, 9011, where 'p[raef. et] proc. Aug. A[lpium]' is restored in a second century inscription.
⁶³ Philo, *Leg. ad Gaium*, 38, Πίλατος ἦν τῶν ὑπάρχων ἐπίτροπος ἀποδεδειγμένος τῆς 'Ιουδαίας.
⁶⁴ Tac. *Ann.* XII. 60.
⁶⁵ *ILS*, 231, *AE*, 1924, 66, *ILS*, 1348, 1349.
⁶⁶ Philo, *in Flaccum*, 2, *Leg. ad Gaium*, 20, Pliny, *NH*, XXXVI. 57, *PSI*, 1160, *P. Lond.* 1912 (H. I. Bell, *Jews and Christians in Egypt*). For the date of *PSI*, 1160, see Musurillo, *Acts of the Pagan Martyrs*, pp. 83-8. Turner (*JRS*, XLV (1955), 119-20) has since pointed out that the text is a translation from Latin and therefore certainly a copy of an official document, and argued that Καῖσαρ εἶπεν must therefore refer to Augustus. But the papyrus is certainly a later copy, presumably made for propaganda purposes, and the subscript may have been garbled. I cannot agree with Sherwin White (*BSR*, XV (1939), p. 14, note 22) that there were two persons called Vitrasius Pollio in Egypt early in Claudius' reign, one the well-known prefect, the other an unknown procurator.

## VIII. THE DEDITICII AND THE CONSTITUTIO ANTONINIANA

¹ An up-to-date bibliography of the Constitutio Antoniniana will be found in C. Sasse, *Die Constitutio Antoniniana* (Wiesbaden, 1958), 134-43, and a list of suggested supplements to *P. Giessen*, 40, in the same work, pp. 12-14.
² By J. Keil in *Anz. Ak. Wien (Phil. Hist. Kl.)*, LXXXV (1948), 143.
³ Other examples of supplements which in effect attach the exception of the *dediticii* to the main verb are [μ]ένοντος [οὐδενὸς τῶν ἄλλων πολιτευμ]άτων ('none of the other statuses being preserved except the *dediticii*'), suggested by Kunkel (Jörs-Kunkel, *Geschichte und System des römisches Rechtes³*, 57, note 10), or [μ]ένοντος [ἔξω οὐδενὸς τῶν πολιτευμ]άτων ('none of the statuses being excluded except the *dediticii*'), proposed by J. Keil, *Anz. Ak. Wien*, LXXXV (1948), 146. The chief objection to these supplements is that they cannot be translated into Latin; for πολίτεια must represent *civitas*, and if so what does πολίτευμα represent?
⁴ By Bickermann, *Das Edikt des Kaisers Caracalla in P. Giess. 40* (Diss. Berlin, 1926).
⁵ Gaius, I. 14.
⁶ For the terms of a typical *deditio* see Livy, I. 38, VII. 31.
⁷ *Staatsrecht³*, III. 138-42, 716 ff.
⁸ Pliny, *Ep.* X. 79, 80, 112, 114-5.

[9] Cic. II *Verr.* II. 90.

[10] Pliny, *Ep.* X. 49-50.

[11] Amm. Marc. XX. viii. 13, XXI. iv. 8. Cf. *Corp. Gloss. Lat.* IV. 51, V. 188, 'dediticius si barbarus tradat se Romanis'.

[12] *ILS*, 9184. See Rowell, *Yale Classical Studies*, VI (1939), 73-108, for a more accurate reading and a discussion of this inscription.

[13] Gaius, I. 13.

[14] Ib. I. 27.

[15] Ib. III. 74-6.

[16] Ib. I. 25, Ulpian, *Reg.* xxii. 2.

[17] Gaius, III. 75.

[18] Ulpian, *Reg.* xx. 14.

[19] Gaius, I. 26.

[20] Ib. I. 67-8, Ulpian, *Reg.* vii. 4.

[21] Suet. *Aug.* 40.

[22] Gaius, I. 13.

[23] Under the Republic Roman citizenship had been given to *dediticii*, e.g. to the Campanians in 334, if this story is historical (Livy, VII. 31, VIII. 14) and again in 189 (Livy, XXXVIII. 28) and to the defeated Italian allies in 87 B.C. (Gran. Licin. XXXV). The doctrine of the incapacity of *dediticii* for the citizenship may have been a learned construction from the regulation of the status of the Campanian *dediticii* in 210 B.C., 'liberos esse iusserunt, ita ut nemo eorum civis Romanus aut Latini nominis esset' (Livy, XXVI. 34).

[24] Pliny, *Ep.* X. 6-7, 10. Sasse, *Die Constitutio Antoniniana*, 79, objects that examples occur in the papyri (e.g. *P. Oxy.* 574, 727, *P. Lond.* II. 348, III. 1231) of Egyptians who have the Roman citizenship. But these may be descendants of Egyptians who had served in the Misenum fleet, or may not have recorded their nominal Alexandrian citizenship. Sasse also tries to explain away the Pliny-Trajan letters, arguing that the bar to Harpocras' citizenship was the fact that he was the freedman of an Egyptian. This is flatly contrary to Pliny's own statement that Harpocras required a prior grant of Alexandrian citizenship 'quoniam esset Aegyptius'.

[25] Jos. *c. Ap.* II. 4, μόνοις Αἰγυπτίοις οἱ κύριοι νῦν ʻΡωμαῖοι τῆς οἰκουμένης μεταλαμβάνειν ἡστινοσοῦν πολιτείας ἀπειρήκασιν.

[26] *P. Gnomon*, 55.

[27] As in the case of Harpocras, Pliny's candidate (see note 24 above). Egyptians who served in the fleet of Misenum and received citizenship on discharge (*P. Gnomon*, 55) must presumably have profited by a similar device: perhaps they were given Latin status on recruitment.

[28] Bickermann, *Archiv Pap.* IX. 24 ff.

[29] Cited in Sasse, op. cit. 9-11.

[30] Bickermann, *Das Edikt des Kaisers Caracalla in P. Giess.* 40.

[31] *Cod. Just.* VII. v. 1, vi. 1: cf. Just. *Inst.* I. v. 3, *Nov.* 78. *Latini Juniani* still survived in the Burgundian kingdom in the early sixth century (*Lex Rom. Burg.* xliv. 5).

³² See above notes 11 and 12 and *Cod. Theod.* VII. xiii. 16 (406), 'eorum servos quos militia armata detentat, foederatorum nihilominus et dediticiorum'.

³³ Gaius does not deduce the incapacity of criminous slaves to receive the Roman citizenship from their status *dediticiorum numero.* He merely states: 'huius ergo turpitudinis servos . . . numquam aut cives Romanos aut Latinos fieri dicemus, sed omni modo dediticiorum numero constitui intelligemus' (I. 15), and later (I. 26), 'nec ulla lege aut senatus consulto aut constitutione principali aditus illis ad civitatem Romanam datur'. That is he merely records the fact that under the Lex Aelia Sentia criminous slaves did not become Latins or Romans on manumission, and the fact that no other enactment gave them access to the citizenship subsequently. Elsewhere he complains of the obscurity of the Lex Aelia Sentia: 'nec me praeterit non satis in ea re legis latorem voluntatem suam verbis expressisse'.

³⁴ The controversy is summarised by Jolowicz, *Historical Introduction to Roman Law*², 545-7, who cites the voluminous literature.

³⁵ Some examples are cited in my *Greek City*, p. 174; the councils likewise retained their peculiarities and were not assimilated to the *ordines* of Roman or Latin cities (op. cit., p. 176).

³⁶ Supplements in this sense have been proposed, e.g. [μ]ένοντος [πάντος γένους πολιτευμ]άτων, by Paul Meyer in the original publication of P. Giessen, or [μ]ένοντος [ἑκάστου ὧν ἄν ᾖ πολιτευμ]άτων, by Wilhelm, cited by Schonbauer in *Atti. Congr. intern. dir. Rom. Verona* IV (1951), 134; or [μ]ένοντος [ἀκεραίου τοῦ δικαίου τῶν πολιτευμ]άτων, suggested by Kübler, *PW*, s.v. 'Peregrinus', XIX. 642. To these the same objection applies as to those cited in note 3.

³⁷ See the literature cited in Taubenschlag, *The law of Greco-Roman Egypt*², p. 586, note 24.

³⁸ See Mommsen, *Staatsrecht* ³, III. 765 ff.

³⁹ Strabo, XII. p. 542, Jos. *Ant. Jud.* XIV. 115, *IGR*, III. 69.

⁴⁰ *IGR*, IV. 289, *SIG*³, 742.

⁴¹ *IGR*, III. 801. This inscription is of particular interest, in that it shows that not only ἀπελεύθεροι (freedmen manumitted under local law by Greek citizens of Syllium) but οὐινδικτάριοι (freedmen manumitted under Roman law by Romans, that is by citizens of Syllium who held Roman citizenship), who would be Roman citizens, were excluded from the citizen register.

⁴² P. *Gnomon*, 49.

⁴³ Riccobono, *Fontes*², III. 19, μὴ ὢν δὲ νόμιμος υἱὸς τοῦ πατρὸς ὄντος Ἀλεξανδρέως Ἀλεξανδρεὺς οὐ δύναται εἶναι.

⁴⁴ It is nowhere expressly stated in the various municipal laws (or rather the sections of them which survive) that only *municipes* (*coloni*) were eligible for the magistracies or the decurionate. It was probably taken for granted and is implied in the final clause of the Lex Tarentina (Riccobono, *Fontes* ², I. 18. § 6): 'quei pecuniam municipio Tarentin[o] non debebit, sei quis eorum quei municeps erit neque eo sexennio [p]roximo quo exeire volet duovirum a[edilisve fuerit ex municipio exeire volet id ei sine fraude sua facere liceto].' Anyone might owe money to the municipality; only a *municeps* could have been duovir or aedilis. It

also appears from *ILS*. 6680 that its *attributi* could not hold office in Tergeste. For Greek cities the rule is implied by Pliny, *Ep*. X. 114-15. The Bithynian cities had evidently been enrolling citizens of other Bithynian cities on their registers, and then putting them on their councils: the enforcement of the Lex Pompeia, which prohibited the first practice, would have involved ejecting the persons involved from the council.

The rule for *munera* was different, *incolae* being liable to them (Gaius cited in *Dig*. L. i. 29), but *incolae* were residents in the town and not in the territory (*Dig*. L. i. 35), so that the cities would not be able to impose their *munera* on rural *attributi*, etc. The distinction between *honores* and *munera* was gradually extinguished, as the former became burdensome and compulsory (see my *Greek City*, pp. 339-40, note 38). *Honores* are already implied to be obligatory on *incolae* in *Cod. Just*. X. xxxix. 1 (a law of Caracalla).

⁴⁵ *ILS*, 6680.

⁴⁶ I at one time (*JRS*, XXVI (1936), 227 ff.) thought that Wilhelm's supplement (*AJA*, XXXVIII (1934), 180), [μ]ένοντος [οὐδενὸς ἐκτὸς τῶν πολιτευμ]άτων ('no one remaining outside the citizen bodies'), would convey the required meaning. The restoration is too long, and while this can be remedied by omitting τῶν and substituting ἔξω for ἐκτός (Schönbauer, *Archiv. Pap.* XIII (1939), 184), the difficulty remains that it cannot be satisfactorily translated into Latin (see above note 3). Oliver's suggestion (*A. J. Phil.* LXXVI (1955), 296), [μ]ένοντος [τοῦ καταλόγου τῶν ὀνομ]άτων χωρ[ὶς] τῶν [δε]δειτικίων ('the register of the names of the *dediticii* remaining separate'), might also give the required meaning; but the order is unnatural. It is on the whole unlikely that so complex a matter as *origo* could have been regulated in a brief genitive (ablative) absolute clause; more probably the rules were laid down by separate edicts.

⁴⁷ *Dig*. L. i. 1, 6, 7, 9, 15 § 3, 16, 22 § 1-2, 23, 27.

⁴⁸ *ad Edictum*. lxi. cited in *Dig*. L. i. 30. The Constitutio Antoniniana is mentioned in *ad Edictum*, xxii (*Dig*. I. v. 17).

⁴⁹ *Dig*. L. vi. 5 §§ 10-11.

⁵⁰ Keil and Premerstein, *Denkschr. Ak. Wien*, LVII (1914-15), 37 (reprinted in Abbot and Johnson, *Municipal Administration in the Roman Empire*, pp. 478-9).

⁵¹ See my *Cities of the Eastern Roman Provinces*, pp. 329 ff. It may be noted that the metropoleis are styled *civitates* in official Latin documents (*P. Oxy.* 1114 of 237 A.D. and *SB*, 1016 of 249 A.D.).

⁵² *JEA*, 1935, 224 ff.

⁵³ Isid. Pelus. *Ep*. I. 489 (Migne, *P.G.* LXXVIII. 448-9). Schönbauer (*J. Jur. Pap*. VI (1952), 17 ff.) has inferred from this that the *dediticii* were excluded from the *ius honorum*, and has proposed the supplement [μ]ένοντος [αὐτοῖς τοῦ δικαίου ἀξιωμ]άτων (cf. *J. Jur. Pap*. VII (1954), 138, for variants on this theme). But it is very doubtful whether such a concept as *ius honorum* existed (see Ph. Fabia, *La Table Claudienne de Lyon*), and if it did, it applied to the magistracies of the Roman people, and not to imperial appointments. Moreover the clause as reconstructed by Schönbauer is illogical; it could not be said that the newly created citizens retained the *ius honorum*.

[54] Cassius Dio, LXXVII. 9.
[55] See pp. 63-5.

## IX. 'IN EO SOLO DOMINIVM POPVLI ROMANI EST VEL CAESARIS'

[1] *JRS*, XVII (1927), 141-161.
[2] Frontinus, Bruns, *Fontes*[7], ii. 86.
[3] Gaius, III, 145.
[4] *Dig.* XLIX. xiv. 45 § 12.
[5] *Cod. Just.* VII. xxv. 1.
[6] Ib. VII. xxxi. 1.
[7] Just. *Inst.* II. 6 pr.
[8] Theophilus, *Comm. in Inst.* II. i. 40.
[9] Gaius, II. 7.
[10] Gaius, II. 14*a*, 21, 27, 31, 46.
[11] Gaius, II. 5, 6.
[12] Gaius, II. 7.
[13] Pliny, *Ep.* X. 50.
[14] Cic. *pro Flacco*, 80.
[15] Gaius, II. 40-2.
[16] Bruns, *Fontes*[7], 11, ll. 53 ff.
[17] P-W, s.v. 'Coloniae', IV. 580 f., 'Ius Italicum', X. 1240. It must be remembered that our list of *coloniae iuris Italici* is far from exhaustive, since it depends on such *obiter dicta* of the classical jurists as Justinian's compilators have preserved and on the chance that a colony issued coins and used the Marsyas type on them.
[18] Stobi (*Dig.* L. xv. 8 § 8) and Coela (Head, *Hist. Num.*[2] p. 259, for a Marsyas statue) seem to be the only *municipia* possessing *ius Italicum*, and of these Stobi is not known to be earlier than Flavian and Coela is Hadrianic. Nothing is known of the four Dalmatian communities stated to be *iuris Italici* in Pliny, *NH*, III. 139.
[19] Mitteis, *Grundzüge*, 172.
[20] Gaius, II. 21.
[21] See above, pp. 130-33.
[22] Cic. II *Verr.* II. 90.
[23] Jos. *Bell. Iud.* VII. 216-17.

## X. THE ROMAN CIVIL SERVICE (CLERICAL AND SUB-CLERICAL GRADES)

[1] The story is told in varying forms in Livy, IX. 46, Pliny, *NH*, XXXIII. 17, *Dig.* I. ii. 2 § 27 and Gellius, VII. ix. He is sometimes called a *scriba* of the aediles (Livy and Gellius), sometimes the *scriba* of Appius Claudius the Censor (Pliny and the *Digest*): as will be seen the two versions are not contradictory.

For the first part of this paper, which deals with the *apparitores*, the basic study is still Mommsen, *Staatsrecht*, I³, 332-71, though the work of J. H. Krause, 'De scribis publicis Romanorum' (*Jahrbuch des Pädagogiums zum Kloster Unser Lieben Frauen in Magdeburg*, Heft 22, 1858), is still of value, especially for the social status of *scribae* during the Republic. I differ from Mommsen on a few points, but my account is mainly a summary of his, where further references may be found.

² Mommsen's assumption that the tenure of *apparitores* was originally and always in principle annual, like that of the magistrates whom they served, seems to be arbitrary. *Apparitores* (except for *accensi*) are always described as serving a college of magistrates, and not any individual magistrate. Long tenure appears to have been already the rule in the early second century B.C., when L. Petilius, appointed *scriba* by Q. Petilius as quaestor, is still holding this post when his patron is praetor (Livy, XL. 29).

³ According to tradition citizens were employed from the earliest days of the Republic (Livy, II. 55). The rule is explicitly recorded in Bruns, *Fontes*⁷, 12, I. 7-8, 12, 'de eis quei cives Romanei sunt'.

⁴ Mommsen, *Staatsrecht*, I³, 320-32.

⁵ Verres' *medicus* and *haruspex* are frequently classed with the *apparitores* by Cicero (II *Verr*. II. 27, III. 28, 54, 137). *Architecti* and *pullarii* are among the staff allocated to Rullus' proposed decemvirs (Cic. *de lege agr*. II. 31-2). Only the last grade are known to have been organised on a regular basis in *decuriae* (*ILS*, 1886, 1907, cf. 1926).

⁶ *Viatores* traditionally go back to the earliest days of the Republic (Livy, II. 56. 13, III. 56. 5, Cic. *de sen*. 56, Festus, p. 371, Pliny, *NH*, XVIII. 20). They are recorded as serving dictators (Livy, VI. 15. 1, XXII. 11. 3), consuls (Gellius, IV. x. 8, Livy, XLI. 15), praetors (Bruns, *Fontes*⁷, 10, l. 50), aediles (Livy, XXX. 38. 7), quaestors (Bruns, *Fontes*⁷, 12) and in particular tribunes of the plebs (Livy II., 56, III. 56, XXXVIII. 51. 12, Gellius, XIII. xii. 6, Cicero, *pro Fonteio*, 29, *pro Cluentio*, 74, *in Vatin*. 22).

⁷ *Praecones* are recorded for censors (Varro, *L.L*. VI. 86-7, Livy, XXIX. 37), dictators (Livy, IV. 32, VIII. 32-3), consuls (Varro, *L.L*. VI. 95, Livy, XXIV. 8. 20), quaestors (Bruns, *Fontes*⁷, 12) and tribunes of the plebs (Livy, XXXVIII. 51. 8, Asconius, *in Cornel*. p. 51, Auctor ad Herenn. IV. 68).

⁸ Lictors, of course, by tradition go back to the regal period (Livy, I. 26. 7).

⁹ II *Verr*. V. 118 ff.; cf. *ad Q.f*. I. 1. 13, 'sit lictor non suae sed tuae lenitatis apparitor: maioraque praeferant fasces illi et secures dignitatis insignia quam potestatis'.

¹⁰ Cicero states this as the traditional practice in *ad Q.f*. I. 1. 13. Timarchides, Verres' *accensus*, was his freedman (II *Verr*. III. 154, 157). Cicero himself, however, employed another man's freedman (*ad Fam*. III. 7), and so apparently did C. Nero as proconsul of Asia (II *Verr*. I. 71). *Accensi* are said to go back to the decemvirate of 450 B.C. (Livy, III. 33. 8). They served consuls (Varro, *L.L*. VI. 88, 95, Suet. *Julius*, 20) and praetors (Varro, *L.L*. VI. 89).

¹¹ *Scribae* are recorded as serving aediles (Gellius, VII. ix, Livy, IX. 46, XXX. 39. 7, Cic. *pro Cluentio*, 126), quaestors (Bruns, *Fontes*⁷, 12, Livy, XL. 29, Plutarch,

*Cato Minor*, 16) and tribunes of the plebs (Livy, XXXVIII. 51, Asconius, *in Cornel.* 51).

[12] Cic. II. *Verr.* III. 182.

[13] Cic. *de domo*, 74.

[14] Cic. II *Verr.* III. 185.

[15] This is implied by 'in secundum ordinem civitatis' in Cic. II *Verr.* III. 184 *Scribae* are placed immediately after the equestrian *tribuni* and *praefecti* and before the unofficial *comites* of a provincial governor in Cic. *pro Rabirio Postumo*, 13.

[16] Many inscriptions (e.g. *ILS*, 1894-5, 1898, 1926, 2748, 9036) speak of *scribae librarii quaestorii III decuriarum* and Bruns, *Fontes*[7], 12, proves that the three *decuriae* of *viatores* and *praecones quaestorii* served in annual rotation.

[17] Lictors: *ILS*, 1904, 'l[ict.] III decuriarum, qui Ca[es.] et magistratibus a[ppar.],' 1908, 1911-12, 9037, 'lict. III decur., qui imp. et cos. et pr. apparuit,' *CIL*, VI. 1874. Praecones: *ILS*, 1933, 'praeco ex tribus decuris qui cos. cens. pr. apparere solent, apparuit Caesari Augusto' (the only mention of censorial *apparitores* in the inscriptions). Viatores: *ILS*, 331, 'viatores qui Caesarib. et pr. apparent,' 1915, 1920, 1922, 1944, 'viat. honor. dec. cos. et pr.,' 5052, *CIL*, VI. 1916.

[18] Lictors: *ILS*, 1908, 'decuriali decuriae lictor. cos. trium decuriar.,' 1910, *CIL*, VI. 1879. Praecones: *ILS*, 1934, 'ordo decuriae Iuliae praec. cos.,' 1935, 3878. Viatores: *ILS*, 1534, 1910, 'exercuit decurias duas viatoria(m) et lictoria(m) consulares,' 1919, *CIL*, VI. 1917, cf. *ILS*, 1921, 6141, 'decuriae viatoriae equestris cos.'

[19] The following table shows the *scribae*, *viatores*, and *praecones* of the lesser magistracies:

| | Scribae | Viatores | Praecones |
|---|---|---|---|
| aed. cur | *ILS*, 1879-82, 1886, 1893, 1898-9, 2727, 3593, 6188 | | *ILS*, 1879, 1908 |
| aed. pleb. | *ILS*, 1893, CIL, VI. 1855 | *ILS*, 1923, 3593, CIL, X. 530 | |
| aed. Cer. | *ILS*, 1893 | | |
| aediles (unspecified) | *ILS*, 1883-5, 1899, 1900, 6283, 6953-4 | | *ILS*, 1936 |
| trib. pl. | *ILS*, 1885-6, 1898-9, 1926 | *ILS*, 1924-5, 1950, 7489, 9039 | CIL, VI. 1949 |
| quaestors | *ILS*, 1886-95, 1898, 1926, etc. | *ILS*, 382, 1926-7, 3416, 3434, 6172 | *ILS*, 1899 |
| X viri stl. iud. | *ILS*, 1900 | *ILS*, 1911 | |
| III viri cap. | | *ILS*, 1898, 1929-30 | |
| IIII viri viar. cur. | | CIL, VI. 1937-8 | |
| XXVI viri (unspecified) | *ILS*, 1901 | | |

It would seem that some *decuriae* were, perhaps at a later stage, doubled. This is the simplest explanation of *ILS*, 1883, 'scribae decur. aedilic. mai.', 1896, 'scr. libr. quaestorius e tribus decuriis minoribus ab aerario', 7489, 'viatori tribunicio decuriae maioris', 1886, 'scrib. tribunicio maior.', and *CIL*, VI. 1848, '[scrib. dec. ae]diliciae maior[is]'. Mommsen explains them otherwise (op. cit., 345).

²⁰ Promagistrates are recorded with *scribae* (Livy, XLV. 29, Cic. II *Verr*. III. 181 ff.), lictors (Cic. II *Verr*. V. 118, 140-2, *ad Q.f.* I. 1. 13), *viatores* (Cic. II *Verr*. III. 154, 183), *praecones* (Livy, XLV. 29, Cic. II *Verr*. II. 27, 75, III. 40, 54, 137, 183), *accensi* (see note 10) and other grades (see note 5). Verres as *legatus* had a *scriba* (Cic. II *Verr*. III. 187) and a lictor (ib. I. 67, 72).

²¹ *Scribae* are mentioned as attending a praetor or *iudex quaestionis* in court in Cic. II *Verr*. III. 26, *pro Cluentio*, 147 (cf. II *Verr*. III. 187), as serving a censor in Val. Max. IV. i. 10, and Varro, *L.L.* VI. 87. They were assigned to Rullus' decemvirs (*de lege agr.* II. 32).

²³ Pliny, *Ep*. IV. 12, cf. schol. on Cic. *in Clod. et Cur*. 'apud aerarium sortiri provincias et quaestores solebant et scribae'.

²³ Cic. II *Verr*. III. 187, 'quandoque tu nulla umquam mihi in cupiditate ac turpitudine defuisti omnibusque in isdem flagitiis mecum et in legatione et in praetura et hic in Sicilia versatus es'. Mommsen ignores this passage, which seems to me the clue to the appointment of provincial *apparitores*.

²⁴ Cic. II *Verr*. III. 181-4.

²⁵ It appears from the *Verrines* that Verres had, as propraetor, one *scriba* in his employ (III. 181-7), and had employed the same man as *legatus* in Cilicia, while Caecilius, his quaestor, had another *scriba* of his own (*Div*. 29). This is my explanation of the two *scribae* with whom Cicero worked as quaestor (II. *Verr*. III. 182), and the two on Scipio's staff as proconsul in 187 B.C. (Livy, XXXVIII. 55). Mommsen's view was that each quaestor had two *scribae* allotted to him, who were also at the disposal of his chief. My explanation is borne out by *AE*, 1921, 38-9, 'L. Marius Perpetuus scriba quaestorius, Sex. Serius Verus haruspex, L. Pomponius Carisianus scriba librarius, P. Papienus Salutaris scriba librarius'. Here the first *scriba* is the man officially allotted to the quaestor, the other two might be serving the proconsul or one of his *legati*. The latter might presumably be drawn from any *decuria* of *scribae* at Rome: this would account for a *scriba* *aedilicius* dying in Britain (*ILS*, 1883), presumably on the legate's staff.

²⁶ *pace* Mommsen the 'dec. lictor Fufid. Pollionis leg. Gal.' of *ILS*, 1914, was a member of the *decuriae* of lictors at Rome; the 'decurialis lictor cives urbicus' who died at Burdigala (*ILS*, 1906) and the 'lictor decur.' at Nicomedia (*CIL*, III. 6987) would also be members of the urban *decuriae* serving in the provinces.

²⁷ Cic. II *Verr*. III. 184, cf. Suetonius, *Vita Horatii*, 'scriptum quaestorium comparavit', and schol. on Juvenal, V. 3.

²⁸ Livy, XL. 29. In Bruns, *Fontes*⁷, 12, the exceptional nominations to the newly created places are made by the consuls, but normally quaestors appoint *viatores* and *praecones quaestorii*.

²⁹ Plutarch, *Cato minor*, 16, cf. Cic. *pro Cluentio*, 126 (the trial of a *scriba* *aedilicius* by a disciplinary court consisting of the aediles and praetors). Momm-

sen points out that the clause in Bruns, *Fontes*[7], 12, II. 14-8, 'dum ni quem in eis viatoribus praeconibus legundeis sublegundeis in eius viatoris praeconis locum viatorem praeconem legant sublegant quoius in locum per leges plebeive scita viatorem praeconem legei sublegei non licebit', gives security of tenure to *apparitores* by defining the causes for which they may be replaced.

[30] Bruns, *Fontes*[7], 12, II. 24-30. Cf. *ILS*, 1936, 'hoc monimentum apparitorum praeconum aedilium veterum vicarium est', *CIL*, VI. 1947, 'appar. aedilic. praec. vicar. veteribus'.

[31] Cic. II *Verr*. III. 182, 'tuus apparitor parva mercede populi conductus'. Other allusions to salary are Bruns, *Fontes*[7], 12, I. 1-6, II. 31-7, Plutarch, *Cato minor*, 16, and under the Principate, Frontinus, *de aqu.* 100, and Pliny, *Ep.* IV. 12.

[32] Cic. II *Verr*. III. 181.

[33] Plutarch, *Cato minor*, 16-18.

[34] Cicero in the *Verrines* is mainly interested in the financial side of a *scriba*'s work, but in *CIL*, VI. 1853, a *scriba* of the aediles claims to be 'iuris prudens', and in *ILS*, 1896, a *scriba quaestorius* boasts 'vixi iudicio sine iudice'.

[35] Cic. II *Verr*. III. 28, 57, 137.

[36] *AE*, 1921, 38-9. Cf. *Dig.* V. i. 82 (Ulpian, *de officio consulis*), 'Nonnumquam solent magistratus populi Romani viatorem nominatim vice arbitri dare, quod raro et non nisi re urgente faciendum est'.

[37] Frontinus, *de aqu.* 100.

[38] *ILS*, 366, 504, 1534, 1909, 1940, 5021; they formed a *decuria*.

[39] E.g. *ILS*, 1942-4, 1946, 1948-50, 1952.

[40] E.g. *ILS*, 1902-3, 1910, 1915, 1918, 1923, 1926, 1932, 1938. A number of *scribae* also were freedmen, e.g. *ILS*, 1877-9, 1899, 1926.

[41] E.g. *ILS*, 1429, 1885, 1893, 2699, 2706, 4951a, *CIL*, VI. 1806, 1817, 1837, 1841, *AE*, 1925, 44, 1934, 107.

[42] E.g. *ILS*, 1883, 2727, 2748, 6188, 6954, *CIL*, VI. 1832.

[43] E.g. *ILS*, 1886, 1889, 1898a, 1901, *AE*, 1927, 125.

[44] *munere functi*: *ILS*, 1033, 1893. *honore usi*: *ILS*, 331, 504, 2727, 9036, *CIL*, VI. 967a, 1008, 1854. Also *honore functi*: *ILS*, 1891. For the sale of *decuriae* under the Empire see *Frag. Vat.* 272.

[45] This is to be inferred from the inclusion of the title '*de decuriis urbis Romae*' by Justinian in the *Codex* (XI. xiv); cf. Cassiodorus, *Variae*, V. 22 (appointment of a *decuriarum rector*).

[46] *Cod. Theod.* VIII. ix. 1 (335), 'ordines decuriarum scribarum librariorum et lictoriae consularis oblatis precibus meruerunt, ut in civilibus causis et editionibus libellorum officiorum sollemnitate fungantur ita ut vetusta aetate servatum est'. The heading of the title, 'de lucris officiorum', supplies the motive. The privileges of the *decuriales* are confirmed in XIV. i. 2 (386), 3 (389), 4 (404), 5 (407), and 6 (409). Their fees are alluded to in laws 4 ('neque ab his commodis quae rationibus adprobentur audeat separare') and 6 ('emolumenta omnia per diversos erepta redhiberi decernimus').

[47] This is implied by *Cod. Theod.* VIII. ix. 1, which is addressed to a praetorian prefect and ends with the words 'rectores itaque quae iussimus observabunt',

by XIV. i. 4, addressed *Exsuperantio Iulio et ceteris decurialibus*, which warns *singulos iudices* to observe their privileges, and by XIV. i. 6, where the *vicarius Africae* is instructed to take proceedings against those who have violated the rights of the *decuriae*. Among the officials attending the *Collatio Carthaginiensis* of 411 is the *scriba officii v.c. legati almae Carthaginis* (Mansi, *Concilia*, IV. 51, 167, 181). John Lydus (*de mag.* II. 30) records that at Constantinople in his day the *praetor Constantianus* had a *scriba*.

⁴⁸ *Cod. Theod.* XIV. i. 3 (389), 'decurialibus quos binos esse ex singulis quibusque urbibus omnium provinciarum veneranda decrevit antiquitas'.

⁴⁹ Frontinus, *de aqu.* 101, 'apparitores et ministeria quamuis perseueret adhuc aerarium in eos erogare, tamen esse curatorum videntur desisse inertia et segnitia non agentium officium'.

⁵⁰ There are several studies of the imperial civil service, notably Hirschfeld's *Verwaltungsbeamten*, but these have concentrated mainly on the functions of the various officials, and the recruitment and promotion of the equestrian grades. I know of no recent study of the humbler personnel from the social aspect: it would be a promising subject for a thesis.

⁵¹ For the reason given in the text I forbear to give references, which to be of any statistical value would have to be exhaustive.

⁵² *CIL*, VI. 8450 a, *ILS*, 1521, 1522.

⁵³ *ILS*, 1514.

⁵⁴ Hirschfeld, *Verwaltungsbeamten*, 108-9.

⁵⁵ See note 51; for the *SC Claudianum* see Buckland, *The Roman Law of Slavery*, 417.

⁵⁶ The basic study is here von Domaszewski, *Die Rangordnungen des römischen Heeres*, hereinafter cited as Dom.

⁵⁷ Caesar, *BC*, I. 75, III. 88.

⁵⁸ Tac. *Hist.* IV. 48.

⁵⁹ *Beneficiarii* (*beneficia*) seem to be used in Tacitus (loc. cit.) and Pliny, *Ep.* X. 21, 27, to cover all grades, for all the *officia* in question would have included *cornicularii*, and those of the proconsul and legate in Africa other grades as well. Cf. *ILS*, 2073, 'Sex. Cetri Severi spec. beneficiarii Getae ab comentaris custodiaru.' and *CIL*, III. 6754, 'Bb. et corniculari eius.'

⁶⁰ *IGR*, III. 1230, *AE*, 1916, 29: a centurion of the *officium* is recorded in Pliny, *Ep.* X. 21, *Dig.* XLVIII. ii. 73, *ILS*, 1880, *AE*, 1946, 227.

⁶¹ Dom. 29-31, *ILS*, 1093, 2382, *CIL*, XIII. 6803.

⁶² Dom. 31, *ILS*, 2382, *CIL*, XIII. 6803.

⁶³ Dom. 32, *ILS*, 2375, 2382, 2648, *CIL*, VI. 4122.

⁶⁴ *ILS*, 2381 and *AE*, 1918, 57, both show thirty *beneficarii* in the legate's *officium*. Tacitus' words 'aequatus inter duos beneficiorum numerus' seem to be literally correct, for in *ILS*, 2381, the legate has two *cornicularii*, two *commentarienses*, and four *speculatores* out of a total of three plus three plus ten. To judge by their frequency in the inscriptions *beneficiarii consularis* must have been numerous.

⁶⁵ *Adiutor principis*: *ILS*, 2448, 4837, *CIL*, II. 6111, *AE*, 1916, 29. *Adiutor corn.*:

*ILS*, 2391, 2586, 3035, 9170, *IGR*, III, 1008. *Adiutor comm.*: *ILS*, 9076, *AE*, 1933, 61.

⁶⁶ *Speculatores*: Seneca, *de benef.* III. 25, *de ira* I. 18. 4, Mark, vi. 27, Firm. Mat. *Math.* VIII. 26, *Dig.* XLVIII. xx. 6. This last passage speaks first of *speculatores* and *optiones* and then of *optiones siue commentarienses*, but the last two words may well be an interpolation. A *commentariensis* appears in the *Acta S. Pionii*, 21, and a *speculator* executed Cyprian (*Acta proconsularia*, 5).

⁶⁷ *ILS*, 1162, 2381, 2383, 4496.

⁶⁸ Dom. 37.

⁶⁹ *ILS*, 1357a, 1358, 2418, 2419a, 2587, *CIL*, III. 10315, *AE*, 1935, 100. 'Unus strator officii Galeri Maximi proconsulis' and 'alius equistrator a custodiis eiusdem officii' arrested Cyprian (*Acta Proconsularia*, 2).

⁷⁰ *ILS*, 486, 2416-8, 2588, 3456, *CIL*, III. 14387 f., VIII. 9763, *AE*, 1935, 100.

⁷¹ See note 64. A *speculator* executed Cyprian when he was condemned by the proconsul of Africa (*Acta proconsularia*, 5).

⁷² *Dig.* I. xvi. 1, cf. note 69.

⁷³ *Acta S. Pionii*, 21.

⁷⁴ Dom. 6 ff., 17, 20-22; for the *praefectus annonae*, *ILS*, 2082.

⁷⁵ Pliny, *Ep.* X. 21, 27; for epigraphic references see Dom. 66-7, and *ILS*, 1389, 1428, *AE*, 1937, 87, 1939, 60, 1944, 38 (*cornicularii*), *ILS*, 4071, 6146, 9127, 9129, 9130 (*beneficiarii*).

⁷⁶ *ILS*, 2118: so also did the procurator, *AE*, 1935, 16.

⁷⁷ Dom. 64-6.

⁷⁸ *ILS*, 2118, *CIL*, III. 9908, VIII. 17635 (*bf.* to *corn.*), *ILS*, 2379, *CIL*, III. 4179 and 4145, XIII. 1732 (*spec.* to *comm.*).

⁷⁹ *ILS*, 2118.

⁸⁰ *ILS*, 8880.

⁸¹ *ILS*, 2173.

⁸² *Dig.* XLVIII. xx. 6. This passage unfortunately cannot be used to prove that proconsuls had *speculatores*, etc., as Ulpian, though writing *de officio proconsulis*, is clearly thinking of a legate with troops under him on the frontier.

⁸³ *Dig.* XII. i. 34.

⁸⁴ *ILS*, 2173. Probably the *scriniarius praeff. praetor.* of *AE*, 1933, 248 (cf. *CIL*, III. 13201, 'Ael Aelianus eq. praet. et Ulp. Licinius a scr. praef.') and the *primiscrinius castrorum praeff.* (*ILS*, 9074) are financial officers; for, though *scrinium* is a general term covering any department on the judicial as on the financial side, *scriniarius* was in later times the technical term for a finance clerk (see note 111) and in the urban prefecture the *primiscrinius* was the head of the finance branch (see Appendix).

⁸⁵ *ILS*, 2392, 2424, *CIL*, III. 7979.

⁸⁶ Lactantius, *de mort. pers.*, 31. The most important work on the Byzantine *officia* is Ernst Stein, *Untersuchungen uber das Officium der Prätorianerpräfektur seit Diokletian* (Wien), hereinafter cited as Stein.

⁸⁷ Eusebius, *Mart. Pal.* pr. §1, τοὺς μὲν τιμῆς ἐπειλημμένους ἀτίμους, τοὺς δὲ ἐν οἰκετίαις εἰ ἐπιμένοιεν τῇ τοῦ Χριστιανισμοῦ προθέσει ἐλευθερίας στερίσκεσθαι.

[88] Cyprian, *Ep.* LXXX, 'senatores vero et egregii viri et equites Romani dignitate amissa etiam bonis spolientur et si ademptis facultatibus Christiani perseveraverint capite quoque multentur . . . Caesariani autem quicumque vel prius confessi fuerant vel nunc confessi fuerint confiscentur et vincti in Caesarianas possessiones descripti mittantur.' For *Caesariani* under the principate see *IGR*, IV. 598.

[89] *Cod. Theod.* VI. xxxv. 3. Seeck in the *Regesten* rightly rejects Mommsen's doubts as to the date.

[90] *Cod. Theod.* VI. xxxvi. 1, 'sed nec alieni sunt a pulvere et labore castrorum qui signa nostra comitantur, qui praesto sunt semper actibus, quos intentos eruditis studiis itinerum prolixitas et expeditionum difficultas exercet.'

[91] *Proximi*: *Cod. Theod.* VI. xxvi, *passim*. *Melloproximi*: VI. xxvi. 16, 17; *AE*, 1941, 101 gives 'v(ir) p(erfectissimus) ex prox(imis) mem(oriae)' for which see A. Degrassi, *Doxa* II, 1949, 105. For these ranks among the imperial freedmen of the Principate, see *ILS*, 1477, 1485, 3703 (*proximi*), 1478 (*melloproximus*).

[92] *Cod. Theod.* VI. xxx. 7 (= *Cod. Just.* XII. xxiii. 7).

[93] *Cod. Theod.* VI. xxxii. 2.

[94] *Cod. Just.* X. i. 5 (Diocletian and Maximian), *Cod. Theod.* X. vii. 1 (317), viii. 2 (319), IX. xlii. 1 (321), X. i. 5 (326), vii. 2 (364); also Bruns, *Fontes*[7], 95. That they served *rationales* appears from the law of 319, which is addressed 'ad Priscum rationalem' and from *Cod. Just.* IX. xlix. 9 (= *Cod. Theod.* IX. xlii. 1), where the by then obsolete term *Caesariani* is explained as *catholiciani* (καθολικός = *rationalis*).

[95] Amm. Marc. XXVIII. ii. 13.

[96] *Cod. Just.* X. i. 5, and *Cod. Theod.* X. viii. 2, show that *Caesariani* dealt with confiscations, which were the province of the *res privata*.

[97] Eus. *Mart. Pal.* 11 § 24.

[98] *Cod. Theod.* VIII. i. 1, 'Dudum sanximus, ut nullus ad singula officia administranda ambitione perveniat, vel maxime ad tabularios, nisi qui ex ordine vel corpore officii uniuscuiusque est.' The date is confirmed, as against Mommsen and Seeck, by the use of the term *tabularii*, which was soon superseded by *numerarii* (see next note): Ensslin has noted this (PW, XVII. 1297).

[99] *Numerarii* is used from 334 (*Cod. Theod.* VIII. i. 4, cf. 6, 7, 8) in all offices. In 365 (*tit. cit.* 9) *numerarii* of *consulares* and *praesides* were ordered to be called *tabularii*. This rule still prevailed in the West in the early fifth century, as the *Notitia Dignitatum* (*Occ.* xliii, xliv, xlv) shows. In the East it still prevailed in 382 (*Cod. Theod.* VIII. i. 12) but in the *Notitia* (*Or.* xliii, xliv) *numerarii* has again become the title in provincial offices.

[100] *Cod. Theod.* VIII. i. 4.

[101] *tit. cit.* 6, 7, 8.

[102] *tit. cit.* 11.

[103] John Lydus, III. 35. Stein (p. 20) appears to believe John's allegation that the financial officials of the prefecture were civilian employees till Theodosius I gave them their military status. John cites, it is true, αἱ παλαιαὶ μάτρικες for this, but the *Codex* proves that he was mistaken. He may have found some old

*matriculae* of the period 362-5, when the *numerarii* were *condicionales*, and genera-
lised from these.

104 There is a handy comparative table of *officia* at the end of Seeck's edition of
the *Notitia*. The apparent confusion is largely due to the varying position in
which the new posts of the *adiutor* and *numerarius* were inserted in the order of
precedence.

105 In *Cod. Theod.* I. xvi. 7 (331), cited on p. 51, the *princeps officii* appears to
be still called a centurion. See also *P. Oxy.* 1261, ἑκατοντάρχου τάξεως τοῦ
διασημοτάτου καθολικοῦ (325), 1424 (ξ and πρίγκιψ used synonymously c.
318), *P. Flor.* 320, ἀπὸ ξ/ρ τάξεως τοῦ πριουάτου πατριμονίου (373). The *princeps*
of the Praetorian Prefect of the East still carried the centurion's *vitis* in Justinian's
reign (John Lydus, II. 19).

106 *Princeps* and *cornicularius* are mentioned as heads of the *officium* in Bruns,
*Fontes*[7], 103, *Cod. Theod.* VIII. iv. 10, VI. xxvi. 5.

107 *Princeps, cornicularius, commentariensis* (and *numerarius* or *tabularius*) are listed
as the principal officers of every *officium* in *Cod. Theod.* VIII. xv. 3 (364), 5 (368).

108 *Cod. Theod.* IX. xl. 5 (364), VIII. xv. 5 (368), IX. iii. 5 (371), 6 (380),
7 (409), John Lydus, III. 16-17.

109 Athanasius, *Apol. c. Arianos*, 8, καὶ παρῆν σπεκουλάτωρ καὶ κομεντάριος
ἡμᾶς εἰσῆγεν (at the Council of Tyre, 335), 83, ὁ μὲν γράψας αὐτὰ Ῥοῦφός
ἐστιν ὁ νῦν ἐν τῇ Αὐγουσταλιανῇ σπεκουλάτωρ (Rufus who recorded the
minutes of the Mareotic Commission in 335—presumably as an *exceptor*—was
by c. 370 a *speculator* in the office of the Augustal Prefect), *P. Oxy.* 1223 (*speculator*
of the prefect of Egypt, fourth century), *P. Erlangen*, 105 (of the *praeses* of the
Thebaid, early fourth century), *P. Oslo.* 88 (late fourth century), *P. Rendel Harris*,
94 (fifth century), *Cod. Theod.* VIII. iv. 16 (389), 'ordinariorum iudicum apparitores, qui vel speculatorum vel ordinariorum attigerint gradum, nullo annorum
numero, nulla stipendiorum contemplatione laxentur, priusquam primipili
pastum digesta ratione compleverint.' *Ordinarii* are also mentioned in VIII. xv.
3 (364), as high grade *officiales*, and appear in the *Notitia* (Or. xxxvii) in the
praesidial *officium* of the *dux Arabiae* between *cornicularius* and *commentariensis*,
and in *P. Lond.* V. 1701, ὀρδινάριος τῆς ἡγεμονικῆς τάξεως (sixth century), and
*P. Oxy.* 942 (also sixth century).

110 *CIL*, III. 14068 (*bf. cos.* under Diocletian and Maximian), Eus. *HE*, IX. 9
(Maximinus' edict of 311), *Cod. Theod.* VIII. iv. 5 (date uncertain), 7 (361).
Βενεφικιάριοι are fairly common in the fourth century papyri, e.g. *P. Erlangen*,
105, *P. Antinoop.* 33, *P. Thead.* 8, *CPR*, 75, *P. Lips.* 20-23, 33, 36-7, 41, 55 (of
the *praeses* of the Thebaid), *PSI*, 469, 807, *BGU*, 1049 (of the prefect of Egypt),
*CPR*, 117 (of the *praeses* of Arcadia in 411).

111 *Cod. Just.* XII. xlix. 10, John Lydus, III. 31, 35. In the *Notitia scriniarii* are
mentioned only for the proconsul of Asia (Or. XX) in the civil *officia*. *Scriniarii
gloriosae sedis* (of the praetorian prefecture of Italy) appear in Tjäder, *die Nichtliterarischen Lateinischen Papyri Italiens*, nos. 6, ll. 8, 38 (575 A.D.), 8, col. III. 7
(564 A.D.). In *P. Oxy.* 2408 (397) there is a σκρινιάριος, apparently of the
*praefectus annonae Alexandriae*. John ὁ λαμπρότατος σκρινιάριος of *P. Oxy.*

P

1869 presumably served in the *officium* of the *praeses* of Arcadia. An *adiutor numerariorum* of the vicar of Africa is recorded in Mansi, IV. 51, 167, 181 (*Collatio Carthaginiensis* of 411).

[112] John Lydus, III. 4, 5, 21, Cassiodorus, *Variae*, XI. 23. Besides the praetorian and urban prefects and vicars, the *praefectus Augustalis* had a *cura epistularum*, but not the *Comes Orientis*, perhaps because his original functions did not include finance (see note 116).

[113] Stein, 61 ff., arguing from Cassiodorus, *Variae*, XI. 29, and John Lydus, III. 4, 21, corrects the *regerendarius* of *Not. Dig. Or.* ii, iii, *Occ.* ii. iii, to *regendarius*: the office has no connection with the *regerendarius* of the Western military offices.

[114] Stein, pp. 57 seqq.: he is also called *subadiuva* or *primiscrinius*.

[115] John Lydus, III. 20, Cassiodorus, *Variae*, XI. 22, *Cod. Just.* I. xxvii. 1 § 26, II. vii. 26 § 3.

[116] The office is recorded for proconsuls, consulars and *praesides* of the East (*Not. Dig. Or.* xx, xxi, xxvii, xliii, restored in xliv) and for the *Comes Orientis* (op. cit. xxiii), perhaps because he had not originally the ordinary functions of a vicar, but, like other *comites provinciarum*, received the complaints of the provincials (*Cod. Theod.* I. xvi. 6, 7).

[117] The system is explained by John Lydus, III. 9-10, cf. 17, 27. Cf. *Cod. Theod.* I. xvi. 7 (331, *adiutores* of the *princeps*), VIII. iv. 10 (365, of *princeps* and *cornicularius*), IX. iii. 5 (371, of *commentariensis*), *P. Lips.* 40, 'adiut. e comm.' (fourth to fifth century), *P. Oxy.* 1837, 1887, βοηθὸς τῶν κομμέντων (late fifth century), *PSI*, 97 (sixth century), Mansi, IV. 51, 167, 181 (411, of *cornicularius* and *commentariensis*), 181 (of *subadiuva*, i.e. *adiutor*), *Cod. Just.* II. vii. 26 § 3 (524, of *ab actis*). The *adiutores* who appear in the *Notitia* immediately after the *exceptores* in the offices of Western proconsul, vicars, consulars, *correctores*, and *praesides* may be the same. But the *subadiuvae* of the praetorian and urban prefects seem to be the assistants of the *numerarii* or *primiscrinius* whom they follow.

[118] *Cod. Theod.* VIII. i. 2.

[119] Bruns, *Fontes*[7], 103. The office of *a libellis* does not appear in the Western section of the *Notitia* at all. The earliest records of an *adiutor* or *primiscrinius* as an independent official are the *primiscrinius* of the *vicarius urbis Romae* in *Cod. Theod.* VIII. viii. 2 (379), and the *adiutor urbani officii* of Symm. *Rel.* 23, 67 (385).

[120] Found in the praetorian prefecture of Africa as established by Justinian (*Cod. Just.* I. xxvii. 1 §§ 29-35). John Lydus mentions *singulares, cursores, nomenclatores* and *praecones*, as well as other obscurer grades in the praetorian prefecture of the East (III. 7 and 8), and Cassiodorus (*Variae*, XII. 31-2) the *singulares* of the praetorian prefecture of Italy. A *cursor inl. p.* and a *strator inl. p.* (i.e. of the praetorian preferecture of Italy) appear in Marini, *Pap. Dipl.* nos. 114, 138 (sixth century). The *Notitia* records only *singulares* of the praetorian and urban prefects and the proconsul of Africa and Western vicars, and *nomenclatores* and *censuales* of the urban prefect. For lesser *officia* the evidence is scanty. The papyri frequently mention σιγγουλάριοι of provincial governors; *P. Oxy.* 1882, *P. Lond.* II. 153 (prefect of Egypt), *P. Oxy.* 1837, 1880-1, *PSI*, 1365 (*praeses* of Arcadia), *P. Lond.* V. 1679, *P. Flor.* 291, *P. Cairo Masp.* 67054, 67103 (*praeses* of Thebaid).

*P. Oxy.* 1901 records the σχολὴ κουρσόρων and the σχολὴ πραικόνων of the praesidial *officium* of Arcadia, and *P. Oxy.* 2050 mentions not only κούρσορες and πρέκονες but κυεσσιονάριοι (*quaestionarii*), κλαουικουλάριοι (*clavicularii*, cf. John Lydus, III. 16) and κουροπερσονάριοι (*curae personarum?*), with their βοηθοί (*adiutores*). From other sources we hear of *stratores* of a proconsul (*Cod. Theod.* XIII. xi. 6) and of a *rationalis* (IX. iii. 1) and of a δρακωνάρις ἐξ ὀφικίου τοῦ λαμπροτάτου ἡγεμόνος (*ILS*, 8881).

¹²¹ He is second only in Africa (*Not. Dig. Occ.* xxv), and fourth in Tingitana, the Litus Saxonicum, Mauretania and Tripolitania (ib. xxvi, xxviii, xxx, xxxi).

¹²² So in all *magistri militum* of the East except the *magister militum per Orientem* (*Not. Dig. Or.* v, vi, viii, ix); the *magister equitum* of the West has a *primiscrinius* after his *numerarius* (*Not. Dig. Occ.* vi). The *adiutores eorum* who follow the *numerarii* (for the title, cf. note 111 above) in the *officia* of all eastern *duces* (*Not. Dig. Or.* xxx–xlii) are presumably *scriniarii*, who are recorded for the *Dux Thebaidis* in the papyri (e.g. *P. Cairo Masp.* 67023, *P. Lond.* V. 1714).

¹²³ He does not occur in the *officia* of eastern *magistri militum* (except the *magister militum per Orientem*). He is followed by his *subadiuva* in the *officia* of all western *comites* and *duces*.

¹²⁴ *Cod. Just.* XII. xxxvi. 6, lii. 3, John Lydus, III. 3.

¹²⁵ *Cod. Theod.* VI. xxx. 11, attests the issue of *vestes* to officials: the *cingulum* is constantly mentioned.

¹²⁶ *Cod. Theod.* VII. iv. 35. *Annonae* are normally mentioned alone, but the detailed schedule in *Cod. Just.* I. xxvii. 1, shows that *capitum* was also provided. Cf. Amm. Marc. XXII. iv. 9.

¹²⁷ E.g. *Cod. Theod.* VII. i. 5, 6, xxii. 8, 10, VIII. vii. 12.

¹²⁸ We know singularly little about the officials of vicars, proconsuls and other governors of the *spectabilis* grade but it may be inferred that these offices were popular from the fact that their numbers had to be limited (*Cod. Theod.* I. xii. 6, xiii. 1, xv. 5, 12, 13) and that entry to them was regulated by *probatoriae* (*Cod. Theod.* VIII. vii. 21, *Cod. Just.* XII. lix. 10) as in the palatine offices. See also note 130.

¹²⁹ *Cod. Theod.* VII. xxii. 3.

¹³⁰ There is no later allusion to any hereditary obligation except in provincial offices, e.g. *Cod. Theod.* VIII. iv. 7, 8, XII. i. 79, VIII. vii. 16. In the last law the phrase 'quibus vel sponte initiatus est vel suorum retinetur consortio maiorum' refers to the distinction made above to *praefectiani* and *vicariani* on the one hand and *provincialia officia* on the other.

¹³¹ Soz. V. 4.

¹³² *Cod. Theod.* VIII. vii. 9, 16, 19.

¹³³ *Not. Dig. Or.* xliii, xliv, *Occ.* xliii, xliv, xlv, cf. *Cod. Theod.* VIII. iv. 21–5, 28–30.

¹³⁴ *Cod. Just.* XII. lvii. 13, 14.

¹³⁵ E.g. *Cod. Theod.* VI. xxxv. 14, VIII. iv. 28, XVI. v. 48, Theod. *Nov.* iii § 6, vii. 2, 4, x. 1.

¹³⁶ John Lydus, III. 67.

[137] *Cod. Just.* XII. xix. 7, 'melloproximo vero vel adiutori pro consuetudine uniuscuiusque scrinii viginti aut quindecim solidos offerre praecipimus.' This fee is to be distinguished from the price of a place discussed below.

[138] A purge of the palatine finance offices is recorded in *Cod. Theod.* VI. xxx. 15-16, and of the praetorian prefecture of the Gauls in VIII. vii. 10; cf. I. ix. 1, VI. xxvii. 17, 18, for purges of the *agentes in rebus*.

[139] Establishments: *Cod. Theod.* VI. xxx. 7, 15-17 (*largitionales* and *privatiani*), *Cod. Just.* XII. xix. 10 (*sacra scrinia*), *Cod. Theod.* VI. xxvii. 23, *Cod. Just.* XII. xx. 3 (*agentes in rebus*), cf. note 128. Justinian regularly prescribed establishments for all the offices he created (e.g. *Cod. Just.* I. xxvii. 1, 2, Just. *Nov.* 14 § 5, *Edict* 13 § 2, etc.). *Statuti* and *supernumerarii* are recorded also for *castrensiani* (*Cod. Theod.* VI. xxxii. 2), *protectores domestici* (*Cod. Just.* II. vii. 25 § 3), *scholares* (Proc. *Anecd.* 24, Const. Porph. *de Cerim.* I. 86), and *silentiarii* (Const. Porph. loc. cit. cf. *Cod. Theod.* VI. xxiii. 4).

[140] *Cod. Theod.* VI. xxx. 11, Const. Porph. *de Cerim.* I. 86.

[141] *Cod. Just.* XII. xix. 7.

[142] *Cod. Theod.* VIII. vii. 1 (315). In 392 and 395 the *domestici* and *protectores* secured a relaxation of this rule in so far that absentees were struck off the list (*Cod. Theod.* VI. xxiv. 5, 6). For illicit promotion by influence, see for instance, *Cod. Theod.* VI. xxvii. 19.

[143] E.g. *Cod. Theod.* VI. xxvi. 6, 11, 17, xxx. 3, 14, 21.

[144] John Lydus, III. 9, *Cod. Just.* XII. xx. 5.

[145] *Cod. Just.* III. xxviii. 30 § 2, XII. xxxiii. 5 § 3. Apart from the *sacra scrinia* purchase seems to have been official only in the more ornamental palatine services, *scholares* (Proc. *Anecd.* 24, Agathias, V. 15), *domestici* (Proc. *Anecd.* 24, *Cod. Just.* II. vii. 25, Const. Porph. *de Cerim.* I. 86), *silentiarii* (*Cod. Just.* III. xxviii. 30, XII. xvi. 5, Const. Porph. *loc. cit.*), *tribuni et notarii* (*Cod. Just.* II. vii. 23). There is no hint in John Lydus that entry to the praetorian prefecture had to be bought, though profitable posts within it were saleable (III. 27).

[146] *Cod. Just.* XII. xix. 7, 11.

[147] *Cod. Just.* XII. xix. 13, 15, Just. *Nov.* 35.

[148] *Cod. Just.* VIII. xiii. 27, Just. *Nov.* 97 § 4, 136 § 2.

[149] *Cod. Theod.* VII. xii. 2, *Cod. Just.* XII. xvii. 3.

[150] *Cod. Just.* XII. xxxiii. 5, cf. XII. xx. 5 § 1.

[151] *Cod. Just.* I. xxvii. 1.

[152] The *locus classicus* is the *Notitia* appended to Just. *Nov.* 8: cf. also *Cod. Just.* I. xxvii. 2, Just. *Nov.* 24-7.

[153] Justinian fixed a tariff (*Cod. Just.* III. ii. 5) which has not survived, but apparently drastically reduced them; John Lydus (III. 25) bitterly complains that a *postulatio simplex* in the praetorian prefecture, which used to bring in 37 *solidi*, now cost a few coppers only. Reduced tariffs of *sportulae* in favour of privileged classes are given in *Cod. Just.* II. vii. 22, 24, XII. xix. 12, xx. 6, xxi. 8, xxv. 4, xxix. 3.

[154] Maj. *Nov.* 7 § 16.

[155] *Cod. Theod.* I. xvi. 7.

[156] Bruns, *Fontes*[7], 103.

[157] John Lydus, III. 27.

[158] Id. I. 14, 15, II. 6, 13.

[159] Id. III. 22.

[160] The change made by Cyrus, *Praefectus Praetorio Orientis*, 439–441, who is described by John as 'an Egyptian admired even now for his poetic talent . . . who understood nothing except poetry' (II. 12, III. 42). It is one of the counts against John the Cappadocian that he abolished Latin in the *scrinium* of Europe where it had hitherto survived (III. 68).

[161] John Lydus, III. 3, 12.

[162] Id., II. 10, III. 23, 40.

[163] Id., III. 35.

[164] Id., III. 36, 46, 49. He was εὲς τῶν τῆς Συρίας σκρινιαρίων.

[165] Id., III. 57. He started as a *scriniarius* of the *magistri militum*.

[166] Id., III. 26–8.

[167] Id. III. 24–5.

[168] E.g. *Cod. Theod.* XI. xxx. 34, 'iudex . . . ipse quidem notabili sententia reprehensus X librarum auri condemnatione quatietur, officium vero eius, quod non suggesserit nec commonuerit de relationis necessitate, viginti libris auri fiat obnoxium'.

[169] As John Lydus (III. 49) freely admits, καὶ γίνεται μὲν πολύχρυσος, εὔπερ τις ἄλλος, ὁ βασιλεὺς καὶ μετ᾽ αὐτὸν ὁ Μαρῖνος καὶ ὅσοι Μαρινιῶντες ἁπλῶς.

# APPENDIX

THE chief point on which I differ from Stein is on the origin of the *exceptores* and *scriniarii*. Stein held that they were originally 'vom Staate konzessionierte Gewerbetreibende' (p. 20). For the *exceptores* his arguments are (*a*) *Cod. Theod.* VIII. vii. 17 (385),

exceptores omnes iudicibus obsequentes, qui nec militiam sustinent neque a fisco ullas consequuntur annonas, absque metu navare coeptis operam, etiamsi decuriones sunt, minime prohibemus, dummodo munia propriae civitatis agnoscant et peracto secundum morem exceptionis officio ad propriam sibi curiam redeundum esse non nesciant.

This law is reproduced in *Cod. Just.* XII. xlix. 5, where, by inserting 'provincialibus' after 'iudicibus' and 'cohortalem' before 'militiam', it is made plain that the practice was confined to provincial *officia*.   (*b*) The organisation of the *exceptores* in *scholae*, which he calls a 'zunftartige Organisation'. But (*a*) the law merely proves that there were civilians who practised as *exceptores* in the *officia*, like the *supernumerarii* of the palatine offices, making their living by *sportulae*, and implies that normally *exceptores* did hold a *militia* and draw *annonae*; and (*b*) *scholae* were a characteristic organisation of military grades in the Principate, e.g. *ILS*, 2375 (*speculatores*), 2400 (*beneficiarii*), 2445 (*optiones*), 2545 (*decuriones*), 9493 (*pulliones*), and in the Byzantine age are found not only for *exceptores* but for subclerical grades of military origin (*Cod. Just.* I. xxvii. 1 § 29, *singularii*, § 33 *stratores*, § 35, *draconarii*). Since military *exceptores* are recorded for the Principate, it seems simplest to assume that their existence was continuous: *ILS*, 9075 records two young soldiers who were 'ex exceptore praeff. praet.', apparently under the tetrarchy. *Exceptores* were certainly much more numerous in the Byzantine period than under the Principate, when they seem to have been individual private secretaries of the *praeses* (*ILS*, 2173), the *princeps* (*CIL*, III. 5293) and others (*ILS*, 2157). The increase of the *exceptores* is probably to be linked with the disappearance of the *beneficiarii* and *speculatores*: as men of these grades were more and more employed for secretarial duties, they came to be called *exceptores*.

For the *scriniarii* (including *tabularii* and *numerarii*) Stein cites *Cod. Theod.* VIII. i. 11 and John Lydus, III. 35. The first reference is highly misleading for, as I have shown above (p. 166 f.), this law restores to the *numerarii* of the praetorian prefecture the *militia* of which both they and those of the provincial governors had been deprived by Julian. John Lydus cannot be quoted in evidence against the clear testimony of the imperial constitutions of the Code, especially as he has been proved by Stein himself to be grossly misinformed about the earlier history of the prefecture (e.g. the date and circumstances in which *deputati* and *Augustales* were established, and in which the post of *princeps* was transferred to an *agens in rebus*. Stein, pp. 43 ff.). Here again, therefore, since a soldier *tabularius* is attested for the Principate, it is simplest to assume a continuous development. The only other piece of evidence which might be cited for the civilian status of *tabularii* is *Cod. Theod.* VIII. ii. 5 (401), 'generali lege sancimus ut sive solidis provinciis sive singulis civitatibus necessarii fuerint tabularii, liberi homines ordinentur neque ulli deinceps ad hoc officium patiscat aditus qui sit obnoxius servituti'. But the whole title deals with *tabularii* and other officials of the *civitates*, who were not imperial civil servants at all, and the *tabularii* appointed *solidis provinciis* in this law cannot therefore be identical with *tabularii* of the provincial *officium*; the *interpretatio* of the law bears this out, for it paraphrases 'sive in solida provincia sive per singules civitates tabularii fuerint ordinati . . . ingenui a provincialibus ordinentur': the *tabularii* of the provincial *officium* were certainly not appointed by the provincials. The provincial *tabularii* mentioned in this law must presumably have been employed by the *concilium provinciae*.

I also differ from Stein's explanation of the origin of the *adiutor* (pp. 57 ff.).

According to Stein the *adiutor* was in origin the principal assistant of the *princeps* and *cornicularius* who shared a joint *scrinium*. But under the Principate there were separate *adiutores principis* and *adiutores corniculariorum*, and there is no reason to believe that the two *scrinia* were merged. That the *adiutor* had belonged to the *princeps* is, I think, proved (*a*) by the fact that in the *officia* of the *magistri militum, comites rei militaris* and *duces* in the *Notitia*, which possess a *princeps* but nearly all lack a *cornicularius*, there is an *adiutor*, (*b*) by the *Collatio Carthaginensis* which records an *adiutor cornicularii* as still existing in the *officium* of the proconsul of Africa in 411, when the *adiutor* certainly existed as an independent post. Stein appears to base his view on the fact that there was in the sixth century no *scrinium* attached to either the *princeps* or the *cornicularius* in the praetorian prefectures of Africa and the East. The case of Africa is not very cogent, as the *princeps* and the *cornicularius* have themselves been abolished (*Cod. Just.* I. xxvii. 1). In the East the language of John Lydus is by no means decisive that the *cornicularius* had no *adiutores*. In III. 4, he says that *exceptores* were attached to various κατάλογοι, which he enumerates as those of the *cornicularius*, the two *primiscrinii*, the two *commentarienses*, the two *regendarii* and the two *curae epistularum* of Pontica (it may be noted that he omits the *ab actis*). In III. 9, he says that the heads of the office each choose three *adiutores*, whence there are six in the *scrinium* of the *ab actis, commentariensis* and *primiscrinius*. It is possible that the *cornicularius* is not mentioned in the second list because he had only three *adiutores* and John is enumerating the *scrinia* which had six, or it may be that the *scrinium* of the *ab actis* had originally belonged to the *cornicularius* and was still reckoned as his κατάλογος.

Stein also so strongly insisted that the two titles of *adiutor* and *primiscrinius* must denote the same office that he proposed to delete one or the other when both occurred in one *officium*, as in *Not. Dig. Occ.* iv (the urban prefect), xviii (the proconsul of Africa), and also vi (*Magister Equitum*). His argument is that since the *adiutor* of the urban prefecture was also officially called *primiscrinius* (as in *Coll. Avell.* 16 and 31) it would have led to confusion if there had been another officer entitled *primiscrinius* in the same office. In view of the pervading ambiguity of Byzantine official terminology, I do not find this argument altogether convincing. In the urban prefecture there are good reasons for believing that besides the *adiutor* (also called *primiscrinius*) whose duties were judicial, there was a *primiscrinius* whose duties were financial, and who corresponded with the *numerarius* of other offices. The evidence is the *Notitia Dignitatum*, which records a *primiscrinius sive numerarius*, and Symmachus, *Rel.* 34, and *Cod. Theod.* XIV. iv. 10, which show a *primiscrinius* of the prefecture exercising financial functions. I do not find Stein's explanation convincing, that the urban prefect had so little financial business that it was assigned, in addition to his judicial duties, to the *adiutor* of his office. Stein's objection that in *Cod. Theod.* XIV. iv. 10, the *primiscrinii* 'tam inl. urbanae sedis quam spectabilis vicariae potestatis' are mentioned and that, as there is no *primiscrinius* other than the *adiutor* recorded in the vicarial offices, the *adiutor* must be meant in both cases, is not valid. It is scarcely conceivable that in the vicar's office, where there was a *numerarius*, financial matters would be handled by the *adiutor*. The law is a typical piece of loose Byzantine drafting, and the phrase means the *primiscrinius* of the urban prefecture, and the corresponding official (actually the *numerarius*) of the vicarial office. There is no exact parallel to a *primiscrinius* being the chief financial officer of an *officium*, but there are the *primiscrinii qui numerarii fiunt* of the *Magistri Militum* in the East (*Not. Dig. Or.* v. vi, viii, ix), and the *primiscrinius* who immediately follows the *numerarius* (*numerarii*) in the offices of the *Magister Equitum* in the West and the proconsul of Africa (*Not. Dig. Occ.* v, xviii).

# INDEX OF PASSAGES CITED

I. LITERARY AUTHORITIES

II. LEGAL AUTHORITIES

III. INSCRIPTIONS

IV. PAPYRI

# INDEX OF PASSAGES CITED

## I. LITERARY AUTHORITIES

*Acta S. Pionii*
21     p. 207 n. 73

*Acts of the Apostles*
x. 1     p. 187 n. 50
xvi. 37     p. 184 n. 14
xxii. 25     p. 184 n. 15
xxv. 9-12     p. 184 n. 16
11-12     p. 191 n. 83
xxvi. 32     p. 184 n. 16
xxvii. 1     p. 184 n. 16
xxviii. 16     p. 184 n. 16

Aelius Aristides
XXVI. 37     p. 191 n. 82
L. 74     p. 191 n. 82

Agathias
V. 15     p. 212 n. 145

Ammianus Marcellinus
XX. viii. 13     p. 198 n. 11
XXI. iv. 8     p. 198 n. 11
XXII. iv. 9     p. 211 n. 126
XXVIII. ii. 13     p. 208 n. 95

Appian
*Bella Civilia*
V. 132     p. 178 n. 22

*Mithradatica*
94     p. 192 n. 13
97     p. 177 n. 5

Asconius
*in Cornelianam*
51     p. 202 n. 7
    p. 203 n. 11

*in Milonianam*
41     p. 189 n. 18

*in Pisonianam*
94     p. 182 n. 63

Athanasius
*Apologia contra Arianos*
8     p. 209 n. 109
83     p. 209 n. 109

Auctor ad Herennium
II. 19     p. 188 n. 17
IV. 68     p. 202 n. 7

Caesar
*de Bello Gallico*
I. 39     p. 195 n. 21
II. 18     p. 195 n. 25
III. 7     p. 195 n. 21
    p. 195 n. 22

*de Bello Civili*
I. 7     p. 178 n. 33
21     p. 195 n. 21
75     p. 206 n. 57
III. 12     p. 195 n. 25
20     p. 188 n. 12
32     p. 196 n. 29
88     p. 206 n. 57
108     p. 195 n. 1

*de Bello Africano*
68. 4     p. 195 n. 25
76. 1     p. 195 n. 25

Cassiodorus
*Variae*
V. 22     p. 205 n. 45
XI. 22     p. 210 n. 115
XI. 23     p. 210 n. 112
XII. 31-2     p. 210 n. 120

Cassius Dio

| | | |
|---|---|---|
| XXXIX. 33. 2 | p. 177 n. 5 | |
| XL. 56. 1 | p. 177 n. 3 | |
| XLVI. 44-5 | p. 181 n. 53 | |
| XLIX. 15. 5-6 | p. 178 n. 22 | |
| LI. 19 | p. 184 n. 13 | |
| | p. 191 n. 76 | |
| 19. 6 | p. 178 n. 23 | |
| 20. 4 | p. 178 n. 23 | |
| LII. 20 | p. 180 III n. 20 | |
| 22 | p. 191 n. 82 | |
| | p. 186 n. 44 | |
| | p. 187 n. 51 | |
| 42 | p. 179 n. 6 | |
| | p. 180 II n. 16 | |
| LIII. 1 | p. 179 n. 11 | |
| 2 | p. 192 n. 23 | |
| | p. 181 n. 39 | |
| 11 | p. 177 n. 6 | |
| 12. 1 | p. 177 n. 2 | |
| 12-13 | p. 177 n. 1 | |
| 13 | p. 186 n. 42 | |
| 13. 1 | p. 177 n. 14 | |
| 14 | p. 191 n. 72 | |
| 14. 2 | p. 177 n. 3 | |
| 16. 2 | p. 177 n. 14 | |
| 17. 5-6 | p. 178 n. 40 | |
| 21 | p. 181 n. 41 | |
| 23 | p. 191 n. 84 | |
| 24 | p. 181 n. 22 | |
| 28 | p. 181 n. 23 | |
| 30. 1-2 | p. 177 n. 12 | |
| 30 | p. 192 n. 19 | |
| 31. 1 | p. 177 n. 10 | |
| 32 | p. 181 n. 24 | |
| | p. 192 n. 23 | |
| 32. 5 | p. 177 n. 13 | |
| | p. 178 n. 29 | |
| LIV. 1 | p. 180 II n. 18 | |
| | p. 181 n. 43 | |
| 1. 3-5 | p. 178 n. 35 | |
| 2 | p. 181 n. 43 | |
| | p. 181 n. 21 | |
| 2. 1 | p. 178 n. 35 | |
| 3. 1-3 | p. 177 n. 9 | |
| 3. 3 | p. 178 n. 29 | |
| 3. 4 | p. 177 n. 11 | |
| 3 | p. 191 n. 73 | |
| | p. 192 n. 85 | |
| | p. 192 n. 86 | |
| 6. 1-2 | p. 178 n. 36 | |

| | | |
|---|---|---|
| LIV. 6. 4-5 | p. 179 n. 47 | |
| 6. 6 | p. 179 n. 48 | |
| 6 | p. 181 n. 44 | |
| 10 | p. 180 n. 20 | |
| | p. 181 n. 44 | |
| | p. 181 n. 37 | |
| 10. 1-3 | p. 178 n. 37 | |
| 10. 5 | p. 178 n. 38 | |
| 12. 4-5 | p. 177 n. 14 | |
| 13-14 | p. 179 n. 7 | |
| 16 | p. 181 n. 46 | |
| 17 | p. 180 n. 3 | |
| 18 | p. 183 n. 85 | |
| 19. 6 | p. 179 n. 49 | |
| 21 | p. 196 n. 46 | |
| 26 | p. 179 n. 8 | |
| | p. 180 n. 4 | |
| | p. 180 n. 8 | |
| | p. 180 III n. 16 | |
| | p. 180 III n. 17 | |
| 28 | p. 180 n. 21 | |
| 28. 1 | p. 179 n. 55 | |
| 30 | p. 180 n. 4 | |
| | p. 180 n. 23 | |
| | p. 180 III n. 17 | |
| 35 | p. 179 n. 8 | |
| | p. 179 n. 13 | |
| | p. 183 n. 85 | |
| LV. 1 | p. 181 n. 22 | |
| 3 | p. 183 n. 85 | |
| 5 | p. 181 n. 47 | |
| 13 | p. 179 n. 8 | |
| | p. 182 n. 66 | |
| | p. 179 n. 14 | |
| | p. 180 n. 24 | |
| | p. 180 n. 5 | |
| 24 | p. 180 III n. 18 | |
| 26. 4 | p. 178 n. 39 | |
| 34 | p. 181 n. 38 | |
| | p. 181 n. 54 | |
| | p. 181 n. 49 | |
| LVI. 23. 2-3 | p. 179 n. 43 | |
| 25 | p. 181 n. 25 | |
| | p. 181 n. 27 | |
| 26 | p. 191 n. 62 | |
| 26. 2 | p. 179 n. 57 | |
| 27 | p. 180 III n. 17 | |
| 28. 2 | p. 179 n. 57 | |
| LVII. 17 | p. 195 n. 16 | |
| 20 | p. 191 n. 80 | |
| 23 | p. 196 n. 51 | |

Cassius Dio (contd.)
LVIII. 20     p. 183 n. 101
    p. 183 n. 113
LIX. 8     p. 191 n. 82
9     p. 180 n. 12
    p. 183 n. 114
    p. 192 n. 22
20     p. 183 n. 114
LX. 23. 4     p. 179 n. 54
24. 1-3     p. 192 n. 24
LXIV. 2     p. 184 n. 21
LXXII. 33     p. 193 n. 56
LXXVII. 8     p. 191 n. 82
9     p. 201 n. 54

Cicero
Academica
I. 11     p. 195 n. 1
II. 97     p. 188 n. 16

ad Atticum
III. 24. 1     p. 192 n. 4
IV. 1. 6     p. 195 n. 1
V. 17. 2     p. 195 n. 21
V. 21     p. 195 n. 26
21. 10     p. 196 n. 53
VI. 1. 2     p. 195 n. 21
1. 4-6     p. 196 n. 53
2. 8     p. 196 n. 53
3. 5-6     p. 196 n. 53
7     p. 192 n. 5
VII. 1. 6     p. 192 n. 7
7. 4     p. 178 n. 20
VIII. 15. 3     p. 177 n. 7

ad familiares
I. 9. 25     p. 177 n. 2
    p. 178 n. 16
II. 17     p. 192 n. 5
17. 4     p. 192 n. 17
III. 5     p. 192 n. 16
6. 5     p. 195 n. 24
8. 7     p. 195 n. 21
IV. 6. 2     p. 195 n. 1
V. 20     p. 192 n. 5
20. 7     p. 195 n. 21
20. 9     p. 192 n. 17
VII. 5. 3     p. 195 n. 21
VIII. 4. 4     p. 192 n. 10

XII. 14. 5     p. 195 n. 1
XIII. 26     p. 189 n. 23
26. 3     p. 177 n. 7

ad Quintum fratrem
I. 1. 13     p. 202 n. 9
    p. 202 n. 10
    p. 204 n. 20
II. 3. 1     p. 192 n. 4
III. 9. 3     p. 195 n. 1

de domo sua
74     p. 203 n. 13

de imperio Cn. Pompei
14     p. 192 n. 18

de lege agraria
I. 21     p. 178 n. 32
II. 10     p. 178 n. 32
II. 31-2     p. 202 n. 5

de officiis
I. 85     p. 195 n. 1

de provinciis consularibus
28     p. 192 n. 11

de republica
II. 51     p. 195 n. 1

de senectute
56     p. 202 n. 6

in Pisonem
5     p. 192 n. 4
50     p. 178 n. 18
86     p. 192 n. 8

in Vatinium
22     p. 202 n. 6

Philippics
I. 21     p. 191 n. 79
I. 23     p. 191 n. 65
IV. 9     p. 177 n. 7
    p. 189 n. 24
V. 45     p. 196 n. 28

Cicero (contd.)
 pro Balbo
  61                    p. 192 n. 11

 pro Cluentio
  74                    p. 202 n. 6
  99                    p. 195 n. 21
  120                   p. 188 n. 1
  121                   p. 182 n. 70
  126                   p. 202 n. 11

 pro Flacco
  49                    p. 188 n. 2
                        p. 188 n. 3
                        p. 188 n. 6
  80                    p. 201 n. 14

 pro Fonteio
  29                    p. 202 n. 6

 pro Quinctio
  29                    p. 188 n. 10
  63                    p. 188 n. 10
  65                    p. 188 n. 10

 pro Rabirio Postumo
  13                    p. 195 n. 21
                        p. 203 n. 15
  19                    p. 195 n. 21

 pro Sestio
  29-30                 p. 179 n. 42

 pro Tullio
  38-9                  p. 188 n. 11

 Verrines, Divinatio
  29                    p. 204 n. 25

 Actio Secunda
  I. 36                 p. 192 n. 6
     67                 p. 204 n. 20
     71                 p. 202 n. 10
     72                 p. 204 n. 20
     73                 p. 195 n. 21
     119                p. 188 n. 13
  II. 19-20             p. 189 n. 30
      25-6              p. 189 n. 30
      27                p. 204 n. 20

II. 27                  p. 202 n. 5
    30                  p. 189 n. 21
    62-3                p. 188 n. 3
    75                  p. 204 n. 20
    90                  p. 201 n. 22
                        p. 198 n. 9
III. 26                 p. 204 n. 21
     28                 p. 202 n. 5
                        p. 205 n. 35
     40                 p. 204 n. 20
     54                 p. 204 n. 20
                        p. 202 n. 5
     57                 p. 205 n. 35
     75                 p. 196 n. 53
     134                p. 195 n. 21
     137                p. 204 n. 20
                        p. 202 n. 5
                        p. 205 n. 35
     138                p. 189 n. 22
     154                p. 202 n. 10
                        p. 204 n. 20
     157                p. 202 n. 10
     163                p. 192 n. 15
     181                p. 205 n. 32
     181-4              p. 204 n. 24
     181-7              p. 204 n. 25
     181 ff.            p. 204 n. 20
     182                p. 203 n. 12
                        p. 204 n. 25
                        p. 205 n. 31
     183                p. 204 n. 20
     184                p. 203 n. 15
                        p. 204 n. 27
     185                p. 203 n. 14
     187                p. 204 n. 20
                        p. 204 n. 21
                        p. 204 n. 23
     197                p. 192 n. 14
V. 39-41                p. 178 n. 20
   118 ff.              p. 202 n. 9
   118                  p. 204 n. 20
   139-73               p. 184 n. 8
   140-2                p. 204 n. 20
   146                  p. 184 n. 11
   161                  p. 184 n. 11
   165                  p. 184 n. 11

Collectio Avellana
 16                     p. 215 App.
 31                     p. 215 App.

Constantine Porphyrogenitus
*de Cerimoniis*
  I. 86             p. 212 n. 139
                  p. 212 n. 140
                  p. 212 n. 145

*Corpus Glossarum Latinarum*
  IV. 51           p. 198 n. 11
  V. 188          p. 198 n. 11

Cyprian
*Acta Proconsularia*
  2               p. 207 n. 69
  5               p. 207 n. 66
                  p. 207 n. 71

  *epistulae*
  LXXX          p. 208 n. 88

Dionysius of Halicarnassus
*Antiquitates Romanae*
  V. 19. 4        p. 191 n. 83
     70. 2        p. 191 n. 83
  VII. 41. 1     p. 191 n. 83
  IX. 39. 2      p. 191 n. 83

Eusebius
*Historia Ecclesiastica*
  V. 1             p. 184 n. 18
  IX. 9           p. 209 n. 110

  *de Martyribus Palaestinis*
  pr. § 1         p. 207 n. 87
  11 § 24        p. 208 n. 97

Festus
  p. 371          p. 202 n. 6

Firmicus Maternus
*Mathesis*
  VIII. 26       p. 207 n. 66

Frontinus
*de aquaeductis*
  100             p. 205 n. 31
                  p. 205 n. 37
  101             p. 206 n. 49
  118             p. 193 n. 60

  *de agrorum qualitate*
  Bruns, Fontes[7],
        II. 86  p. 201 n. 2

Gellius
  VII. ix        p. 201 X n. 1
                  p. 202 n. 11
  X. iii. 3     p. 184 n. 4
  XIII. xii.    p. 189 n. 18
     xii. 6     p. 202 n. 6

Granius Licinianus
  XXXV        p. 198 n. 23

Horace
*Epodes*
  IV. 15–16    p. 182 n. 60

*Satires*
  I. iv. 121–3  p. 182 n. 70
  II. vii. 53    p. 182 n. 59

Isidore of Pelusium
*epistulae*
  I. 489        p. 200 n. 53

John Lydus
*de Magistratibus*
  I. 14           p. 213 n. 158
    15           p. 213 n. 158
  II. 6           p. 213 n. 158
    10           p. 213 n. 162
    12           p. 213 n. 160
    13           p. 213 n. 158
    19           p. 209 n. 105
    30           p. 206 n. 47
  III. 3          p. 211 n. 124
                  p. 213 n. 161
    4            p. 210 n. 112
                  p. 215 App.
    5            p. 210 n. 112
    7            p. 210 n. 120
    8            p. 210 n. 120
    9            p. 212 n. 144
                  p. 215 App.
    9–10         p. 210 n. 117
    12           p. 213 n. 161
    16           p. 211 n. 120
    16–17      p. 209 n. 108
    17           p. 210 n. 117
    20           p. 210 n. 115
    21           p. 210 n. 112
    22           p. 213 n. 159
    23           p. 213 n. 162

John Lydus—contd.

| | | |
|---|---|---|
| 24-5 | p. 213 n. 167 | |
| 25 | p. 212 n. 153 | |
| 26-8 | p. 213 n. 166 | |
| 27 | p. 213 n. 157 | |
| | p. 210 n. 117 | |
| 31 | p. 209 n. 111 | |
| 35 | p. 208 n. 103 | |
| | p. 209 n. 111 | |
| | p. 213 n. 163 | |
| 36 | p. 213 n. 164 | |
| 42 | p. 213 n. 160 | |
| 46 | p. 213 n. 164 | |
| 49 | p. 213 n. 164 | |
| | p. 213 n. 169 | |
| 57 | p. 213 n. 165 | |
| 67 | p. 211 n. 136 | |
| 68 | p. 213 n. 160 | |

Josephus
*Antiquitates Iudaicae*

| | | |
|---|---|---|
| XIV. 115 | p. 199 n. 39 | |
| XVI. 162-5 | p. 177 n. 15 | |
| 166 | p. 177 n. 8 | |
| 169-70 | p. 178 n. 15 | |
| 171 | p. 177 n. 8 | |
| XVIII. 2 | p. 195 n. 20 | |
| 31-3 | p. 195 n. 20 | |
| 55 | p. 195 n. 20 | |
| 60 | p. 197 n. 59 | |
| 158 | p. 196 n. 57 | |
| | p. 196 n. 52 | |
| 237 | p. 195 n. 20 | |
| XIX. 363 | p. 195 n. 20 | |
| XX. 2 | p. 195 n. 20 | |

*Bellum Iudaicum*

| | | |
|---|---|---|
| II. 117 | p. 187 n. 49 | |
| | p. 195 n. 20 | |
| 167 | p. 196 n. 52 | |
| 169 | p. 195 n. 20 | |
| 175 | p. 197 n. 59 | |
| 308 | p. 184 n. 19 | |
| VII. 216-17 | p. 201 n. 23 | |

*contra Apionem*

| | | |
|---|---|---|
| II. 4 | p. 198 n. 25 | |

Juvenal

| | | |
|---|---|---|
| IV. 55 | p. 193 n. 42 | |
| V. 3 | p. 204 n. 27 | |
| VII. 228 | p. 189 n. 18 | |

Lactantius
*de Mortibus Persecutorum*

| | | |
|---|---|---|
| 31 | p. 207 n. 86 | |

Livy

| | | |
|---|---|---|
| I. 26. 7 | p. 202 n. 8 | |
| 38 | p. 197 n. 6 | |
| II. 56 | p. 202 n. 6 | |
| III. 33. 8 | p. 202 n. 10 | |
| 56. 5 | p. 202 n. 6 | |
| IV. 32 | p. 202 n. 7 | |
| VI. 15. 1 | p. 202 n. 6 | |
| VII. 31 | p. 197 n. 6 | |
| | p. 198 n. 23 | |
| VIII. 14 | p. 198 n. 23 | |
| 32-3 | p. 202 n. 7 | |
| IX. 46 | p. 201 X n. 1 | |
| | p. 202 n. 11 | |
| XXII. 11. 3 | p. 202 n. 6 | |
| XXIV. 8. 20 | p. 202 n. 7 | |
| XXVI. 34 | p. 198 n. 23 | |
| XXIX. 37 | p. 202 n. 7 | |
| XXX. 38. 7 | p. 202 n. 6 | |
| 39. 7 | p. 202 n. 11 | |
| XXXVIII. 28 | p. 198 n. 23 | |
| 51 | p. 203 n. 11 | |
| 51. 8 | p. 202 n. 7 | |
| 51. 12 | p. 206 n. 6 | |
| 55 | p. 204 n. 25 | |
| XL. 29 | p. 202 n. 2 | |
| | p. 204 n. 28 | |
| XLI. 15 | p. 202 n. 6 | |
| XLV. 29 | p. 204 n. 20 | |
| Epit. LVII | p. 184 n. 6 | |

Mansi
*Concilia*

| | | |
|---|---|---|
| IV. 51 | p. 206 n. 47 | |
| | p. 210 n. 111 | |
| | p. 210 n. 117 | |
| 167 | p. 206 n. 47 | |
| | p. 210 n. 111 | |
| | p. 210 n. 117 | |
| | p. 206 n. 47 | |
| 181 | p. 210 n. 111 | |
| | p. 210 n. 117 | |

Mark
*Gospel*

| | | |
|---|---|---|
| VI. 27 | p. 207 n. 66 | |

*Notitia Dignitatum*
  *Orientis*
    ii          p. 210 n. 113
    iii         p. 210 n. 113
    v           p. 211 n. 122
                p. 216 App.
    vi          p. 211 n. 122
                p. 216 App.
    viii        p. 211 n. 122
                p. 216 App.
    ix          p. 211 n. 122
                p. 216 App.
    xx          p. 210 n. 116
    xxi         p. 210 n. 116
    xxiii       p. 210 n. 116
    xxvii       p. 210 n. 116
    xxx–xlii    p. 211 n. 122
    xliii       p. 208 n. 99
                p. 211 n. 133
                p. 210 n. 116
    xliv        p. 208 n. 99
                p. 211 n. 133

  *Occidentis*
    ii          p. 210 n. 113
    iii         p. 210 n. 113
    iv          p. 215 App.
    v           p. 216 App.
    vi          p. 211 n. 122
                p. 215 App.
    xviii       p. 215–6 App.
    xxv         p. 211 n. 121
    xxvi        p. 211 n. 121
    xxviii      p. 211 n. 121
    xxx         p. 211 n. 121
    xxxi        p. 211 n. 121
    xliii       p. 211 n. 133
                p. 208 n. 99
    xliv        p. 211 n. 133
                p. 208 n. 99
    xlv         p. 211 n. 133
                p. 208 n. 99

Orosius
  VI. 18. 34    p. 178 n. 22

Ovid
  *ex Ponto*
    IV. v. 17   p. 190 n. 47
        ix. 43  p. 190 n. 47

*Tristia*
    II. 131–2   p. 190 n. 59
        132     p. 182 n. 71
        135     p. 178 n. 42
    IV. x. 29–37 p. 180 n. 13

*Passio S. Perpetuae*
    6           p. 187 n. 57
                p. 187 n. 53

Philo
  *in Flaccum*
    2           p. 197 n. 66
    3–4         p. 196 n. 58

  *Legatio ad Gaium*
    20          p. 197 n. 66
    30          p. 196 n. 52
    38          p. 195 n. 19
                p. 197 n. 63
    40          p. 177 n. 8

Philostratus
  *Vitae Sophistarum*
    568         p. 191 n. 78

Pliny the Elder
  *Natural History*
    III. 139    p. 201 n. 18
    VI. 84      p. 193 n. 31
        90      p. 191 n. 83
    X. 134      p. 195 n. 3
    XII. 113    p. 193 n. 32
         123    p. 193 n. 32
    XIV. 145    p. 179 n. 57
    XVIII. 20   p. 202 n. 6
           114  p. 193 n. 36
    XXXIII. 17  p. 201 X n. 1
            29  p. 182 n. 59
            29–31 p. 182 n. 68
            30  p. 183 n. 91
                p. 181 n. 56
            32  p. 182 n. 59
    XXXVI. 57   p. 197 n. 66

Pliny the Younger
  *epistulae*
    II. 9       p. 180 III n. 15
                p. 183 n. 107

Q

Pliny the Younger, *epistulae—cont*

II. 11          p. 184 n. 22
                p. 191 n. 71
    11. 2       p. 191 n. 64
III. 20         p. 183 n. 109
                p. 183 n. 110
IV. 9. 17       p. 191 n. 64
    12          p. 204 n. 23
                p. 205 n. 31
    25          p. 183 n. 110
VI. 6           p. 183 n. 107
    19          p. 183 n. 108
VII. 16         p. 178 n. 19
    32          p. 178 n. 19
VIII. 2;        p. 180 III n. 15
                p. 183 n. 107
X. 6–7          p. 198 n. 24
    10          p. 198 n. 24
    21          p. 206 n. 59
    27          p. 206 n. 59
                p. 196 n. 50
                p. 196 n. 55
    49–50       p. 198 n. 10
    50          p. 201 n. 13
    56–7        p. 186 n. 38
    58          p. 184 n. 23
    72          p. 186 n. 39
    79          p. 197 n. 8
    80          p. 197 n. 8
    96. 4       p. 184 n. 17
    99          p. 177 n. 15
    112         p. 197 n. 8
    114–5       p. 197 n. 8
                p. 200 n. 44

*Panegyricus*
    36          p. 193 n. 59
    42          p. 193 n. 58
    63. 2       p. 183 n. 101
    64. 1       p. 183 n. 101

Plutarch
*Caesar*
    28          p. 192 n. 9

*Cato Minor*
    16          p. 192 n. 1
                p. 203 n. 11
                p. 204 n. 29
                p. 205 n. 31

*Crassus*
    10          p. 184 n. 7

*C. Gracchus*
    9           p. 184 n. 2

*Marcellus*
    2           p. 191 n. 82

*Pompey*
    25          p. 192 n. 12

Polybius
VI. 12          p. 192 n. 3
    13          p. 192 n. 2
                p. 192 n. 3
    37–38       p. 184 n. 7

Procopius
*Anecdota*
    24          p. 212 n. 139
                p. 212 n. 145

Quintilian
*de Institutione Oratoria*
III. vi. 70     p. 190 n. 45
                p. 190 n. 50

Sallust
*Bellum Iugurthinum*
    14. 1       p. 195 n. 1
    69          p. 184 n. 5

Scriptores Historiae Augustae
*Vita Severi*
    12          p. 194 n. 80

Seneca
*Apocolocyntosis*
    6           p. 196 n. 46

*Consolatio ad Marciam*
    15          p. 180 n. 22

*de Beneficiis*
III. 7          p. 182 n. 80
    25          p. 207 n. 66
IV. 39. 3       p. 193 n. 30
VII. 6. 3       p. 193 n. 35

*de Ira*
I. 18. 4        p. 207 n. 66

*epistulae*
83. 14          p. 179 n. 57
98. 13          p. 180 III n. 15

Sozomenus
V. 4            p. 211 n. 131

Strabo
III. p. 167     p. 196 n. 48
     p. 169     p. 182 n. 62
IV. p. 203      p. 195 n. 3
V. p. 213       p. 182 n. 62
XII. p. 542     p. 199 n. 39
XVII. p. 797    p. 196 n. 33
     p. 840     p. 177 n. 1
                p. 177 n. 4

Suetonius
*Julius*
18              p. 192 n. 4
20              p. 202 n. 10
41. 2           p. 182 n. 64

*Augustus*
19. 1           p. 177 n. 11
24. 1           p. 179 n. 43
27              p. 179 n. 2
28              p. 192 n. 19
28. 1           p. 177 n. 12
29. 3           p. 183 n. 89
30. 1           p. 181 n. 22
32. 1           p. 178 n. 39
32. 3           p. 182 n. 65
                p. 182 n. 67
                p. 183 n. 84
                p. 183 n. 88
                p. 183 n. 89
                p. 183 n. 92
33              p. 190 n. 61
33. 3           p. 189 n. 25
34              p. 179 n. 4
35              p. 179 n. 3
                p. 180 n. 26
37. 1           p. 179 n. 9
37              p. 178 n. 38
38. 2           p. 180 n. 11
38. 3           p. 179 n. 10
                p. 181 n. 55
38. 3-40. 1     p. 179 n. 5
40              p. 198 n. 21

40. 1           p. 181 n. 46
                p. 182 n. 61
40. 2           p. 181 n. 40
                p. 181 n. 48
41. 1           p. 180 n. 2
45. 4           p. 178 n. 41
45              p. 186 n. 45
46              p. 183 n. 96
49. 1           p. 178 n. 39
51              p. 190 n. 61
54              p. 179 n. 3
56. 1           p. 181 n. 34
56. 4           p. 177 n. 11
66. 2           p. 191 n. 84
66. 3           p. 177 n. 11
67. 1           p. 196 n. 46
93              p. 190 n. 51
94. 10          p. 180 n. 14
97              p. 179 n. 12
101             p. 192 n. 19

*Tiberius*
8               p. 177 n. 11
                p. 192 n. 86
21. 1           p. 179 n. 56
21              p. 179 n. 12
37. 1           p. 178 n. 39
41              p. 182 n. 83
                p. 183 n. 89
42. 1           p. 179 n. 57
75              p. 191 n. 80

*Caligula*
16. 2           p. 182 n. 72
16              p. 192 n. 22

*Claudius*
14              p. 188 n. 5
                p. 190 n. 47
15              p. 190 n. 51
23. 1           p. 190 n. 44
23. 2           p. 190 n. 46
24              p. 192 n. 24

*Nero*
10. 2           p. 191 n. 81
15              p. 190 n. 51
17              p. 189 n. 29

*Galba*
9               p. 184 n. 20

Suetonius—contd.
Vespasianus
2. 3          p. 183 n. 106
4. 3          p. 180 n. 10
16           p. 194 n. 63
23           p. 193 n. 42

Domitianus
8. 1          p. 190 n. 51
12           p. 193 n. 48

vita Horatii     p. 204 n. 27

Symmachus
Relationes
23           p. 210 n. 119
34           p. 215 App.
67           p. 215 n. 119

Tacitus
Annals
I. 2         p. 178 n. 34
7            p. 178 n. 30
             p. 178 n. 39
             p. 179 n. 57
11           p. 192 n. 19
14           p. 179 n. 50
             p. 181 n. 26
             p. 181 n. 29
             p. 183 n. 104
15           p. 181 n. 31
             p. 183 n. 99
             p. 183 n. 103
31           p. 179 n. 43
72           p. 191 n. 63
             p. 190 n. 58
75           p. 180 n. 6
77           p. 186 n. 45
81           p. 179 n. 50
             p. 181 n. 29
             p. 183 n. 112
II. 36        p. 183 n. 104
37           p. 180 n. 6
47           p. 194 n. 61
48           p. 193 n. 39
59           p. 196 n. 32
79           p. 190 n. 56
III. 10       p. 190 n. 56
12           p. 190 n. 56
29           p. 180 III n. 19

III. 30       p. 180 n. 25
             p. 182 n. 83
             p. 183 n. 90
50           p. 191 n. 65
51           p. 191 n. 80
56           p. 178 n. 31
68           p. 190 n. 57
70           p. 178 n. 24
IV. 6         p. 196 n. 51
15           p. 196 n. 54
             p. 196 n. 47
20           p. 193 n. 37
             p. 194 n. 64
21           p. 190 n. 58
27           p. 178 n. 39
VI. 2         p. 193 n. 38
             p. 194 n. 64
11           p. 179 n. 44
             p. 179 n. 57
17           p. 194 n. 62
XI. 25        p. 179 n. 1
XII. 41       p. 179 n. 53
49           p. 195 n. 16
60           p. 189 n. 34
             p. 197 n. 64
             p. 196 n. 39
XIII. 4       p. 189 n. 29
28           p. 189 n. 18
28-9         p. 192 n. 23
             p. 192 n. 24
             p. 193 n. 25
31           p. 193 n. 46
XIV. 28       p. 183 n. 105
             p. 189 n. 26
             p. 191 n. 83
31-2         p. 196 n. 56
48           p. 191 n. 65
             p. 178 n. 24
XV. 18        p. 193 n. 45
44           p. 195 n. 2
XVI. 11       p. 178 n. 24

Histories
I. 11         p. 196 n. 32
46           p. 193 n. 40
58           p. 193 n. 41
77           p. 183 n. 111
IV. 48        p. 206 n. 58

Dialogus
7            p. 180 III n. 15

Theodoret
  *epistulae*
    42            p. 194 n. 81

Valerius Maximus
  IV. i. 10        p. 204 n. 21
  VI. ii. 11       p. 193 n. 29
  VII. vii. 3      p. 190 n. 41
                   p. 190 n. 48
    4              p. 190 n. 42
                   p. 190 n. 49
    6              p. 188 n. 14
  IX. v. 1         p. 184 n. 1

Varro
  *de lingua Latina*
    VI. 86-7       p. 202 n. 7
       87          p. 204 n. 21

VI. 88           p. 202 n. 10
   89            p. 202 n. 10
   95            p. 202 n. 7
                 p. 202 n. 10

Velleius Paterculus
  II. 39. 2        p. 192 n. 21
     89            p. 181 n. 24
     91            p. 177 n. 11
     91-2          p. 181 n. 22
     92            p. 181 n. 30
                   p. 181 n. 45
     95            p. 180 II n. 19
     111           p. 181 n. 20
     121           p. 179 n. 56
     124           p. 181 n. 20
     124           p. 183 n. 95

## II. LEGAL AUTHORITIES

Bruns
  *Fontes Iuris Romani*[7]
    10, l. 50           p. 202 n. 6
    10, ll. 76-9        p. 184 n. 3
    11, ll. 53 ff.      p. 201 n. 16
    12                  p. 202 n. 6
                        p. 202 n. 7
                        p. 203 n. 16
                        p. 204 n. 28
    12, I. 1-6          p. 205 n. 31
       I. 7-8, 12       p. 202 n. 3
       II. 14-18        p. 205 n. 29
       II. 24-30        p. 205 n. 30
       II. 31-7         p. 205 n. 31
    16, cap. xxi,
              xxii      p. 189 n. 19
    17                  p. 189 n. 20
    18, l. 119          p. 190 n. 52
    95                  p. 208 n. 94
    103                 p. 210 n. 119
                        p. 213 n. 156

*Collatio Mosaicarum et Romanarum*
    *Legum*
    XII. v. 1           p. 186 n. 37
    XIII. iii           p. 187 n. 69
    XIV. iii. 2-3       p. 185 n. 36
                        p. 191 n. 68

*Codex Justinianus*
  I. xxvii. 1 §26       p. 210 n. 115
            §29-35      p. 210 n. 120
            §29         p. 214 App.
            §33         p. 214 App.
            §35         p. 214 App.
            1           p. 211 n. 126
                        p. 212 n. 139
                        p. 212 n. 151
                        p. 215 App.
            2           p. 212 n. 139
                        p. 212 n. 152
  II. vii. 22           p. 212 n. 153
       23               p. 212 n. 145
       24               p. 212 n. 153
       25               p. 212 n. 145
       26 §3            p. 210 n. 115
                        p. 210 n. 117
  III. ii. 5            p. 212 n. 153
       xxviii. 30       p. 212 n. 145
  VII. v. 1             p. 198 n. 31
       vi. 1            p. 198 n. 31
       xxv. 1           p. 201 n. 5
       xxxi. 1          p. 201 n. 6
  VIII. xiii. 27        p. 212 n. 148
  IX. xlix. 9           p. 208 n. 94
  X. i. 5               p. 208 n. 94
                        p. 208 n. 96

*Codex Justinianus—cont.*

| | |
|---|---|
| X. xxxix. 1 | p. 200 n. 44 |
| XI. xiv | p. 205 n. 45 |
| lxviii | p. 194 n. 81 |
| lxix | p. 194 n. 81 |
| lxxi-lxxiv | p. 194 n. 81 |
| XII. xvii. 3 | p. 212 n. 149 |
| xvi. 5 | p. 212 n. 145 |
| xix. 7 | p. 212 n. 146 |
| | p. 212 n. 137 |
| 10 | p. 212 n. 139 |
| 11 | p. 212 n. 146 |
| 12 | p. 212 n. 153 |
| 13 | p. 212 n. 147 |
| 15 | p. 212 n. 147 |
| xx. 3 | p. 211 n. 139 |
| 5 §1 | p. 212 n. 150 |
| 6 | p. 212 n. 153 |
| xxi. 8 | p. 212 n. 153 |
| xxiii. 7 | p. 208 n. 92 |
| xxv. 4 | p. 212 n. 153 |
| xxix. 3 | p. 212 n. 153 |
| xxxiii. 5 | p. 212 n. 150 |
| 5 §3 | p. 212 n. 145 |
| xxxvi. 6 | p. 211 n. 124 |
| xlix. 5 | p. 213 App. |
| 10 | p. 209 n. 111 |
| lii. 3 | p. 211 n. 124 |
| lvii. 13 | p. 211 n. 134 |
| 14 | p. 211 n. 134 |
| lix. 10 | p. 211 n. 128 |

*Codex Theodosianus*

| | |
|---|---|
| I. ix. 1 | p. 212 n. 138 |
| xii. 6 | p. 211 n. 128 |
| xiii. 1 | p. 211 n. 128 |
| xv. 5 | p. 211 n. 128 |
| 12 | p. 211 n. 128 |
| 13 | p. 211 n. 128 |
| xvi. 6 | p. 210 n. 116 |
| 7 | p. 212 n. 155 |
| | p. 209 n. 105 |
| | p. 210 n. 116 |
| | p. 209 n. 117 |
| VI. xxiii. 4 | p. 212 n. 139 |
| xxiv. 6 | p. 212 n. 142 |
| xxvi. 5 | p. 209 n. 106 |
| 6 | p. 212 n. 143 |
| 11 | p. 212 n. 143 |
| 16 | p. 208 n. 91 |

| | |
|---|---|
| VI. xxvi. 17 | p. 208 n. 91 |
| | p. 212 n. 143 |
| xxvii. 17 | p. 212 n. 138 |
| 18 | p. 212 n. 138 |
| 19 | p. 212 n. 142 |
| 23 | p. 212 n. 139 |
| xxx. 3 | p. 212 n. 143 |
| 7 | p. 208 n. 92 |
| | p. 212 n. 139 |
| 11 | p. 211 n. 125 |
| | p. 212 n. 140 |
| 14 | p. 212 n. 143 |
| 15-16 | p. 212 n. 138 |
| 15-17 | p. 212 n. 139 |
| 21 | p. 212 n. 143 |
| xxxii. 2 | p. 208 n. 93 |
| | p. 212 n. 139 |
| xxxv. 3 | p. 208 n. 89 |
| 14 | p. 211 n. 135 |
| xxxvi. 1 | p. 208 n. 90 |
| VII. i. 5 | p. 211 n. 127 |
| iv. 35 | p. 211 n. 126 |
| xii. 2 | p. 212 n. 149 |
| xiii. 16 | p. 199 n. 32 |
| xxii. 3 | p. 211 n. 129 |
| 8 | p. 211 n. 127 |
| 10 | p. 211 n. 127 |
| VIII. i. 1 | p. 208 n. 98 |
| 2 | p. 210 n. 118 |
| 4 | p. 208 n. 99 |
| | p. 208 n. 100 |
| 6 | p. 208 n. 99 |
| | p. 208 n. 101 |
| 7 | p. 208 n. 99 |
| | p. 208 n. 101 |
| 8 | p. 208 n. 99 |
| | p. 208 n. 101 |
| 11 | p. 208 n. 102 |
| | p. 214 App. |
| 12 | p. 208 n. 99 |
| iv. 5 | p. 209 n. 110 |
| 7 | p. 209 n. 110 |
| | p. 211 n. 130 |
| 8 | p. 211 n. 130 |
| 10 | p. 209 n. 106 |
| | p. 210 n. 117 |
| 16 | p. 209 n. 109 |
| 21-5 | p. 211 n. 133 |
| 28-30 | p. 211 n. 133 |
| 28 | p. 211 n. 135 |
| vii. 1 | p. 212 n. 142 |

VIII. vii. 9    p. 211 n. 132
10    p. 212 n. 138
12    p. 211 n. 127
16    p. 211 n. 130
17    p. 213 App.
19    p. 211 n. 132
21    p. 211 n. 128
ix. 1    p. 205 n. 46
         p. 205 n. 47
xv. 3    p. 209 n. 107
         p. 209 n. 109
5    p. 209 n. 107
     p. 209 n. 108
IX. iii. 1    p. 211 n. 120
5    p. 209 n. 108
6    p. 209 n. 108
7    p. 209 n. 108
xl. 5    p. 209 n. 108
xlii. 1    p. 208 n. 94
X. i. 5    p. 208 n. 94
vii. 1    p. 208 n. 94
2    p. 208 n. 94
viii. 2    p. 208 n. 96
           p. 208 n. 94
XI. xxx. 34    p. 213 n. 168
XII. i. 79    p. 211 n. 130
XIV. i. 2    p. 205 n. 46
3    p. 205 n. 46
3    p. 206 n. 48
4    p. 205 n. 46
     p. 206 n. 47
5    p. 205 n. 46
6    p. 205 n. 46
     p. 206 n. 47
iv. 10    p. 215-6 App.
XVI. v. 48    p. 211 n. 135

*Digest*
I ii. 2 §27    p. 201 X n. 1
2 §32    p. 190 n. 45
v. 17    p. 129
         p. 200 n. 48
x    p. 188 n. 15
xvi. 1    p. 207 n. 72
          p. 178 n. 17
2    p. 196 n. 45
     p. 178 n. 19
3    p. 196 n. 45
4 §6    p. 178 n. 17

I. xvi. 6    p. 185 n. 31
6 pr.    p. 191 n. 72
11    p. 185 n. 31
       p. 191 n. 72
xvii. 1    p. 196 n. 34
xviii. 6 §8    p. 185 n. 34
xxi. 1    p. 185 n. 35
          p. 195 n. 27
          p. 191 n. 66
          p. 185 n. 31
          p. 191 n. 72
5 §1    p. 185 n. 31
        p. 195 n. 27
II. i. 3    p. 185 n. 32
viii. 9    p. 189 n. 33
IV. iv. 7 §4    p. 188 n. 5
38    p. 188 n. 9
39    p. 188 n. 9
V. i. 12    p. 179 n. 45
15    p. 188 n. 7
16    p. 188 n. 7
58    p. 190 n. 38
82    p. 205 n. 36
ii. 2    p. 190 n. 40
5    p. 190 n. 40
13    p. 190 n. 40
17    p. 190 n. 40
XXVI. v. 1    p. 196 n. 42
1 §1    p. 196 n. 44
XXVIII. iii. 6 §7    p. 185 n. 28
                     p. 185 n. 29
6 §8-9    p. 185 n. 27
          p. 187 n. 63
6 §9    p. 185 n. 25
        p. 187 n. 62
6 §10    p. 187 n. 64
XL. i. 14    p. 196 n. 41
ii. 1    p. 196 n. 41
8    p. 196 n. 41
17    p. 196 n. 43
18 §1    p. 196 n. 41
20 §4    p. 196 n. 41
21    p. 196 n. 40
XLIV. vii. 5 §4    p. 188 n. 7
XLVII. vi. 8    p. 191 n. 74
xxi. 2    p. 187 n. 69
XLVIII. i. 1    p. 185 n. 36
ii. 6    p. 185 n. 30
ii. 73    p. 206 n. 60
iii. 3    p. 186 n. 39
iii. 9    p. 186 n. 44

*Digest—contd.*

| | |
|---|---|
| XLVIII. iii. 9 | p. 187 n. 51 |
| | p. 187 n. 52 |
| v. 38 §8 | p. 187 n. 67 |
| vi. 7 | p. 184 n. 12 |
| | p. 190 n. 55 |
| 10 §2 | p. 186 n. 37 |
| viii. 1 §5 | p. 187 n. 67 |
| 3 §5 | p. 186 n. 37 |
| 16 | p. 185 n. 28 |
| | p. 186 n. 37 |
| x. 1 §13 | p. 186 n. 37 |
| 33 | p. 186 n. 37 |
| xiii. 11 §6 | p. 104 |
| xiv. | p. 181 n. 46 |
| 1 §4 | p. 183 n. 86 |
| xix. 2 §1 | p. 185 n. 29 |
| 2 §2 | p. 185 n. 27 |
| 9 §11-15 | p. 187 n. 64 |
| 10 §2 | p. 185 n. 30 |
| 15 | p. 187 n. 66 |
| 27 §1-2 | p. 185 n. 28 |
| 28 §2-5 | p. 185 n. 30 |
| 28 §13 | p. 186 n. 38 |
| 38 §7-9 | p. 186 n. 37 |
| 43 §1 | p. 187 n. 64 |
| xx. 2 | p. 185 n. 27 |
| 6 | p. 207 n. 82 |
| | p. 207 n. 66 |
| xxi. 2 §1 | p. 185 n. 28 |
| | p. 185 n. 29 |
| xxii. 6 §1 | p. 185 n. 29 |
| 6 §2 | p. 187 n. 68 |
| 7 §§1, | |
| 6-17 | p. 178 n. 42 |
| XLIX. i. 6 | p. 187 n. 60 |
| 10 §1 | p. 187 n. 58 |
| 16 | p. 185 n. 25 |
| | p. 187 n. 62 |
| 21 pr. §1 | p. 190 n. 39 |
| iv. 1 | p. 185 n. 28 |
| | p. 185 n. 29 |
| 1 §§5-15 | p. 185 n. 27 |
| 2 | p. 185 n. 26 |
| 2 §3 | p. 185 n. 27 |
| v. 2 | p. 185 n. 26 |
| vi. 1 pr. | p. 194 n. 79 |
| vii. 1 §3 | p. 185 n. 27 |
| viii. 1 | p. 188 n. 8 |
| ix. 1 | p. 185 n. 26 |
| | p. 187 n. 63 |

| | |
|---|---|
| XLIX. xiii. 1 | p. 185 n. 26 |
| xiv. 3 §10 | p. 194 n. 78 |
| 6 §1 | p. 194 n. 77 |
| 45 §12 | p. 201 n. 4 |
| L. i. 1 | p. 200 n. 47 |
| 6 | p. 200 n. 47 |
| 7 | p. 200 n. 47 |
| 9 | p. 200 n. 47 |
| 15 §3 | p. 200 n. 47 |
| 16 | p. 200 n. 47 |
| 22 §1-2 | p. 200 n. 47 |
| 23 | p. 200 n. 47 |
| 27 | p. 200 n. 47 |
| 29 | p. 200 n. 44 |
| 30 | p. 200 n. 48 |
| 35 | p. 200 n. 44 |
| ii. 2 §2 | p. 187 n. 64 |
| | p. 185 n. 30 |
| vi. 5 §10-11 | p. 200 n. 49 |
| 6 §9 | p. 194 n. 68 |
| xiii. 6 | p. 188 n. 7 |
| xv. 8 §8 | p. 201 n. 18 |
| xvi. 178 | p. 190 n. 50 |

*Fragmenta Vaticana*

| | |
|---|---|
| 197-8 | p. 183 n. 87 |
| 272 | p. 205 n. 44 |

Gaius

| | |
|---|---|
| I. 13 | p. 198 n. 13 |
| | p. 198 n. 22 |
| 14 | p. 197 n. 5 |
| 15 | p. 199 n. 33 |
| 25 | p. 198 n. 16 |
| 26 | p. 198 n. 19 |
| | p. 199 n. 33 |
| 27 | p. 198 n. 14 |
| 67-8 | p. 198 n. 20 |
| II. 5, 6 | p. 201 n. 11 |
| 7 | p. 201 n. 9 |
| 14a | p. 201 n. 10 |
| 21 | p. 201 n. 10 |
| | p. 201 n. 20 |
| 27 | p. 201 n. 10 |
| 31 | p. 201 n. 10 |
| 40-2 | p. 201 n. 15 |
| 46 | p. 201 n. 10 |
| 278 | p. 189 n. 31 |
| | p. 190 n. 45 |

III. 74-6    p. 198 n. 15
    75    p. 198 n. 17
    145    p. 201 n. 3
IV. 9    p. 188 n. 2
    30    p. 183 n. 87
    52    p. 188 n. 7
    53    p. 188 n. 5
    57    p. 188 n. 5
    102    p. 188 n. 2
    103-9    p. 190 n. 37
    109    p. 189 n. 32

Justinian
  Institutes
    I. v. 3    p. 198 n. 31
       20 §3    p. 190 n. 46
    II. 6 pr.    p. 201 n. 7
       25 pr.    p. 190 n. 43
       23 §1    p. 190 n. 43

  Novels
    2    p. 194 n. 81
    8    p. 212 n. 152
    14 §5    p. 211 n. 139
    24-7    p. 212 n. 152
    78    p. 198 n. 31
    97 §4    p. 212 n. 148
    136 §2    p. 212 n. 148

  Edicts
    13 §2    p. 211 n. 139

Lex Romana Burgundionum
  xliv. 5    p. 198 n. 31

Lex Romana Visigothorum, Appendix
  II. 6    p. 188 n. 2
    9    p. 188 n. 2
    10    p. 188 n. 2

Majorian
  Novels
    7 §16    p. 212 n. 154

Marcian
  Novels
    2    p. 194 n. 81

Paulus
  Sententiae
    IV. vii. 1    p. 186 n. 37
    V. va. 6a    p. 188 n. 2
       7    p. 188 n. 2
       8    p. 188 n. 2
       xxi. 1    p. 185 n. 30
          p. 190 n. 54
       xxiii. 1    p. 186 n. 37
          13    p. 186 n. 37
          14    p. 186 n. 37
          16    p. 186 n. 37
       xxv. 1-2    p. 186 n. 37
          7-13    p. 186 n. 37
       xxvi. 1    p. 184 n. 12
          2    p. 186 n. 43
       xxxiii    p. 187 n. 59
       xxxv    p. 187 n. 61
          p. 189 n. 27

Riccobono
  Fontes Iuris Romani Antejustiniani[2]
    I. 18 §6    p. 199 n. 44
    III. 19    p. 189 n. 34
          p. 199 n. 43
       64    p. 189 n. 34
       101    p. 191 n. 82

Theodosius II
  Novels
    iii. §6    p. 211 n. 135
    vii. 2    p. 211 n. 135
    vii. 4    p. 211 n. 135
    x. 1    p. 211 n. 135

Theophilus
  Commentarius in Institutiones
    II. i. 40    p. 201 n. 8

Ulpian
  Regulae
    I. 7    p. 188 n. 15
    VII. 4    p. 198 n. 20
    VIII. 2-5    p. 196 n. 42
    XI. 18-20    p. 196 n. 42
    XX. 14    p. 198 n. 18
    XXII. 2    p. 198 n. 16
    XXV. 12    p. 190 n. 45
          p. 190 n. 50

R

## III. INSCRIPTIONS

*Année Epigraphique*

| | |
|---|---|
| 1916. 29 | p. 206 n. 60 |
| | p. 206 n. 65 |
| 1918. 57 | p. 206 n. 64 |
| 1921. 38–9 | p. 204 n. 25 |
| | p. 205 n. 36 |
| 1924. 66 | p. 195 n. 18 |
| | p. 197 n. 60 |
| | p. 197 n. 65 |
| 1925. 44 | p. 205 n. 41 |
| 1927. 125 | p. 205 n. 43 |
| 1932. 58 | p. 193 n. 47 |
| 1933. 61 | p. 207 n. 65 |
| 248 | p. 207 n. 84 |
| 1934. 107 | p. 205 n. 41 |
| 1935. 16 | p. 207 n. 76 |
| 100 | p. 207 n. 69 |
| 1936. 83 | p. 195 n. 15 |
| 1937. 87 | p. 207 n. 75 |
| 1938. 173 | p. 196 n. 30 |
| 1939. 60 | p. 207 n. 75 |
| 1941. 105 | p. 196 n. 52 |
| 1944. 38 | p. 207 n. 75 |
| 1945. 80 | p. 194 n. 70 |
| 1946. 227 | p. 206 n. 60 |
| 1952. 80 | p. 183 n. 100 |

*Corpus Inscriptionum Latinarum*

| | |
|---|---|
| II. 3271 | p. 195 n. 8 |
| 6111 | p. 206 n. 65 |
| III. 1919 | p. 186 n. 47 |
| 4145 | p. 207 n. 78 |
| 4179 | p. 207 n. 78 |
| 5293 | p. 214 App. |
| 6754 | p. 206 n. 59 |
| 6987 | p. 204 n. 26 |
| 7979 | p. 207 n. 85 |
| 9908 | p. 207 n. 78 |
| 10315 | p. 207 n. 69 |
| 13201 | p. 207 n. 84 |
| 14068 | p. 209 n. 110 |
| 14387 | p. 207 n. 70 |
| VI. 967a. | p. 205 n. 44 |
| 1008 | p. 205 n. 44 |
| 1495 | p. 193 n. 55 |
| 1806 | p. 205 n. 41 |
| 1817 | p. 205 n. 41 |
| 1832 | p. 205 n. 42 |
| 1837 | p. 205 n. 41 |

| | |
|---|---|
| VI. 1841 | p. 205 n. 41 |
| 1848 | p. 204 n. 19 |
| 1853 | p. 205 n. 34 |
| 1854 | p. 205 n. 44 |
| 1855 | p. 203 n. 19 |
| 1937–8 | p. 203 n. 19 |
| 1947 | p. 205 n. 30 |
| 1949 | p. 203 n. 19 |
| 2104b, 40 | p. 194 n. 76 |
| 3962 | p. 193 n. 28 |
| 4122 | p. 206 n. 63 |
| 5744 | p. 193 n. 52 |
| 8409 | p. 193 n. 26 |
| 8450a | p. 206 n. 52 |
| 8506 | p. 193 n. 28 |
| 8519 | p. 193 n. 51 |
| 8521–2 | p. 193 n. 51 |
| 8540a | p. 193 n. 43 |
| 8573 | p. 193 n. 52 |
| 37744 | p. 193 n. 51 |
| VIII. 2702 | p. 193 n. 51 |
| | p. 194 n. 76 |
| 9367 (=20995) | p. 187 n. 55 |
| 9763 | p. 207 n. 70 |
| 17635 | p. 207 n. 78 |
| 18250 | p. 193 n. 51 |
| | p. 194 n. 76 |
| 20996 | p. 187 n. 55 |
| X. 530 | p. 203 n. 19 |
| 7351 | p. 195 n. 7 |
| 8023–4 | p. 197 n. 62 |
| XII. 2455 | p. 195 n. 6 |
| XIII. 1732 | p. 207 n. 78 |
| 1800 | p. 193 n. 53 |
| 6803 | p. 206 n. 61 |
| XV. 4102 | p. 194 n. 69 |
| 4111 | p. 194 n. 69 |
| 4114 | p. 194 n. 69 |
| 7974 a, b | p. 193 n. 52 |

*Denschrift der Akademie den Wissenschaften in Wien*

| | |
|---|---|
| LVII. 55 | p. 194 n. 67 |

*Documents illustrating the Reigns of Augustus and Tiberius*[2] (V. Ehrenberg, A. H. M. Jones)

| | |
|---|---|
| pp. 32–43 | p. 181 n. 28 |

| 30 | p. 178 n. 28 |
| 94a | p. 178 n. 26 |
| 166 | p. 195 n. 4 |
| 224 | p. 195 n. 12 |
| 225 | p. 196 n. 52 |
| 232a | p. 195 n. 5 |
| 233 | p. 196 n. 30 |
| 234 | p. 196 n. 30 |
| 243 | p. 195 n. 4 |
|  | p. 195 n. 15 |
|  | p. 195 n. 9 |
| 244 | p. 195 n. 11 |
| 278 | p. 178 n. 28 |
| 279 | p. 178 n. 27 |
| 307 | p. 178 n. 28 |
| 311 | p. 178 n. 28 |

*Ephemeris Epigraphica*
| VIII. 744 | p. 195 n. 5 |

*Greek Inscriptions in the Rijksmuseum Van Oudheden at Leyden* (H.W. Pleket)
| p. 49 ff. | p. 177 n. 8 |

*Inscriptiones Graecae*
| II-III.² 1100 | p. 191 n. 82 |
| V. 21 | p. 191 n. 82 |

*Inscriptiones Graecae ad res Romanas pertinentes* (R. Cagnat)
| III. 69 | p. 199 n. 39 |
| 801 | p. 199 n. 41 |
| 1008 | p. 207 n. 65 |
| IV. 289 | p. 199 n. 40 |
| 598 | p. 208 n. 88 |
| 914 | p. 196 n. 50 |
| 1057 | p. 187 n. 54 |

*Inscriptiones Latinae Selectae* (H. Dessau)
| 94 | p. 195 n. 4 |
| 212 | p. 180 n. 7 |
| 231 | p. 195 n. 17 |
|  | p. 197 n. 65 |
| 244 | p. 177 n. 4 |
|  | p. 178 n. 29 |
| 309 | p. 193 n. 57 |
| 331 | p. 203 n. 17 |
|  | p. 205 n. 44 |
| 366 | p. 205 n. 38 |
| 382 | p. 203 n. 19 |

| 478 | p. 194 n. 83 |
| 486 | p. 207 n. 70 |
| 504 | p. 205 n. 38 |
|  | p. 205 n. 44 |
| 530 | p. 197 n. 62 |
| 847 | p. 195 n. 13 |
| 914-5 | p. 180 III n. 16 |
| 944 | p. 181 n. 33 |
| 966-7 | p. 192 n. 24 |
| 1005 | p. 193 n. 55 |
| 1022 | p. 181 n. 32 |
| 1033 | p. 205 n. 44 |
| 1039 | p. 181 n. 32 |
| 1043 | p. 181 n. 32 |
| 1045 | p. 181 n. 32 |
| 1051 | p. 181 n. 32 |
| 1056 | p. 181 n. 32 |
| 1061-2 | p. 181 n. 32 |
| 1068 | p. 181 n. 32 |
| 1086 | p. 181 n. 32 |
| 1093 | p. 206 n. 61 |
| 1096 | p. 181 n. 32 |
| 1111 | p. 187 n. 48 |
| 1162 | p. 207 n. 67 |
| 1330 | p. 194 n. 72 |
|  | p. 194 n. 75 |
| 1347 | p. 194 n. 73 |
|  | p. 194 n. 82 |
| 1348 | p. 197 n. 65 |
|  | p. 195 n. 14 |
|  | p. 197 n. 60 |
| 1349 | p. 197 n. 65 |
|  | p. 195 n. 4 |
|  | p. 195 n. 15 |
| 1352 | p. 197 n. 61 |
| 1353 | p. 197 n. 61 |
| 1356 | p. 187 n. 55 |
| 1357a | p. 207 n. 69 |
| 1368-60 | p. 197 n. 62 |
| 1358 | p. 207 n. 69 |
| 1368 | p. 186 n. 47 |
| 1370 | p. 194 n. 73 |
| 1371 | p. 194 n. 72 |
| 1372 | p. 186 n. 47 |
| 1387 | p. 194 n. 70 |
| 1389 | p. 207 n. 75 |
| 1422 | p. 194 n. 73 |
| 1428 | p. 207 n. 75 |
| 1429 | p. 205 n. 41 |
| 1439 | p. 194 n. 72 |
|  | p. 194 n. 75 |

*Inscriptione Latinae Selectae* (H. Dessau)
—*contd.*

| | |
|---|---|
| 1452 | p. 194 n. 82 |
| 1477 | p. 208 n. 91 |
| 1478 | p. 208 n. 91 |
| 1485 | p. 208 n. 91 |
| 1487 | p. 193 n. 27 |
| 1491 | p. 194 n. 74 |
| 1507 | p. 193 n. 53 |
| 1514 | p. 192 n. 20 |
| | p. 206 n. 53 |
| 1515-17 | p. 193 n. 53 |
| 1518 | p. 193 n. 52 |
| 1519 | p. 193 n. 48 |
| 1521 | p. 206 n. 52 |
| 1522 | p. 206 n. 52 |
| 1534 | p. 203 n. 18 |
| | p. 205 n. 38 |
| 1540-4 | p. 193 n. 49 |
| 1570 | p. 193 n. 50 |
| 1643 | p. 193 n. 28 |
| 1648 | p. 193 n. 51 |
| 1650 | p. 193 n. 51 |
| 1651 | p. 193 n. 50 |
| 1660 | p. 193 n. 50 |
| 1738 | p. 194 n. 71 |
| 1740 | p. 194 n. 82 |
| 1877-9 | p. 205 n. 40 |
| 1879 | p. 203 n. 19 |
| 1879-82 | p. 203 n. 19 |
| 1880 | p. 206 n. 60 |
| 1883 | p. 204 n. 25 |
| | p. 205 n. 42 |
| 1883-5 | p. 203 n. 19 |
| 1885-6 | p. 203 n. 19 |
| 1885 | p. 205 n. 41 |
| 1886 | p. 202 n. 5 |
| | p. 205 n. 43 |
| | p. 203 n. 19 |
| 1886-95 | p. 203 n. 19 |
| 1889 | p. 205 n. 43 |
| 1891 | p. 205 n. 44 |
| 1893 | p. 203 n. 19 |
| | p. 205 n. 41 |
| | p. 205 n. 44 |
| 1894-5 | p. 203 n. 16 |
| 1896 | p. 205 n. 34 |
| 1898 | p. 203 n. 16 |
| | p. 203 n. 19 |
| 1898a | p. 205 n. 43 |
| 1898-9 | p. 203 n. 19 |

| | |
|---|---|
| 1899 | p. 205 n. 40 |
| | p. 203 n. 19 |
| 1900 | p. 203 n. 19 |
| 1901 | p. 203 n. 19 |
| | p. 205 n. 43 |
| 1902-3 | p. 205 n. 40 |
| 1904 | p. 205 n. 17 |
| 1906 | p. 204 n. 26 |
| 1907 | p. 202 n. 5 |
| 1908 | p. 203 n. 17 |
| | p. 203 n. 18 |
| | p. 203 n. 19 |
| 1909 | p. 205 n. 38 |
| 1910 | p. 203 n. 18 |
| | p. 205 n. 40 |
| 1911 | p. 203 n. 19 |
| 1911-12 | p. 203 n. 17 |
| 1914 | p. 204 n. 26 |
| 1915 | p. 203 n. 17 |
| | p. 205 n. 40 |
| 1918 | p. 205 n. 40 |
| 1919 | p. 203 n. 18 |
| 1920 | p. 203 n. 17 |
| 1921 | p. 203 n. 18 |
| 1922 | p. 203 n. 17 |
| 1923 | p. 203 n. 19 |
| | p. 205 n. 40 |
| 1924-5 | p. 203 n. 19 |
| 1926 | p. 203 n. 16 |
| | p. 203 n. 19 |
| | p. 205 n. 40 |
| 1926-7 | p. 203 n. 19 |
| 1929-30 | p. 203 n. 19 |
| 1932 | p. 205 n. 40 |
| 1933 | p. 203 n. 17 |
| 1934 | p. 203 n. 18 |
| 1935 | p. 203 n. 18 |
| 1936 | p. 205 n. 30 |
| 1938 | p. 205 n. 40 |
| 1940 | p. 205 n. 38 |
| 1942-4 | p. 205 n. 39 |
| 1944 | p. 203 n. 17 |
| 1946 | p. 205 n. 39 |
| 1948-50 | p. 205 n. 39 |
| 1950 | p. 203 n. 19 |
| 1952 | p. 205 n. 39 |
| 2073 | p. 206 n. 59 |
| 2082 | p. 207 n. 74 |
| 2118 | p. 207 n. 76 |
| | p. 207 n. 78 |
| | p. 207 n. 79 |

| | | | |
|---|---|---|---|
| 2120-3 | p. 187 n. 53 | 4837 | p. 206 n. 65 |
| 2157 | p. 214 App. | 4951a | p. 205 n. 41 |
| 2173 | p. 207 n. 81 | 5006 | p. 182 n. 73 |
| | p. 207 n. 84 | 5016 | p. 182 n. 76 |
| | p. 214 App. | 5021 | p. 205 n. 38 |
| 2375 | p. 206 n. 63 | 5319 | p. 195 n. 25 |
| | p. 214 App. | 5350 | p. 197 n. 62 |
| 2379 | p. 207 n. 78 | 5526 | p. 197 n. 62 |
| 2381 | p. 206 n. 64 | 5920 | p. 194 n. 70 |
| | p. 207 n. 67 | 6123 | p. 180 II n. 17 |
| 2382 | p. 206 n. 61 | 6141 | p. 203 n. 18 |
| | p. 206 n. 62 | 6172 | p. 203 n. 19 |
| | p. 206 n. 63 | 6188 | p. 203 n. 19 |
| 2383 | p. 207 n. 67 | | p. 205 n. 42 |
| 2391 | p. 206 n. 65 | 6283 | p. 203 n. 19 |
| 2392 | p. 207 n. 85 | 6286 | p. 195 n. 23 |
| 2400 | p. 214 App. | 6333 | p. 194 n. 82 |
| 2416-8 | p. 207 n. 70 | 6523 | p. 182 n. 77 |
| 2418 | p. 207 n. 69 | 6572-3 | p. 182 n. 73 |
| 2419a | p. 207 n. 69 | 6680 | p. 200 n. 44 |
| 2424 | p. 207 n. 85 | 6744 | p. 182 n. 74 |
| 2445 | p. 214 App. | 6747 | p. 182 n. 58 |
| 2448 | p. 206 n. 65 | 6772 | p. 182 n. 78 |
| 2487 | p. 187 n. 53 | 6862 | p. 182 n. 75 |
| 2545 | p. 214 App. | 6870 | p. 194 n. 65 |
| 2586 | p. 207 n. 65 | 6948 | p. 195 n. 8 |
| 2587 | p. 207 n. 69 | 6953-4 | p. 203 n. 19 |
| 2588 | p. 207 n. 70 | 6954 | p. 205 n. 42 |
| 2648 | p. 206 n. 63 | 7122 | p. 182 n. 74 |
| 2677 | p. 196 n. 30 | 7489 | p. 203 n. 19 |
| 2678 | p. 196 n. 30 | 8852 | p. 194 n. 73 |
| 2689 | p. 195 n. 11 | 8880 | p. 207 n. 80 |
| 2699 | p. 205 n. 41 | 8881 | p. 211 n. 120 |
| 2706 | p. 205 n. 41 | 8902 | p. 195 n. 10 |
| 2727 | p. 205 n. 44 | 9007 | p. 195 n. 12 |
| | p. 205 n. 42 | 9011 | p. 197 n. 62 |
| | p. 203 n. 19 | 9036 | p. 203 n. 16 |
| 2748 | p. 203 n. 16 | 9037 | p. 203 n. 17 |
| | p. 205 n. 42 | 9039 | p. 203 n. 19 |
| 2927 | p. 185 n. 24 | 9074 | p. 207 n. 84 |
| 2942 | p. 194 n. 82 | 9075 | p. 214 App. |
| 3035 | p. 207 n. 65 | 9127 | p. 207 n. 75 |
| 3416 | p. 203 n. 19 | 9129 | p. 207 n. 75 |
| 3434 | p. 203 n. 19 | 9130 | p. 207 n. 75 |
| 3456 | p. 207 n. 70 | 9184 | p. 198 n. 12 |
| 3593 | p. 203 n. 19 | 9196 | p. 195 n. 10 |
| 3703 | p. 208 n. 91 | 9200 | p. 186 n. 46 |
| 3878 | p. 203 n. 18 | | p. 186 n. 47 |
| 4071 | p. 207 n. 75 | 9483 | p. 180 II n. 25 |
| 4093 | p. 182 n. 79 | 9493 | p. 214 App. |
| 4496 | p. 207 n. 67 | | |

*Journal of Roman Studies*
XIV (1924) 180    p. 193 n. 55

*Notizie degli Scavi*
1892, 289         p. 195 n. 5
1901, 20          p. 193 n. 52

*Orientis Graeci Inscriptiones Selectae*
(W. Dittenberger)
458              p. 191 n. 82
689              p. 193 n. 34

*Res Gestae Divi Augusti*
5                 p. 178 n.. 35
                   p. 181 n. 43
6                 p. 21
                   p. 178 n. 25

8                 p. 21
                   p. 179 n. 51
10              p. 178 n. 21
11              p. 178 n. 37
12              p. 178 n. 37

*Supplementum Epigraphicum Graecum*
IX. 8            p. 183 n. 86
                   p. 177 n. 15
                   p. 190 n. 60
                   p. 191 n. 69
                   p. 191 n. 70

*Sylloge Inscriptionum Graecarum*[3]
(W. Dittenberger)
742              p. 199 n. 40
800              p. 193 n. 33

## IV. PAPYRI

*Berliner Griechische Urkunden (BGU)*
114             p. 189 n. 34
1049           p. 209 n. 110

*Corpus Papyrorum Raineri (CPR)*
75              p. 209 n. 110
117             p. 209 n. 110

*Journal of Egyptian Archaeology*
1935, 224 ff.      p. 200 n. 52

Marini, *Papiri Diplomatici*
114             p. 210 n. 120
138             p. 210 n. 120

*P. Antinoopolis*
33             p. 209 n. 110

*P. Cairo Maspero*
67023         p. 211 n. 122
67054         p. 210 n. 120
67103         p. 210 n. 120

*P. Erlangen*
105             p. 209 n. 109
                   p. 209 n. 110

*P. Flor.*
291             p. 210 n. 120
320             p. 209 n. 105

*P. Giessen*
40             p. 129-30, 133 ff.
                   p. 197 n. 1

*P. Gnomon*
49             p. 199 n. 42
55             p. 198 n. 27
                   p. 198 n. 26

*P. Lips.*
20-23         p. 209 n. 110
33             p. 209 n. 110
36-7           p. 209 n. 110
40             p. 210 n. 117
41             p. 209 n. 110
55             p. 209 n. 110

*P. Lond.*
II. 153         p. 210 n. 120
   348         p. 198 n. 24
III. 1231       p. 198 n. 24
V. 1679       p. 210 n. 120
   1701       p. 209 n. 109
   1714       p. 211 n. 122
   1912       p. 197 n. 66

*P. Michigan*
III. 159        p. 189 n. 34

*P. Oslo.*
88      p. 209 n. 109

*P. Oxy.*
574      p. 198 n. 24
727      p. 198 n. 24
942      p. 209 n. 109
1114      p. 200 n. 51
1223      p. 209 n. 109
1261      p. 209 n. 105
1424      p. 209 n. 105
1837      p. 210 n. 117
     p. 210 n. 120
1869      p. 210 n. 111
1880-2      p. 210 n. 120
1887      p. 210 n. 117
1901      p. 211 n. 120
2050      p. 211 n. 120
2408      p. 209 n. 111

*P. Rendal Harris*
94      p. 209 n. 109

*P. Thead.*
8      p. 209 n. 110

*PSI*
97      p. 210 n. 117
469      p. 209 n. 110
807      p. 209 n. 110
1160      p. 197 n. 66
1365      p. 210 n. 120

*Sammelbuch (SB)*
1016      p. 200 n. 51

Tjäder, *die nichtliterarischen Lateinischen Papyri Italiens*
6.      p. 209 n. 111
8.      p. 209 n. 111

*Wilcken, Chrestomathie*
I. 174      p. 194 n. 66

# GENERAL INDEX

*Ab actis*, 167, 174
*Accensi*, 154, 157-8
*Actio iudicati*, 70
*Adiutores*, 159, 161, 164, 167-8, 170-1, 173
Aediles, election of, 32; *scribae* of, 155
Aerarium, 101 ff.
Agrippa, 6, 12, 16, 21, 24
*A libellis*, 167-8, 171
Alps, prefects of, 117-8
*Apparitores*, 153-8
*Appellatio*, 57-8, 63-5, 69-83, 93 ff.
*A rationibus*, 106, 113-4
Asturia, prefect of, 118
*Attributi*, 136-7
*Auctoritas*, Augustus' use of his, 13-4, 33-5, 79, 84
Augustus, constitutional position of, 3 ff., see also *auctoritas, censoria potestas, consulare imperium, maius imperium, tribunicia potestas;* regulation of elections by, 29 ff.; jurisdiction of, 77 ff., 83-5, 88-9, 94-8; financial position, 104-6; use of prefects by, 117 ff.; procurators of, 123
*Auxilium*, 4, 10, 69, 72, 94-5

Balearic Isles, prefects of, 118
*Beneficiarii*, 161-3, 167
Bribery, electoral, 36, 47

Caepio, conspiracy of, 7; trial of, 98
Caesar (Julius), 97
*Caesariani*, 165-6
Cappadocia, procurators of, 118
Cappadocians, legal status of, 139
Cato (Minor), 156-7
*Censoria potestas* of Augustus, 24-6
Census, of Augustus, 15-6, 21, 23-5
*Chartularii*, 167, 174
Christians, trials of, 55-7, 59
Claudius, 15, 106, 125
*Coercitio*, 59-62, 94
*Cognitio*, 58, 79-80, 85-6, 89
*Cohortales*, 168-9

*Commendatio*, 34-5, 48
*Commentarienses*, 161-3, 167, 171
Constitutio Antoniniana, 62-5, 129 ff.
*Consulare imperium* of Augustus, 5-6, 13-6, 25, 33, 78, 84
Consuls, election of, 33-4, 37-9, 45, 48; *imperium* of, 6, 76; civil jurisdiction of, 73-8, 83-6; capital jurisdiction of, 86 ff.
Cornelius Gallus, 97, 121
*Cornicularii*, 161-3, 167, 171-4
Corsica, prefect of, 118
*Cura epistularum*, 167
*Cura morum*, 21, 24-5
*Cursores*, 167
Cyprus, *pro legato* of, 118

*Decuriae, iudicum*, 40-3, *apparitorum*, 154-8
Decurions, legal privileges of, 57, 64-5
*Dediticii*, 130 ff.
*Destinatio*, 37-8
*Draconarii*, 167
*Ducenarii, decuria* of, 23, 41

Egnatius Rufus, 32-3, 36
Egypt, prefect of, 121-5
Egyptians, legal status of, 132-4, 138-9
Elections, 29 ff.
Emperor, appellate jurisdiction of, 77 ff., 94-7; civil jurisdiction of, 83-6; capital jurisdiction of, 88-90
Equites, 22-3, 39-44
*Exceptores*, 162-3, 167, 171, 173
*Exercitio publici iudicii*, 58-9, 90-3

Festus, 55
*Fideicommissa*, 84-5
Fiscus, 102 ff., *libertatis et peculiorum*, 109, 160; *castrensis*, 110-1, 113; *Alexandrinus*, 110-1; *Asiaticus*, 110-1
Flavius Archippus, 56, 59
Flavius, Gnaeus, 153
Fonteius Capito, 56
Formulary procedure, 70 ff., 79 ff.

Freedmen, *dediticiorum numero*, 131-3; *Latini Juniani*, 133; imperial, 123, 158-61, 164-6, as *apparitores*, 154, 158

Gaius (Caligula), 49
Galba, 56
Gallaecia, prefect of, 118
*Geruli*, 158
*Gladii, ius* or *potestas*, 58-63

Hereditary service in *officia*, 168-9
Herennius Capito, 123-4
*Honestiores*, 57, 64-5
*Humiliores*, 64-5

*Imperium*, of consuls, 6, 76; of proconsuls, 9; of prefects, 120; of the prefect of Egypt, 121-2. See also *maius imperium*, *merum imperium*, and *consulare imperium*
*Intercessio*, 10, 72
*Iudex extra ordinem datus*, 79
*Iudex privatus*, 70-1; appeal from, 80-3
*Iudicia publica*, 58-9, 86 ff.
*Ius gladii*, 58-63
*Ius Italicum*, 146

John Lydus, 172 ff.
Judaea, prefects and procurators of, 119, 124-5

Latin, official use of, 172
Latins, and *provocatio*, 53-4; Junian, 133
*Latus clavus*, 30-2
*Lectio senatus*, 21-6
*Legati Augusti*, 5; jurisdiction of, 59-60, 122; *officia* of, 161-2
*Legati* of proconsuls, jurisdiction of, 58-9, 122
*Legis actiones*, 121-2
Lex Acilia, 53
   Aelia Sentia, 131-3
   Cornelia de provinciis, 5, 8
   Cornelia de XX quaestoribus, 156
   de imperio Vespasiani, 5, 10-1, 34-5
   Gabinia, 102
   Iulia de vi publica, 54, 58, 60, 86-7, 90-3, 97-8
   Iunia, 133
   Manilia, 5

Pompeia de provinciis, 5
Saenia, 21
Trebonia, 5, 101
Valeria Cornelia, 36-9, 44-5
Licinus, 123
Lictors, 154-7
Lucilius Capito, 124

*Maius imperium*, of Augustus, 8; of Agrippa, 16
Marius Priscus, 56
Mauretania, *procurator et pro legato* of, 119, 125
*Merum imperium*, 58, 60-3
Messalla Corvinus, 14
Metropoleis, Egyptian, 138-9
*Mittendarii*, 167
Moesia and Treballia, prefect of, 118
Murena, 6-7, 98

*Nobiles*, 3, 45, 49-50
*Nomenclatores*, 167
*Nominatio*, 14, 33, 48
Noricum, procurator of, 118
*Numerarii*, 166-8

*Officia, officiales*, 161 ff.
*Origo*, 136 ff.
Ovid, 14, 31

*Patrimonium*, 106, 112-4
Paul, 54-5
Perpetua, 62-3
Piso, prefect of the city, 17
Piso, trial of, 87
Pliny, 55-7
Pontius Pilate, 119, 124-5
*Praecones*, 154, 156-7, 167
*Praefecti*, 117 ff., *imperium* of, 120
*Praefecti aerarii*, 106, 110
*Praefectus Aegypti*, 121-5
*Praefectus fabrum*, 119
*Praefectus Urbi*, 14, 17
Praetors, election of, 33-5, 37-9, 47; jurisdiction of, 72-5, 77, 80-3; *praetores aerarii*, 106, 110
*Primiscrinii*, 168
Primus, trial of, 6, 98
*Princeps officii*, 161, 167-8, 171, 174
Proconsuls, *imperium* of, 9; capital jurisdiction of, 56-9; civil jurisdiction of, 121-2; *officia* of, 162

Procurators, 117 ff.; *officia* of, 162, 164
*Procurator a patrimonio*, 106, 112, 114
*Procurator rei privatae*, 112-4
*Professio*, see *Nominatio*
*Pro legato*, 118, 120, 124
Provincial land, legal quality of, 143 ff.
Provincials, legal status of, 130-1
*Provocatio*, 53-4, 58-9, 86 ff., 96 ff.
*Publicani*, 102-4
Purchase of offices, 156, 169-70

*Quaestionarii*, 161
Quaestors, shortage of, 32; of the *aerarium*, 101, 106; *apparitores* of, 154-7

Raetia, prefects and procurators of, 118, 125
*Recognitio equitum*, 22-3, 25
*Regendarius*, 167
*Regerendarius*, 168
*Res Gestae Divi Augusti*, credibility of, 13, 25
*Res privata*, 112-4
*Restitutio in integrum*, 70-1
*Revocatio Romae*, 75-7

*Sacrosanctitas*, 4, 10
Salaries of civil servants, 156, 161, 163, 170
Sardinia, *pro legato* and prefects of, 118; *procurator et praefectus* of, 125
*Scribae*, 101, 154-8
*Scrinia, sacra*, 169-70
*Scriniarii*, 167-8
*Selecti iudices*, 41-3

Senate, elections transferred to, 46-50; appellate civil jurisdiction of, 77 ff; capital jurisdiction of, 87 ff.
Senators, property qualification, 22, 29-30
Septimius Severus, 112-4
*Singulares*, 162, 167
*Speculatores*, 161-3, 167
*Sportulae*, 170-2
Statilius Taurus, 14
*Statuti*, 169
*Stratores*, 162, 167
*Subscribendarius*, 168
*Summae rationes*, 114
Supernumeraries, 169

Tabula Hebana, 29, 37-9
*Tabularii*, 159, 163-4, 166-7
Thrace, procurator of, 118-9
Tiberius, 16-7, 45-9, 87-9, 96
*Tribuni aerarii*, 43
*Tribuni militum*, 119
Tribunes of the plebs, 11; election of, 32-3, 47; intervention in jurisdiction by, 72, 74
*Tribunicia potestas*, 9-12, 16, 21, 33, 94-5
Turpilius, execution of, 53-4
Tutors, appointment of, 85

Velius Paulus, 56
Verres, 9, 54, 72-3, 101, 154-7
Vespasian, 110-1
*Viatores*, 154-6
*Vigintiviri*, 22, 32
Vindelicia, see Raetia
Vitrasius Pollio, 125